MW01001716

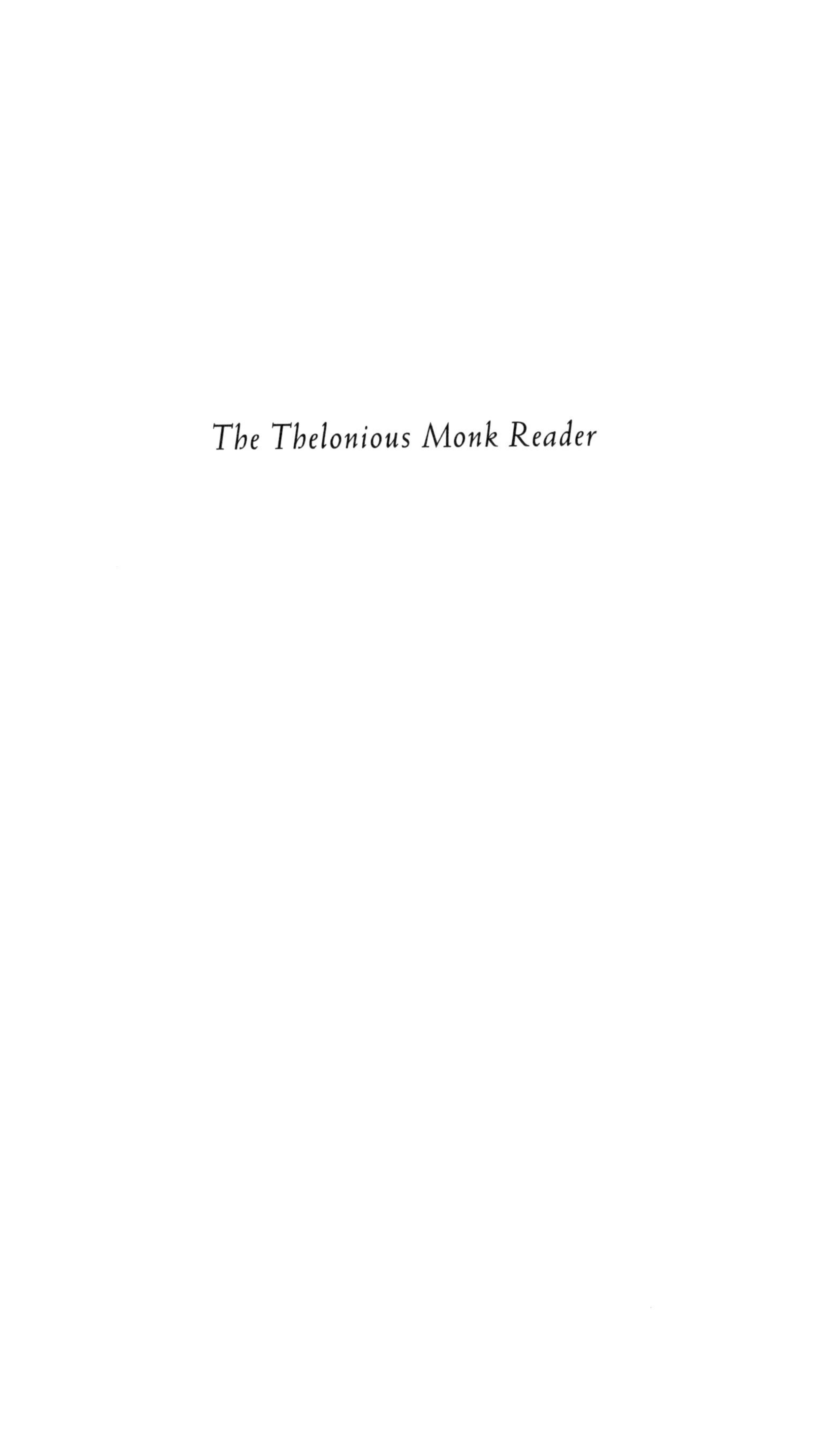

The Thelonious Monk Reader

Readers on American Musicians
Scott DeVeaux, Series Editor

The Thelonious Monk Reader

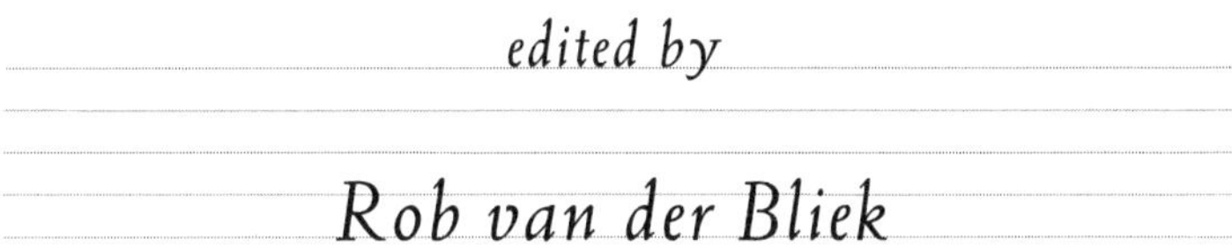

2001

OXFORD
UNIVERSITY PRESS

Oxford New York
Athens Auckland Bangkok Bogotá
Buenos Aires Calcutta Cape Town Chennai Dar es Salaam
Delhi Florence Hong Kong Istanbul Karachi
Kuala Lumpur Madrid Melbourne
Mexico City Mumbai Nairobi Paris São Paulo Shanghai
Singapore Taipei Tokyo Toronto Warsaw

and associated companies in
Berlin Ibadan

Published by Oxford University Press, Inc.
198 Madison Avenue, New York, New York 10016

Library of Congress Cataloging-in-Publication Data
The Thelonious Monk reader / edited by Rob van der Bliek
p. cm. — (Readers on American Musicians)
Includes index.
ISBN 0-19-512166-X
1. Monk,Thelonious. 2. Jazz musicians—United States—Biography.
I. van der Bliek, Rob. II. Readers on American Musicians.
ML417.M846 T54 2000
786.21650923—dc21 00-037475

1 3 5 7 9 8 6 4 2

Printed in the United States of America
on acid-free paper

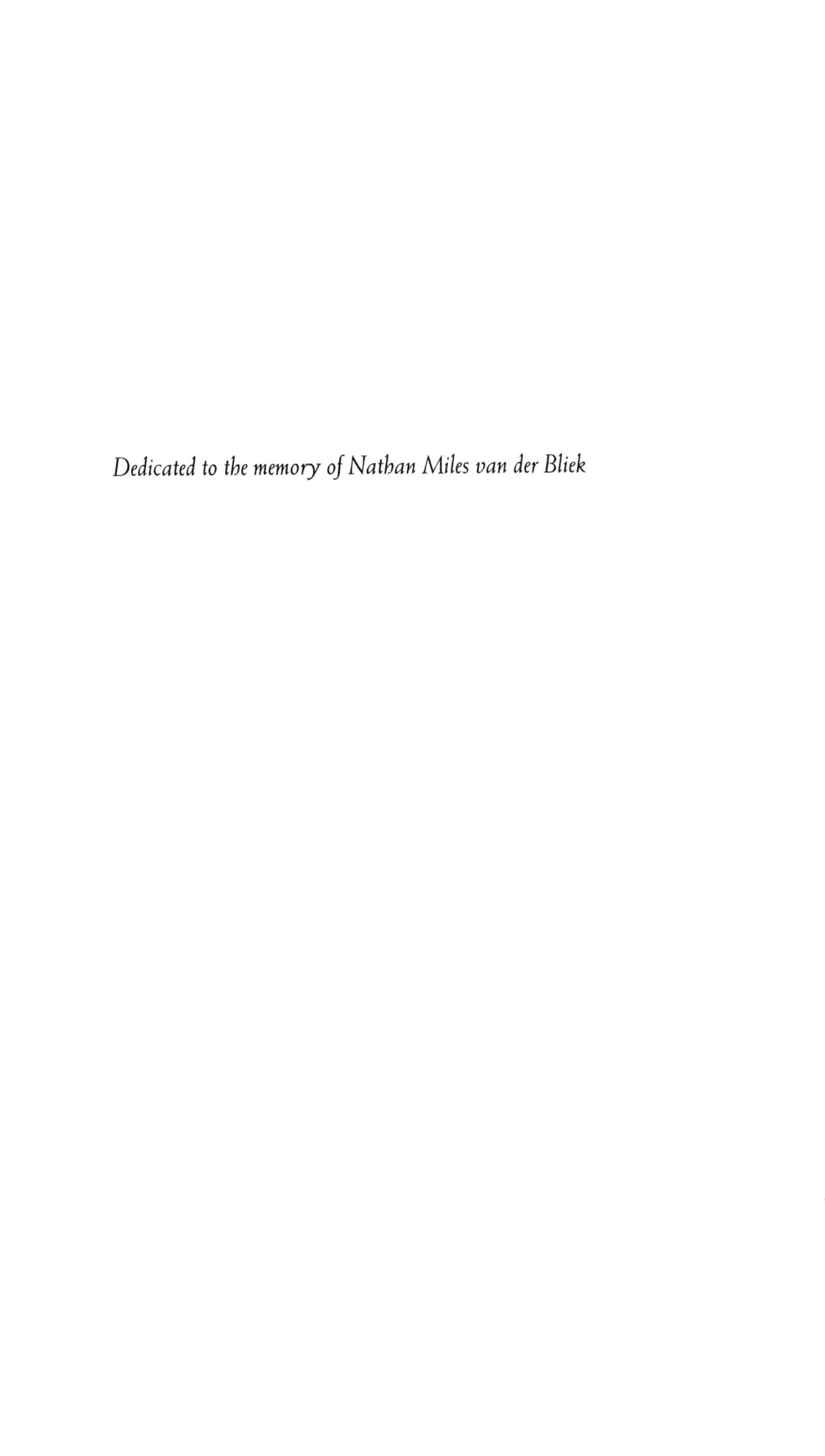

Dedicated to the memory of Nathan Miles van der Bliek

Contents

Acknowledgments

Gathering and assembling material from the vast and untidy universe of published documentation is a laborious task, one that depends greatly on the previous work of others as well as their willingness to help. Numerous individuals and organizations have helped in the compilation of this reader, many anonymously as part of the interlibrary loan system, but many also as independent and not-so-anonymous researchers and aficionados. Compiling may seem like a solitary activity—reading, thinking, organizing—but there is a strong social component (particularly in the permissions stage). I would like to expressly thank the following individuals for their willingness to share information, guidance or critique: Stephen Blum, Fred Canté (author of the meticulously researched *Monk on Records*), Scott DeVeaux, Orrin and Peter Keepnews, Howard Mansfield, Carol Ohlers, Jacques Ponzio, Jim Robbins, Chris Sheridan, Mark Tucker, and Carl Woideck. In addition, thanks to staff from The Hogan Jazz Archive and The Institute of Jazz Studies, two invaluable and readily accessible archives to which much jazz research owes a debt. At Oxford University Press a long string of editors and editorial assistants were burdened with the manuscript and its accompanying administrative problems—thanks to these individuals for keeping the project on track. Lilian Radovac was an exceptional research assistant through much of the project, supported through funding from York University through the Matching Fund Graduate Assistantship program and library research grants. Also thanks to the Resource Sharing Department of York University Libraries, particularly Gladys Fung and Linda Hurley, who handled the bulk of my interlibrary loan requests. The owners of *Down Beat* were particularly generous in the granting of permission to use their material; in fact, the history of post–World War II jazz in general is ready to be culled from the pages of *Down Beat*, where pragmatic, how-to columns stand next to polemical discussions of what jazz should or should not be. Finally, I'd like to thank Lise, Thomas, and Sonja van der Bliek for keeping me involved and interested in things that have nothing to do with Monk, or for that matter, music, musicology, and librarianship.

Toronto, Summer 2000

Introduction

> Make no mistake. This man knows exactly what he is doing in a theoretical way—organized, more than likely, in a personal terminology, but strongly organized nevertheless . . . Monk approaches the piano and, I should say right now, music as well, from an "angle" that, although unprecedented, is just the right "angle" for him.
>
> —Bill Evans, liner notes to *Monk*

Of all the characteristics that a jazz artist requires in order to succeed, musical originality is probably the most desirable, if not the most important. And of all the major jazz artists, Thelonious Monk was one of the most original musical thinkers, in the true sense of being nonconformist, idiosyncratic, imaginative, eccentric, or, in one word, unique. When Monk was hired as house pianist for the Minton's Monday night jam sessions in 1940 at age 23, his original musical thinking acted as a catalyst for the development of bebop, which was subsequently advanced by the likes of Dizzy Gillespie, Kenny Clarke, Charlie Christian, and later, Charlie Parker. Monk was left behind after the Minton's sessions dissipated and he struggled for more than 15 years before he achieved critical and commercial success. In fact, as late as 1964, Columbia Records still felt the need to seek out public endorsements from jazz luminaries such as Bill Evans. This was after Monk had already appeared on the cover of *Time* magazine, made several world tours, and had consistently been receiving laudatory reviews of his concerts and recordings.

In some ways Monk was the original bebopper—in his music, stance, clothing, and aura. But his piano playing developed outside of bebop, remaining partially rooted in an older stride style of playing and eschewing the breakneck-speed runs of bebop in favor of sparse, broken phrases relying on ellipsis and understatement, and a playful experimentation with sound. His compositions, inextricably linked to his playing, charted melodic, harmonic and rhythmic territories differently than those of the bebop players. The characteristic dissonances and chord substitutions of bebop belonged to Monk but the linear melodic lines and normalized rhythmic patterns did not.

Monk's image—his on-stage pirouettes, pacing, dancing, flat-handed playing, floundering footwork, mumbling speech, nodding off or laying out; his goatee, glasses, and hats—was very much a part of his allure, although combined with an idiosyncratic piano technique it may have initially done more harm than good for his reception by the critics. His unusual name inspired appellations like "Melodious Thunk," "The Onliest Monk," and "The Loneliest Monk," all of which had some grain of truth in them. But his sometimes mysterious and eccentric behavior may not have been so much a desire to confound as it was an inability to conform and communicate through normal conventions, whether in an interview, a club date, or a recording session. Monk clearly exhibited symptoms of a psychological disorder and was prone to disconnect from his surroundings, whether drug-related or not. This condition worsened over time, to the point where he no longer communicated with anyone, living in near seclusion for the last decade of his life. His last years were spent living in silence in a room in the house of the Baroness Nica de Koenigswarter, the "jazz baroness" who, along with his wife Nellie, proved to be one of the constants in his personal life.

A chronology of the literature on Monk would begin with profile pieces introducing him to the public (late 1940s), followed by critical appraisals of his music (late 1950s), interviews and descriptions of his career and life (1960s–1970s), retrospectives (1980s), and finally, monographs and analyses (1990s). Reading through this literature—essays, profiles, liner notes, record and concert reviews, interviews—quickly exposes a meager set of facts and stories that are perpetually recycled and restated. Researching and tracing the history and paths of these facts and stories would in itself be a laborious undertaking, with not the least part of the problem being that many jazz writers have a tendency to rework their own writings for alternate forms of publication (e.g., liner notes are revised and collocated to form a book, or an article for one journal is revised and updated for another journal under a slightly different title). Nevertheless, there is a cornucopia of stimulating and informed opinions sprinkled throughout the readings. The great majority of writings on Monk are profiles—pieces that summarize the events of his life, his personal traits (of which there were many), and discuss his music in largely adjectival terms. Analytical articles, at least those discussing his music with the aid of musical transcriptions and musicological concepts, are few and far between, but there are several outstanding and insightful essays describing his music and its significance in critical, literary, or philosophical terms. Only in the last decade have there been books dedicated solely to Monk, beginning with one in German, Thomas Fitterling's *Thelonious Monk: Sein Leben, Seine Musik, Seine Schallplaten* (1987), three in French, Yves Buin's *Monk* (1988), Jacques Ponzio and François Postif's *Blue Monk* (1995), Laurent De Wilde's *Monk* (1996), and finally, one in English, Leslie Gourse's *Straight, No Chaser: The Life and Genius of Thelonious Monk* (1997).[1] Gourse's book is the first to use new material, as she interviewed Monk's manager, family, and selected band members.

Selection of material for this reader has in part been the result of the range and character of the available published material written on Monk, and in part determined by a desire to document the milestones of Monk's career and criticism of his music. The overriding concern was to give a balanced yet representative picture of the literature on Monk. There were over 200 items to choose from, not including the bulk of record and concert reviews, but limited to books, articles, liner notes, and theses.[2] In general, the selection is skewed toward historical material, including early reviews of the Blue Note recordings and the first profiles of Monk, the latter of which are all reprinted here. As this is the first published collection of articles on Monk, it seems almost obligatory to dig up and expose these early profiles, most never having been reprinted, but often cited and difficult to obtain. They are not necessarily all of a high literary standard, but they document how Monk was received early on in his career. With the post-1949 material, literary or critical interest plays a more significant role in the selection. Some interviews also have been included, in several cases clearly demonstrating Monk's aversion to the jazz establishment as represented by well-known critics. Whether he is forthcoming or not, the interviews are a good place to witness Monk's dry sense of humor. Other articles have either instigated some public discourse, are cited

1. Fitterling's book was translated into English in 1997 and published as *Thelonious Monk: His Life and Music* (Berkeley: Berkeley Hills Books), making it the first English language biography of Monk. De Wilde's book was also translated into English in 1997 (New York: Marlowe).
2. Although the focus of the reader is English language material, I also looked at French and German articles.

often enough to be considered significant, or simply have demonstrated a complementary perspective. Representation of record reviews is limited to the Blue Note recordings, which are noteworthy because critics initially did not know what to make of Monk, and the *Brilliant Corners* album for Riverside, which marked a turn in the critical tide.

Very few changes have been made to the articles, with omissions indicated through ellipses in cases where the information (usually biographical) has been covered elsewhere. Obvious factual errors have been footnoted with corrections, and missing references for quotes in articles have been supplied with bibliographic information where possible; as well, original discographical information has been supplied when a specific recording is an essential part of the discussion. In instances where an article has already been reprinted with slight emendations by the author, the latest version has been reprinted here.

Four main sections in the book delineate Monk's life and career: I. 1917–1954: His beginnings and early recordings for Blue Note and Prestige; II. 1955–1961: A period of critical recognition for the recordings made for Riverside; III. 1962–1981: The years of commercial success, recording for Columbia, world tours, and subsequent withdrawal from music and life in general; and IV. 1982–Present: Death, followed by tributes and analyses.[3] These sections are each organized differently, depending on the type, amount and quality of material available in combination with the events covered during the period. Further grouping is on the basis of content or article type, when possible. Admittedly, this somewhat artificial clustering works better in some sections than in others.

Had this reader been conceived in an ideal world, unfettered by the practical limitations of publishing and copyright, then surely Jef Langford's lengthy and insightful discussion of the entire body of Monk's recordings with emphasis on the contributions made by the horn players who took part in the sessions would have been included.[4] Langford is not the only writer missing in this reader: Michael Cuscuna has produced some excellent liner notes to

3. Laurent De Wilde, in his book *Monk* (New York: Marlowe, 1997; translation of original French edition published in 1996) offers a more stratified delineation: "1917–27: Birth of a genius; 1927–37: Childhood of a genius; 1937–47: Apprenticeship; 1947–57: Ascension; 1957–67: Glory; 1967–77: Decline; 1977–82: Silence." In this sequence, Monk's Columbia years, perhaps not his most creative period, is chosen as the apex of his career, whereas many would argue that the artistic apex occurred much earlier with the Blue Note and Riverside recordings.

4. Jef Langford, "Monk's Horns," (Parts 1–3), *Jazz Journal International*, Vol. 23, No. 11 (Nov. 1970), pp. 2–5; Vol. 24, No. 1 (Jan. 1971), pp. 7–8, No. 2 (Feb. 1971), pp. 3–4, 40.

the Mosaic box sets, representing some of the best and most accurate writing on Monk,[5] and there are a slew of French writers who have been promoting Monk since the early 1950s in *Jazz Hot* and *Jazz Magazine*. Another area of writing not represented is the small body of fictional and poetic writings that use themes from Monk's life and titles of his compositions as inspiration: Geoff Dyer's chapter on Monk in *But Beautiful*, Art Lange's *Monk Poems*, and the journal *Brilliant Corners* come to mind as obvious examples.[6] There is another collection waiting to be formed.

Monk has not generated a school of imitators in the way that Charlie Parker or Bud Powell has, but he has inspired and opened our ears to the possibilities inherent in the changes instigated by the bebop players of the 1940s. He undeniably shaped the course of jazz in ways that are only now being realized by other jazz musicians and his stature as a composer continues to grow, as can be witnessed by the rapidly increasing number of albums devoted to playing his compositions. An anecdote by Nellie, Monk's lifelong wife and companion, is telling: "I used to have a phobia about pictures or anything on a wall hanging just a little bit crooked. Thelonious cured me. He nailed a clock to the wall at a very slight angle, just enough to make me furious. We argued about it for two hours, but he wouldn't let me change it. Finally, I got used to it. Now anything can hang at any angle, and it doesn't bother me at all."[7] Gary Giddins astutely comments: "That's about the best description I've heard of what Monk has done for the collective ear."[8] In an era characterized by a musical aesthetic conducive to asymmetry, fragmentation, derivation, and juxtaposition, Monk's music is evidence that he had already thought through these musical problems. It was only a question of us catching up with him.

5. See "Thelonious Monk: The Early Years; The Blue Note Recordings," liner notes to *The Complete Blue Note Recordings of Thelonious Monk*, Mosaic MR4-101 (1983) and "Thelonious Monk: The Final Professional Years," liner notes to *The Complete Black Lion and Vogue Recordings of Thelonious Monk*, Mosaic MR4-112 (1985).
6. Geoff Dyer, *But Beautiful* (London: Jonathan Cape, 1991); Art Lange, *The Monk Poems*, (New York: Frontward Books, 1977).
7. Nat Hentoff, "The Private World of Thelonious Monk," *Esquire*, April 1960, pp. 133–137.
8. Gary Giddins, "Rabbi Monk Reasserts His Mastery, *Village Voice*, April 12, 1976, p. 99.

Beginnings and Early Reception (1917–1954)

Monk's early development as a musician is poorly documented and his remarks on when, where and what he was playing have been few and sometimes cryptic. Before his seminal job as the house pianist at Minton's during 1940–1941, he had toured with an evangelist for two years (although nobody seems to recall the name of the evangelist) and passed through Kansas City where he befriended Mary Lou Williams. Her comments about his playing are one of the few assessments from this period. This would have been between 1934–1936, as Monk left home at age 16. Back in New York between 1936 and 1939, he seems to have worked sporadically at a number of musical jobs, including work with Cootie Williams, and purportedly studied part-time at Juilliard,[1] finally ending up as the house pianist at Minton's in 1940. The earliest recordings of Monk, made in 1941 at Minton's by Jerry Newman on a portable recorder, demonstrate that Monk's modernist ideas were beginning to fall in place by the time he was twenty-four.[2] Later, between 1942 and 1946, he performed briefly with Lucky

1. According to longtime Monk researcher Peter Keepnews, there is no evidence to support the fact that Monk studied at Juilliard. In fact, in George Simon's 1948 interview with Monk (reprinted on page 53), he is quoted as saying "I never studied. I just experimented arranging by experience . . . You fool around and listen."
2. Jerry Newman was a Columbia University student who roamed the Harlem nightclubs with his portable disc recorder, often recording with the permission of the musicians. The recordings with Monk include musicians such as Charlie Christian, Joe Guy, Don Byas, and Roy Eldridge (see George Hoefer's article reprinted on p. 14).

Millinder, Dizzy Gillespie, and Coleman Hawkins. The first known description of Monk in print stems from this period, when he was working the *Downbeat Club* on West 52nd Street in 1944; the writer is Herbie Nichols, a pianist who, musically, actually had a great deal in common with Monk:

> Thelonious Monk is an oddity among piano players. This particular fellow is the author of the weirdest rhythmical melodies I've ever heard. They are very great too. (Don't ever praise Monk too much or he'll let you down). But I will say that I'd rather hear him play a "boston" than any other pianist. His sense of fitness is uncanny. However, when Monk takes a solo, he seems to be partial to certain limited harmonies which prevent him from taking a place beside Art [Tatum] and Teddy [Wilson]. He seems to be in a vise as far as that goes and never shows any signs of being able to extricate himself.[3]

With the little exposure that Monk received during the 1940s, his music was generally not received very well. Leonard Feather's 1949 comments were typical:

> Monk's place in the jazz scene, according to most musicians in the bop movement, has been grossly distorted, as a result of some high-powered publicity work. He has written a few attractive tunes, but his lack of technique and continuity prevented him from accomplishing much as a pianist. In fact, Cootie Williams' original 1944 recording of *'Round Midnight,* arranged for big band, is vastly superior to Monk's own recording as an interpretation of the theme. Monk, who has been touted as a 'genius' and a 'high priest of bebop,' would wander in and out of Minton's, often falling asleep at the piano.[4]

3. Herbie Nichols, "Jazz Milieu," *The Music Dial,* August 1944, Vol. 2, No. 2, p. 24. In an interview with A. B. Spellman, published in Spellman's book *Four Lives in the Bebop Business* [New York: Pantheon, 1966; later retitled *Black Music*], Nichols comments on his writing about Monk: "Monk is a good example of how irresponsible critics are. Now I like Monk. He's a friend of mine and a great composer and musician. I wrote Monk up for a Negro magazine, the *Music Dial,* back in 1946 [sic] before he recorded for Blue Note. I was honest. I knew people hadn't caught on to him, but I raved about him anyway. Leonard Feather and those other people didn't even know what he was doing; they hated him. Nowadays if you say anything against Monk you're a dog. But do you know that Monk's music hasn't changed from 1939 until now? That shows critics haven't been doing what they're responsible to do" (p. 162).
4. Leonard Feather, *Inside Jazz* (New York: Da Capo, 1977 [1949]) p. 10.

It is clear Feather was reacting to the hype generated by Blue Note and people like Orrin Keepnews and Paul Bacon, who were writing about Monk in glowing terms at the time.[5] And he must have been irritated by Monk's image, since he went out of his way to denounce the hype by claiming that "it cannot be too strongly emphasized, for the benefit of those who heard him in person or on records, that he is not a bebop pianist, nor do his solos have any of the mystic qualities attributed to them by some non-musical admirers."[6] Articles by several of these non-musical admirers have been included here.

Until the Riverside recordings in the 1950s, Monk was widely misunderstood by critics, musicians, and listeners alike. He had a brief contract with Prestige, which produced a much-discussed solo on Miles Davis' album *Bag's Groove,* but he lost his cabaret card in 1951 due to a drug-related arrest and was unable to work in a nightclub in New York City until 1957. For Monk, who loved the city and hated leaving it, this proved disastrous. Although there were a few jobs in places outside of Manhattan and in establishments that did not sell alcohol, Monk worked very little during this period. The only performance of any significance before the breakthrough with Riverside Records and his 1957 stay at the Five Spot was a concert performance in the Salle Pleyel as part of the *Salon International du Jazz* in Paris in 1954.[7]

5. These articles have been reprinted in the section "Early Profiles."
6. Feethe, *Inside Jazz,* p. 10.
7. See the article by Raymond Horricks reprinted on p. 63.

Minton's and Before

1. Young Monk

Writer Peter Keepnews, the son of record producer and jazz writer Orrin Keepnews, has been collecting material about Monk's life for several decades. An authority on Monk's life, he has published numerous articles and liner notes on him, as well as other jazz artists. Whereas most writers have relied on the common stock of facts about Monk's childhood and early musical development, Keepnews has reexamined every fact or story about Monk, and in this piece he provides illuminating evidence relating to Monk's early musical development, with new facts (in 1989) drawn from personal interviews with Monk's brother and sister.[1] Monk usually claimed that nobody influenced him, or that he was influenced by every musician he heard and all styles of music, or even that he influenced himself. Here the central question about where his musical style came from is answered through examining and hypothesizing from descriptions of situations and individuals who played a role during Monk's teenage years, with the conclusion

1. Before the publication of Leslie Gourse's *Straight, No Chaser* in 1997 (New York: Schirmer), few primary sources in the form of interviews with friends, family, or other musicians had been used in describing Monk's life.

that much of his musical development occurred before the legendary Minton's sessions in 1940 and 1941.

This article originally appeared as "Young Monk," Peter Keepnews, *The Village Voice*, August 8, 1989, pp. 18, 20–21. It has been slightly revised by the author for this reprint. Used by permission of Peter Keepnews.

Modern jazz was in full bloom when Thelonious Monk's first recording under his own name was released by the enterprising Blue Note label in early 1948. Eager to capitalize on the burgeoning bebop movement by identifying the 30-year-old Monk with it, the company sent out a breathless press release announcing that it had "actually found the person who was responsible for this whole new trend in music." Hyperbole, to be sure—but not entirely inaccurate. Monk may not have invented modern jazz by himself, but he was certainly one of its primary architects, and he was working on the kind of advanced musical ideas that came to characterize bebop years before that word entered the jazz lexicon.

A 1951 news item in the British music magazine *Melody Maker* included the assertion that Monk "claims to have played bop since 1932." Monk was never enamored of such terminology and probably never made that claim. But it's clear that as a pianist and a songwriter he was, as the title of one album put it, "the unique Thelonious Monk" from an early age. According to his younger brother, Thomas Monk, and his older sister, Marion Monk White, his unusual musical style was already taking shape by his teenage years.

The earliest available recorded evidence of Monk's playing comes from his tenure as the house pianist at Minton's Playhouse in the early '40s. Recordings of late-night jam sessions at that legendary Harlem nightclub reveal that Monk was already using many of the off-center accents and idiosyncratic voicings that would eventually be celebrated as profoundly influential and distinctively Monkian. His approach was not celebrated by everyone, however; even some of his fellow modernists were thrown off by it, although such older and supposedly more traditional-minded musicians as Art Tatum had no trouble appreciating it.

Where did his style—with its broken rhythms, its alternately dense and stripped-down chords, and its creative use of silence—come from? After he became famous enough to attract interviewers, Monk dealt coyly with the question of who influenced him. He had three standard answers, all of them variations on the same evasive theme: Nobody influenced him; he was influenced by every musician he heard; he influenced himself. Such answers made it easy for commentators to conclude that Monk invented his style out of whole cloth.

Yet as different as Monk's playing might have sounded, especially in the Minton's days, its antecedents were there for anyone who had ears to discern them. Duke Ellington—whose reaction, the first time he heard a Monk record, was, "Sounds like he's stealing some of my stuff"—was an obvious influence. A less obvious but equally important one was the great stride pianist James P. Johnson, who for a time lived near the Monk family in the San Juan Hill section of Manhattan, and who befriended Monk in the early '30s. (At a 1957 recording session for the solo album *Thelonious Himself*, Monk remarked proudly of his blues improvisation "Functional," "I sound just like James P." In fact, he sounded almost nothing like James P. Johnson, who was not primarily a blues player, on that particular performance—but traces of the Johnson style can be heard on many of Monk's other recordings.)

Of course, the neighborhood in which he grew up was also an influence. San Juan Hill, a primarily black area in Manhattan's West 60s where Monk lived most of his life, was a thriving center of black culture. Eubie Blake and Noble Sissle's pioneering all-black musical *Shuffle Along* had its world premiere just a few blocks from the house where Monk's family lived, and the area was a home for many musicians, writers, and artists. It was a rough neighborhood (Monk and his brother got into their share of fights), but also a very musical one.

Barbara Monk and her three children had moved to New York from Rocky Mount, North Carolina, in 1922. Three years later Monk's father, Thelonious Sr., who had remained in North Carolina, probably for health reasons, rejoined the family. It was also about this time that the Monks moved into an apartment building on West 63rd Street that was part of the Phipps Houses. An early example of subsidized housing built specifically for African Americans, the Phipps Houses were the brainchild of philanthropist Henry Phipps, who referred to them as "model tenements" because they were designed to offer more living space, sunlight, and other advantages than the buildings in which most black New Yorkers were then living.

"They used to call them the new houses, way back then in the '20s," Marion White recalls. "We were lucky to get in. They had steam heat, and each apartment had its own bathroom." Another amenity that the Monks had in their new three-room apartment was a piano, at which Thelonious Sr.—who, after arriving in New York, worked first as a longshoreman and then in the boiler room of a theater—spent much of his spare time. "My father was gifted as far as music was concerned," says Thomas Monk. "He never had the opportunity to study, but he was gifted, really. He just had the ear for music."

The elder Monk was self-taught. He played what his son Thomas recalls as "honky-tonk" piano, which probably contained elements of both ragtime and boogie-woogie. Although Marion White says that her father didn't so much play the piano as "play at it," his playing was pervasive in the Monks' small apartment.

Thelonious Sr. taught his sons to play the Jew's harp—an instrument whose insistent, droning quality offers intriguing parallels to the sound of much of his son's later music. He also was a talented harmonica player; Thomas Monk recalls his father being able to produce a variety of train sounds on that instrument. (Train sounds would later occupy a prominent place in the Thelonious Monk oeuvre; indeed, he built entire compositions around pianistic versions of such sound—notably "Little Rootie Tootie," which he dedicated to his son, also named Thelonious. The open chords characteristic of the harmonica found a frequent echo in Monk's writing and playing.)

A variety of medical problems prompted Thelonious Monk Sr. to move back to the South in the late '20s, but by that time he had left his mark on his older son, who was already beginning to pick out melodies on the family piano. The first instrument young Thelonious studied formally was the trumpet, but he would look over his sister's shoulder as she practiced piano, and when she stopped taking lessons (her enthusiasm for the keyboard was as low as her brother's was high, she says; she really wanted to play the saxophone), their mother made a momentous decision. In those days, remembers Marion White, "Most of the boys took violin or horn and the girls took piano. And that's the way it was [in the Monk family] until we found out that he didn't like the trumpet and I didn't like the piano." When Thelonious Monk was 12, a neighborhood teacher, a Mr. Wolf (or Wolfe), who had worked with Marion, undertook to explain the rules of the keyboard to Thelonious—rules he would, before too long, systematically bend to his own ends.

It was under the tutelage of Mr. Wolf that Monk learned the rudiments of musical notation, with which in later years he would have a love-hate relationship. Although all his compositions were notated, he often refused to let his sidemen see the sheet music, preferring to let them learn his tunes by playing rather than reading them. During his brief tenure as a piano student (probably less than a year), he began to confront the fact that he would never be a virtuoso in the traditional sense.

Thelonious Monk's unorthodox piano style was essentially a matter of inspiration, but also a matter of practical necessity: Monk was tall and muscular, but he had unusually small hands. "He had the smallest hands for a piano player," Thomas Monk recalls. "He had a friend named Louis Taylor who played the piano. Louis had big hands, like the finer piano players. They have that wide stretch. And my brother used to sort of get aggravated because he couldn't stretch like Louis or the other piano players." This meant that the wide left-hand intervals characteristic of stride piano were beyond Monk's reach, and the graceful execution of arpeggios was difficult for him. Armed with the fortuitous combination of an agile imagination and an indomitable stubbornness, Monk didn't so much compensate for those apparent limitations as turn them into advantages.

Gradually, young Monk developed an approach to the piano that, while violating standard ideas of how the instrument should be played, enabled him to express himself. He discovered he could imply certain notes in a chord without playing them, through the judicious use of overtones; he discovered he could hit more of the notes he wanted to hit if he kept his fingers flat on the keyboard rather than curving them the way piano students are invariably taught. Such experimentation may not have gone over with Mr. Wolf, but it represented an early example of Monk's single-mindedness. "He did what he wanted to do," Thomas Monk says. "If somebody would try to make him do something, he would automatically rebel against it. He had his own ideas about things, and once his mind was made up about something nobody could change it."

Not all of the unorthodox elements in Monk's style were in place when he stopped taking piano lessons, but his interest in jazz certainly was. By the time he was 15, he had formed a small band with some friends from the neighborhood, including a drummer named Morris Simpson and a saxophonist remembered only as "Dukey." They played for dances at the neighborhood community center, and Marion White remembers going to the Apollo several times to see her brother's band participate in—and win—the Harlem theater's famous amateur competition. (Monk's victories at the Apollo are a matter of family legend, but not a matter of historical record. No documentation exists of the weekly amateur contest's winners, and the contest didn't begin until shortly after Monk had left New York at the age of 16—which means that if he did ever win the contest, it was probably at a more advanced age than the oft-told story has it.) Monk had absorbed an impressive amount of jazz knowledge in a relatively short time; his unique style was in its formative stages, but his playing was not so far outside the mainstream that it couldn't be grasped by lindy-hoppers and the notoriously critical Apollo audience.

By this time, Thelonious and everyone who knew him well recognized that playing the piano was what he wanted to do with his life. Yet music did not then consume his entire existence. He was an exceptional student, one of the first blacks to be accepted at the highly competitive Stuyvesant High School, where he excelled in math and physics. He played basketball, checkers, and Ping-Pong with a passion retained well into adulthood. Intense, self-absorbed, and so direct in his dealings with other people that his honesty sometimes got him into trouble, Thelonious Monk was hardly the typical teenager. But neither was he the mad genius of jazz mythology, totally obsessed with his music.

Still, music was the center of his life, and his determination to make a living at it was made considerably easier by his mother, who worked for the city as a cleaning woman and who never hesitated to offer him her total support—financial as well as emotional. "My mother never figured I should do anything else," he told Valerie Wilmer in 1965. "She was with me. If I wanted to play music, it was all right with her."[2] His sister, who worked for the telephone company and continued to live at home for several years, also pitched in. "He was lucky that he lived with his mother and his sister," she laughs. "You've got to have somebody behind you when you're following one road, because otherwise you can't make it. All artists have to suffer—unless they're at home."

Thomas Monk—who briefly pursued a career as a prizefighter before becoming first a policeman and then a bridge-and-tunnel worker—remembers only one instance of his brother breaking his vow to do nothing but music for his living. "One time he ventured to work for a guy named Joe, an iceman. He carried ice; it was pretty strenuous work. He worked one day and said he'd never do that again."

His mother's support was put to the test in 1934 when Monk, at age 16, decided he wanted to drop out of Stuyvesant and join some of his musician friends from the neighborhood who were going on the road with a woman evangelist. The evangelist—whose name no one seems to know or remember—undertook to persuade Barbara Monk that it was time to loosen the apron strings. "She had to do a lot of convincing for Mama to let him go," Thomas Monk recalls. "She finally conceded 'cause his heart was so bent on going. She was convinced that it was something that would be beneficial to him, 'cause he was playing the piano and that's what he wanted to do. So she let him go. And when he came back, he had changed his style of playing."

By the time Thelonious hit the road, he was already hard at work on new concepts of harmony, rhythm, and melody. His brother and sister recall him sitting at the piano for hours at a time, often painstakingly working out varia-

2. Valerie Wilmer, "Monk on Monk," *Down Beat,* June 3, 1965, p. 20. *Ed.*

tions on a familiar old song. His mature style was in the process of crystallizing; during his two years on the road, it took shape.

Monk had played hymns and other religious music prior to his departure; he frequently accompanied his mother when she sang at the local Baptist church. But playing in storefront churches and at tent shows, over the course of what turned out to be a two-year road trip, presented new challenges that accelerated his development as a pianist. Faced with the need to make himself heard over noisy crowds, he discovered that through skillful use of the pedals and other techniques, he could get a bigger sound from the instrument. Faced day after day with the simple harmonies of gospel music, Monk found a way to make those harmonies his own, to maintain the integrity of the songs without losing his identity in them. By the time he returned to New York in 1936, his style was unequivocably original.

The protean pianist Mary Lou Williams, who was living in Kansas City in the mid-30s, saw Monk at several after-hours jam sessions during his extended stay there. "He was one of the original modernists all right," she told *Melody Maker* in 1954, "playing pretty much the same harmonies then that he's playing now."[3] Other musicians who saw Monk in upstate New York during the same period have recalled him playing in the traditional stride style, but he may have been acceding to the demands of a paying gig. Williams's recollections indicate that Monk's thinking was already in advance of the mainstream four or five years before Minton's.

During his years with the evangelist or very soon after, Monk began writing music in earnest. He probably wrote his famous composition, "'Round Midnight," in those years. He definitely wrote such cornerstones of his repertoire as "Well, You Needn't" and "Ruby, My Dear." The inspiration for the latter piece, one of his most beautiful ballads, was his sister's best friend, a dietician named Ruby Richardson, whom he met shortly after he returned to New York and who soon became his first serious girlfriend.

As often as not, the first people to hear Monk's new compositions were his brother and sister. Marion White enjoyed the opportunity to sample her brother's creativity; Thomas Monk, who was more interested in sports than music, offered a less receptive ear. "He'd tell me, 'Sit down and listen,'" says Thomas, bemused a half-century after the fact by his own indifference to his brother's budding genius. "And I had to sit there and listen to him play these songs. He'd ask me, 'How's that sound?' and I'd say, 'That sounds all right.' But I didn't know. I wasn't musically inclined. In order for me to get away, I

3. Excerpts from the *Melody Maker* articles are reprinted beginning on p. 11.

had to say, 'Oh, that sounds nice!' Otherwise I'd have to sit there and listen to him play."

Four years elapsed between the time Monk returned from the road and the start of the epochal Minton's engagement. During those years he paid his share of dues. His early professional experience in New York included, as he later told a friend, jobs backing up singers "who sing all kinds of songs and fuck up and blame it on the musicians," as well as at least one brief stint with a polka band.

At Minton's, where Monk had the opportunity to interact with such kindred musical spirits as Kenny Clarke, Charlie Christian, and Dizzy Gillespie, the ideas he was developing began to bear fruit. When he performed on 52nd Street in a group led by Clarke two years later, *Down Beat*, the jazz musician's bible, first mentioned his name—sort of: the magazine referred to him as "The Lonius Monk." Not until two years after that did he enter a recording studio for the first time, as a sideman with Coleman Hawkins. But it wasn't in Monk's nature to be impatient. As he told Grover Sales in 1959, he had always been content to play his music his way and let the public catch up to him, "even if it does take them 15, 20 years," which, of course, it did.[4]

2. *Then Came Zombie Music and The Mad Monk*

Mary Lou Williams, perhaps the most accomplished female jazz musician of the 1930s and 1940s, had a long and varied career, beginning with Andy Kirk's Clouds of Joy and ending as a respected educator. Her account of meeting Monk in Kansas City in the 1930s is probably the most well-known description of Monk from the period, and has often been used by Monk's advocates to prove that he was capable of employing a more conventional and recognizably virtuosic piano technique, but that he simply chose not to. At the time, Williams was pianist and chief arranger with Andy Kirk's Clouds of Joy, which was based in Kansas City. She eventually resigned and started up her own band in New York, in addition to brief stints arranging for Duke

4. See Grover Sales' article on p. 100. *Ed.*

Ellington and Dizzy Gillespie. Her association with the beboppers is described in the second excerpt reprinted here.

This originally appeared as part of a multipart series on Mary Lou Williams' life in *Melody Maker,* as "Then Came Zombie Music" (May 8, 1954, p. 11) and "The Mad Monk" (May 22, 1954, p. 11), by Max Jones. Portions also appeared in *Hear Me Talkin' to Ya: The Story of Jazz as Told by the Men Who Made It* (Rhinehart and Company) in 1955 and Max Jones' *Talking Jazz* (Basingstoke: Macmillan) in 1987. Used with cooperation from *Melody Maker.*

Excerpt from "Then Came Zombie Music"

Thelonious, still in his teens, came into town with either an evangelist or a medicine show—I forget which.

While Monk was in Kaycee [Kansas City] he jammed every night; really used to blow on piano, employing a lot more technique than he does today. Monk plays the way he does now because he got fed up. Whatever people may tell you, I *know* how Monk can play.

He felt that musicians should play something new, and started doing it. Most of us admire him for this.

He was one of the original modernists all right, playing pretty much the same harmonies then that he's playing now. Only in those days we called it "Zombie music" and reserved it mostly for musicians after hours.

Why "Zombie music?" Because the screwy chords reminded us of music from "Frankenstein" or any horror film.

Excerpt from "The Mad Monk"

Now I want to write what I know about how and why bop got started. Monk and some of the cleverest of the young musicians used to complain: "We'll never get credit for what we're doing." They had reason to say it.

In the music business the going is tough for original talent. Everybody is being exploited through paid-for publicity and most anybody can become a great name if he can afford enough of it. In the end the public believes what it reads. So it is often difficult for the real talent to break through.

Anyway, Monk said: "We're going to get a big band started. We're going to create something they can't steal, because they can't play it."

There were more than a dozen people interested in the idea and the band began rehearsing in a basement somewhere. Monk was writing arrangements and Bud Powell and maybe Milt Jackson. Everyone contributed towards the arrangements, and some of them were real tough. Even those guys couldn't always get them right.

It was the usual story. The guys got hungry, so they had to go to work with different bands. Monk got himself a job at Minton's—the house that built bop—and after work the cats fell in to jam, and pretty soon you couldn't get in Minton's for musicians and instruments.

Minton's Playhouse was not a large place, but it was nice and intimate. The bar was at the front, and the cabaret was in the back. The bandstand was situated at the rear of the back room, where the wall was covered with strange paintings depicting weird characters sitting on a brass bed, or jamming, or talking to chicks.

During the daytime, people played the jukebox and danced. I used to call in often and got many laughs. It is amazing how happy those characters were—jiving, dancing, and drinking. It seemed everybody was talking at the same time; the noise was terrific. Even the kids playing out on the sidewalk danced when they heard the records.

That's how we were then—one big family on West 118th Street. Minton's was a room next door to the Cecil Hotel, and it was run by Teddy Hill, the one-time band leader who did quite well in Europe and who now managed for Minton.

Henry Minton must have been a man about fifty, who at one time played saxophone and at another owned the famous Rhythm Club, where Louis, Fats, James P., Earl Hines, and other big names filled the sessions. He had also been a musician's union official at Local 802.

He believed in keeping the place up and was constantly redecorating. And the food was good. Lindsay Steele had the kitchen at one time. He cooked wonderful meals and was a good mixer, who could sing a while during intermission.

When Monk first played at Minton's there were few musicians who could run changes with him. Charlie Christian, Kenny Clarke, Idrees Sulieman, and a couple more were the only ones who could play along with Monk then. Charlie and I used to go to the basement of the hotel where I lived and play and write all night long. I still have the music of a song he started but never completed.

Sometime in 1943 I had an offer to go into Café Society Downtown. I accepted, though fearing I might be shaky on solo piano since I had been so long with Andy Kirk's band and my own combo.

. . . During this period Monk and the kids would come to my apartment every morning around 4 or pick me up at the café after I'd finished my last show and we'd play and swap ideas until noon or later.

Monk, Tadd Dameron, Kenny Dorham, Bud Powell, Aaron Bridges, Bill Strayhorn, plus various disc jockeys and newspapermen would be in and out of my place at all hours, and we'd really ball.

When Monk wrote a new song he customarily played it night and day for weeks unless you stopped him. That, he said, was the only way to find out if it was going to be any good. "Either it grew on [you] or it didn't."

. . . So the boppers worked out a music that was hard to steal. I'll say this for the "leeches," though: they tried. I've seen them in Minton's busily writing on their shirt cuffs or scribbling on the tablecloth. And even our own guys, I'm afraid, did not give Monk the credit he had coming. Why, they even stole his idea of the beret and bop glasses.

I happened to run into Thelonious standing next door to the 802 Union building on Sixth Avenue, where I was going to pay my dues. He was looking at some heavy-framed sun-glasses in a shop window, and said he was going to have a pair made similar to a pair of ladies' glasses he had seen and liked.

He suggested a few improvements in the design, and I remember laughing at him. But he had them made in the Bronx, and several days later came to the house with his new glasses and, of course, a beret. He had been wearing a beret, with a small piano clip on it, for some years previous to this. Now he started wearing the glasses and beret and the others copied him.

3. *Hotbox: Thelonious Monk in the '40s*

George Hoefer first featured Monk in his regular "The Hot Box" column in *Down Beat* in 1948 when the Blue Note 78s were released, beginning with the opening lines: "Thelonious Sphere Monk is one of the most fabulous characters in jazz. You've seen his counterpart [Dizzy Gillespie], the goateed cat with the beret and massive gold rimmed glasses on 52nd Street for the past six years but chances are rare that you've seen the Monk himself."[1] The article goes on to repeat a few of the stories about Monk's lifestyle and particulars of the Blue Note releases. In the article reprinted below, Hoefer elaborates on how Columbia University student Jerry Newman, the owner of a portable disc recorder, ended up documenting one of the most creative and legendary

1. George Hoefer, "The Hot Box: Pianist Monk Getting Long Awaited Break," *Down Beat*, February 11, 1948, p. 11.

musical interactions in the history of jazz—the Minton's sessions. Monk was present on 22 takes, and though his playing is not well represented on the recordings it is the only aural evidence we have of what transpired at Minton's.[2] In addition to *Down Beat,* Hoefer wrote about jazz for *Esquire, Metronome, and Melody Maker.*

This article originally appeared as "Hotbox: Thelonious Monk in the '40s," George Hoefer, *Down Beat,* October 25, 1962, pp. 43–44. Reprinted with permission of *Down Beat.*

Thelonious Sphere Monk's weird individualism tended to defer attention to his artistry for 15 years. When he began to receive notice around 1956, his characteristic isolation was turned around to enhance his image as a jazz genius. As a composer and pianist, he is now accepted as one of the great innovators of modern jazz.

Monk's musical story started at Minton's Playhouse in October, 1940, when former bandleader-tenor saxophonist Teddy Hill installed a house band made up of Joe Guy, trumpet; Monk, piano; Nick Fenton, bass; Kenny Clarke, drums. Guy was the front man, but when clearance was sought to release some amateur recordings made on the spot, it was decided that Guy and Clarke had been co-leaders, the drummer taking credit for music direction.

Minton's in Harlem was noisy, informal, a neighborhood meeting place for night people. It had poor lighting and a run-down appearance (it is still open today, but the room has been renovated and modernized). There was a long bar in front, and a former dining room of the Hotel Cecil, located back of the bar, served as a cabaret. A raised bandstand, placed flush against a side wall, was midway between the Gents and Ladies signs, accounting for the frequency of the sound of slamming doors on some of the recordings made at Minton's.

On weeknights most of the crowd congregated at the bar, but on weekends the couples moved back to the tables, which carried a 50-cent cover charge, in order to dance to the music. No one sat and listened much, except on rare occasions when someone like Helen Humes sang a number with the band. This held true, too, on Monday nights, off-time for musicians, when the sitters-in were Charlie Christian, Dizzy Gillespie, Roy Eldridge, Don Byas, Hot Lips Page, and others.

2. This figure is taken from Dutch discographer Fred Canté's *Monk on Records*, 2nd Ed. (Amsterdam: Fred Canté, 1985), perhaps the most authoritative discography of Monk's recordings available in print.

There was usually a catch-as-catch-can floor show, featuring such entertainers as singer Duke Groner and dancer Baby Lawrence.

Groner brought in a 23-year-old Columbia University student named Jerry Newman one night. Newman, an enthusiastic jazz fan, as well as an amateur recorder, had worked up a little act for himself. He took off the air, and put on acetate, the famous radio voices of Bob Hope and Franklin D. Roosevelt, among others. He would set up his equipment on the bandstand and play his records while "lipping" the words, presenting something new that gained for him a regular spot on the show. His compensation consisted of the privilege of making recordings. Sometimes he made a disc for whoever wanted to hear himself on records. This brought him a slight return over the cost of a 7-cent paper disc. His equipment consisted of a Federal portable recording unit and two stand-by mikes.

Newman became a regular at Minton's. He recalls today, "I was the only ofay around there, except for a few white jazz musicians, and I don't recall seeing any of the jazz writers up there." Guitarist Christian also became a nightly guest after finishing his stint with the Benny Goodman Band downtown.

Christian's playing and Newman's recording machine attracted musicians from all over town, and on some nights there were as many as 18 instrumentalists trying to get their improvisations on Newman's aluminum-based acetates. This state of affairs did not please the regulars. Trumpeter Gillespie has told how he would join pianist Monk in the basement to work out weird harmonies to frustrate and discourage the over-eager musicians. Newman remembers that the only non-regular sideman he ever saw getting the instructions on the changes was alto saxophonist Jimmy Hamilton.

Newman's impressions of Monk at the time were as follows: "He was an exciting player—the released sides don't come anywhere near indicating how good he was in those days—and he was always working on new ideas. He would get an idea, and before he had a chance to try it out, he would have four or five others. There was one half-hour version of 'I Surrender Dear' that Monk made with tenor saxophonist Herbie Fields that he wore out playing back during intermissions. He'd say, 'it's pretty good, and that tenor boy really goes.' I still have it, but it can never be issued on account of its condition, plus the fact I ruined it by playing trombone on it." (Newman was a trombonist in a marching band at Columbia.)

Monk was always practicing; when Newman went up to Minton's in the afternoon to check over his gear, he would see Monk seated alone at the piano, playing for all he was worth. Manager Hill would have to run Monk away from the piano when it came time to close.

The usual format was a free-wheeling jam session where the participants improvised on famous jazz standards such as "Stompin' at the Savoy." The tune titles on the released three tracks of the Eddie Durham-Edgar Battle tune "Topsy" were labeled "Charlie's Choice" by Bill Simon when the Vox 78-rpm album came out in 1947. When Newman put the same sides out on LP in 1953, he called them "Swing to Bop." Since the versions on Newman's records were based only on the chords of the standards, they were not required to pay royalties unless the original titles were used.[3] Actually there is not a great deal of Monk's playing, other than comping on the released sides, for they were selected to showcase Christian's guitar.

The jazz galas at Minton's came to an end with the advent of wartime conditions in December, 1941, although Monk continued to work there, with his own groups, intermittently until 1948. A noteworthy interval came when the pianist had drummer Art Blakey in his group around 1947–48.

After Newman's home-recording sessions at Minton's, Monk didn't play for records again until October, 1944, when he made four sides with the Coleman Hawkins Quartet while a member of Hawkins 52nd St. small combo.

At this time he was unknown and unappreciated. His name was printed in *Down Beat* as "Delonius Monk," and Hawkins recalls that musicians would come up to him and say, "Why don't you get yourself a piano player. What is that guy you've got trying to do?"[4]

The bop scene was passing him by, and the stars of the bop revolution on 52nd St. were the trumpeters and the saxophonists. As Barry Ulanov pointed out in his *History of Jazz* [*sic*], "The piano was used in bop chiefly as an accompanying instrument: it had little place in a music which was essentially a one-line expression, played by a single-line solo instrument or several in unison."[5]

In an interview with *Down Beat* in 1947 Monk, who was miffed at all the credit and attention given to Gillespie and Charlie Parker (Newman said that he never saw Parker at Minton's, though he did hear him at Monroe's and turned off his machine because he disliked Parker's tone), said, "Bebop wasn't developed in any deliberate way. For my part I'll say it was just the style of music I happened to play. I think all styles are built around the piano developments. The piano lays the chord and rhythm foundations."[6]

3. Whether or not royalties were paid, the tunes were released with their original titles on the LP reissues in the 1950s and again in the 1970s. *Ed.*
4. The misprint actually read "The Lonius Monk." See Peter Keepnews's article, reprinted on p. 4. *Ed.*
5. Barry Ulanov, *A History of Jazz in America* (New York: Viking Press, 1952). *Ed.*
6. The interview is reprinted on p. 22. *Ed.*

When his first Blue Note records were released in 1948, Monk told George Simon, "Unless bop is planned and organized, it turns out to be like Dixieland with everybody blowing for themselves. Too many guys don't know what they're doin'!"

Monk's final summation to Simon was, "I don't think I actually play bop the way it's being performed today. My style is more original."[7]

4. *To Be, or Not . . . to Bop*

Dizzy Gillespie's multivaried and lengthy career as a jazz musician provided a rich source for his memoirs, resulting in outstanding firsthand documentation of various significant events in the history of jazz. The book *To Be, or Not . . . to Bop,* compiled by Al Fraser, not only presents Gillespie's story as autobiography, but draws from over 150 interviews with other musicians and individuals in the music business who offer their own versions of events. Here, Gillespie recounts his time with Monk at Minton's, located on West 118th Street in Manhattan, which became known as "the house that built bop" during the 1940s. Former bandleader Teddy Hill became manager in 1940 and instituted a policy of Monday night open jam sessions with a house band consisting of Thelonious Monk and Kenny Clarke. The place became a mecca for musicians wanting to try out new ideas, with jazz luminaries such as Charlie Christian, Lester Young, Roy Eldridge, Coleman Hawkins (who had just returned from spending several years in Europe) and others dropping by regularly. Dizzy Gillespie, Kenny Clarke, Charlie Christian and Monk were instrumental in developing the new music at Minton's. Christian would come uptown after his job with Benny Goodman and jam until the early hours of the morning. Charlie Parker would be playing at Monroe's Uptown House about a year later and eventually join the revolution. Gillespie later teamed up with Parker and brought the new style to a larger audience, more or less leaving Monk behind. The excerpt reprinted here recounts Gillespie's version of Monk's role in the Minton's sessions, with a brief interlude with comments on how Monk viewed Gillespie.

7. George Simon's article is reprinted on p. 53. *Ed.*

In those days we had several means of access to experience: big bands were one, jam sessions were another. I tried to get plenty of both. Musical happenings at that time were an excellent reason to want to stay around New York. Amongst musicians when I came up, we had a very close feeling of camaraderie. We were all trumpet players together—Charlie Shavers, Benny Harris, Bobby Moore, and I—and we were unified socially; not just trumpet players, other musicians too. We traded off ideas not only on the bandstand but in the jam sessions. We had to be as sensitive to each other as brothers in order to express ourselves completely, maintain our individuality, yet play as one. Jam sessions, such as those wonderfully exciting ones held at Minton's Playhouse were seedbeds for our new, modern style of music.

Monk'd be asleep on the piano. To wake him up, I'd mash the quick of his finger and wake him up right quick. He'd say, "What the fuck're you doing, muthafucka!" He'd wake up and go into his thing.

I first met Monk during the early days, 1937 and 1938. Monk used to be with Cootie Williams up at the Savoy, and then, in 1939, he got the gig down at Minton's.[1] I learned a lot from Monk. It's strange with Monk. Our influence on one another's music is so closely related that Monk doesn't actually know what I showed him. But I do know some of the things that he showed me. Like, the minor-sixth chord with a sixth in the bass. I first heard Monk play that. It's demonstrated in some of my music like the melody of "Woody 'n You," the introduction to "Round Midnight," and a part of the bridge to "Manteca."

* * *

There were lots of places where I used that progression that Monk showed me. You see, I give people credit; I don't try to take nothing from nobody. If I get something from someone, and I expand on it, I give them credit for it.

Now in my ending of "I Can't Get Started," there's an expansion of a minor-sixth chord going to the first chord of the ending of that song and also to the introduction of "'Round Midnight." It's the same progression. Those are two of my most well-known solos on ballads, and the first time I heard

1. More likely Monk began in 1940, since Teddy Hill, who was responsible for setting up the Monday night jam sessions, did not become manager at Minton's until then. *Ed.*

that, Monk showed it to me, and he called it a minor-sixth chord with a sixth in the bass. Nowadays, they don't call it that. They call the sixth in the bass, the tonic, and the chord a C-minor seventh, flat five. What Monk called an E-flat-minor sixth chord with a sixth in the bass, the guys nowadays call a C-minor seventh flat five. C is the sixth note of an E-flat chord—the sixth in the bass—the bass plays that note. They call that a C-minor seventh flat five, because an E-flat-minor chord is E-flat, G-flat, and B-flat. So they're exactly the same thing. An E-flat-minor chord with a sixth in the bass is C, E-flat, G-flat, and B-flat. C-minor seventh flat five is the same thing, C, E-flat, G-flat, and B-flat. Some people call it a half diminished, sometimes.

So now, I extended that into a whole series of chords. B minor, E seventh, B-flat minor seventh, E-flat seventh, A minor seventh, D seventh, A-flat minor seventh, D-flat seventh, and into C. We'd do that kind in 1942 around Minton's a lot.[2] We'd been doing that kind of thing, Monk and I, but it was never documented because no records were being made at the time. There was a recording ban.

The union wanted a trust fund for the musicians and wanted the record companies to pay for it, but they refused to pay. So the union stopped us from making recordings.[3] I don't think it was a question of stopping the new style of music from coming out. They just wanted some benefits for the musicians. It was a good move for the musicians trying to get some of the money that was being made by these people who were making records. The recording ban lasted three or four years, I think 1942, 1943, and 1944. I was recording again by 1945.

The only reason some of the new things we were doing musically were never documented is because there were no records made at the time to show what we were doing. So later, when I recorded "I Can't Get Started," I didn't play the regular progressions. I went E seventh to E-flat seventh, D seventh to D-flat seventh, to C. And then we'd do the flatted fifths inside of that. Tadd Dameron used to do those kinds of things too.

I asked Monk one time, "Hey, man, show me something that you learned from me that you used countless times in other works."

2. It was more likely in 1940 or 1941. *Ed.*

3. The recording ban only lasted two years, with different record companies settling with the union at different times, with Victor and Columbia at the end of 1944. See Scott DeVeaux's article "Bebop and the Recording Industry: The 1942 AFM Recording Ban Reconsidered" (*Journal of the American Musicological Society*, Vol. 41, No. 1, pp. 126–165) for further discussion of this topic. *Ed.*

Monk said, "A Night in Tunisia."

"Not a tune." I said, "I'm talking about progressions." Then I showed him what I'd learned from him the first time, that one particular thing that opened up a whole new trail for me. But he couldn't remember one particular thing that he'd heard me do. I was always a piano player, so I was always finding things on the piano and showing them to the guys. I'd show Monk. And I know that there are hundreds of things, because we used to get together. I'd say, "Look, here . . . " and show him something. But Monk is the most unique musician of our crowd. He was the one least affected by any other musician, unless he's affected by piano players like James P. Johnson and Fats Waller or Duke Ellington. I never heard him play like Teddy Wilson. I never heard him play like that. When I heard him play, he was playing like Monk, like nobody else.

Also, by that time, I was getting my chops together. And Roy used to come by Minton's. Roy is the most competitive musician. Roy used to just shower trumpet players with chops and speed. I'll never forget the time, the first time, Roy heard me make an altissimo B-flat. Boy, his eyes went up. I always had my speed, but didn't have too much chops. But I was getting them together at that time. One time, we were playing "Sweet Georgia Brown," in A-flat. I played about two choruses and hit a high B-flat, Roy looked!

"Look, you're supposed to be the greatest trumpet player in the world," Monk used to tell him, "but that's the best." And he'd point at me. Monk will tell you that. Ha! Ha! "You're supposed to be the greatest trumpet player in the world," Monk said, "but that guy is. He'll eat you up." Monk'll tell anybody. He'd tell Coleman Hawkins. Anybody. Monk would tell anybody how he feels about his playing. Monk'll tell you the truth, whatever he thinks about it. He's not diplomatic at all.

THELONIOUS SPHERE MONK (piano):
"I first met him at the Rhythm Club."

How did he sound when you first heard him?
"He sounded good."

Was it different from what you'd been used to hearing?
"Yes, I mean it sounded original."

Did you hear anything of his that you especially liked?
"I heard a lotta things."

Which things?
"Well, I don't know all his tunes, so I can't say which one I like the best."

If there's any great contribution that you think Dizzy's made to our music, what do you think that contribution would be?
"I mean that is hard to answer. That's hard to say, you know."

Are there any incidents you can recall, let's say from the days at Minton's or the Savoy when something Dizzy did or said to you struck you as particularly unique, that really knocked you out?
"I don't know what you mean when you say 'knocked you out.' Well, he was amusing to the people on the stage."

What do you like most about him as a person?
"His musicianship. That's what."

5. *Thelonious Monk—Genius of Bop: Elusive Pianist Finally Caught in an Interview*

The first article devoted to Monk was based on a sketchy interview with Monk and Teddy Hill at Minton's. It was written by writer-photographer Bill Gottlieb, who worked for *Down Beat* magazine in the late 1940s, and who later became renowned for his classic black-and-white portraits of jazz musicians. The article appeared about one month before Monk recorded his first sides for Blue Note. Most of the information seems to come from Teddy Hill, the ex-bandleader who managed Minton's beginning in 1940. Hill instituted the Monday night jam session policy that spawned the experiments leading to the development of bebop. The article captures some of the myths propagated during the six-year period in which Monk had limited exposure to the public, but during which bebop became known through Charlie Parker and Dizzy Gillespie. The last few paragraphs of the article inexplicably change to a description of Gillespie.

This article originally appeared as "Thelonious Monk—Genius of Bop: Elusive Pianist Finally Caught in an Interview," Bill Gottlieb, in *Down Beat*, September 24, 1947, p. 2. Reprinted with permission of *Down Beat*.

New York—I have interviewed Thelonious Sphere Monk. It's not like having seen Pinetop spit blood or delivering the message to Garcia. But, on the other hand, it's at least equal to a scoop on the true identity of Benny Benzedrine or on who killed Cock Robin.

Thelonious, the George Washington of be-bop, is one elusive gent. There's been much talk about him—about his pioneering role at Minton's, where Bebop began . . . about his fantastic musical imagination . . . about his fine piano playing. But few have ever seen him; except for people like Diz and Mary Lou, I didn't know anyone else who had seen very much of him, either.

Come to think of it, I had seen him once, at the club where Dizzy's band was working some time ago. Even without his music, which was wonderful, you could recognize his cult from his be-bop uniform: goatee, beret and heavy shell glasses, only his were done half in gold.

I listened in fascination until he got up from the keyboard. "And who," I finally inquired, "was that bundle of bop?"

"Why, Thelonious Monk."

But by that time the quarry had disappeared.

Meeting Is Arranged

Finally, through the good offices of Mary Lou Williams, I was arranged with Thelonious. In order to take some pictures in the right setting, we went up to Minton's Playhouse at 208 West 118th St.[1]

In the taxi, on the way up, Thelonious spoke with singular modesty. He wouldn't go on record as insisting HE started be-bop; but, as the story books have long since related, he admitted he was at least one of the originators. Yes, he continued, verifying the oft told tale, it all began up at Minton's in early 1941.

Orchestra leader Teddy Hill had broken up his great orchestra because of problems brought on by the draft, poor transportation facilities and the like. He had bought into the tavern owned by Morris Milton (who had been the first colored delegate to the New York local of the musicians' union). Teddy eventually took over active management and instituted a policy of good music.

1. Other sources quote the address as being 210 West 118th St. See *New Grove Dictionary of Jazz*, p. 898. *Ed.*

Guys in Band

As a starter, Teddy called together some of the boys who had played in his last band, including John Birks Gillespie (by then with Calloway), and Joe Guy, trumpets, and Kenny Clarke, drums. There was also Nick Fenton on bass. Monday night was the big night at Minton's. Bandleaders like Goodman, Dorsey and Johnny Long would come in to visit. And practically every jazz man of merit in town sat in at one time or other. Charlie Parker, who had come to New York with the Jay McShann ork [orchestra], appeared often and became a regular at Minton's.

"Be-bop wasn't developed in any deliberate way," continued Thelonious. "For my part, I'll say it was just the style of music I happened to play. We all contributed ideas, the men you know plus a fellow called Vic Coulson, who had been with Parker and Al Hibbler in the McShann band. Vic had a lot to do with our way of phrasing.[2]

Piano Focal Point

"If my own work had more importance than any others, it's because the piano is the key instrument in music. I think all styles are built around piano developments. The piano lays the chord foundation and the rhythm foundation, too. Along with bass and piano, I was always at the spot, and could keep working on the music. The rest, like Diz and Charlie, came in only from time to time, at first."

By the time we'd gotten that far, we had arrived at Minton's where Thelonious headed right for the piano. Roy Eldridge, Teddy Hill and Howard McGhee dropped around.[3] McGhee, fascinated, got Thelonious to dream up some trumpet passages and then conned Thelonious into writing them down on some score sheets that happened to be in the club.

2. The pianist Al Tinney recounts the Minton's days in Ira Gitler's *Swing to Bop: An Oral History of the Transition in Jazz in the 1940s* (New York: Oxford, 1985, p. 79): "Victor was a cornet player, a cornetist. He played beautifully, and in fact, he took the band over after I left Monroe's Uptown House. Very dapper little guy. When I saw him a few years later when I got out of the Army, I couldn't believe it. He had become a wino. . . . Did you hear Fats Navarro? That was Victor Coulson before Fats Navarro." *Ed.*

3. This meeting resulted in the famous photograph that Gottlieb took of the four musicians standing in front of Minton's. The photo accompanied the article and has since been reproduced in numerous books on jazz. *Ed.*

Hill Gives Credit

Teddy Hill began to talk. Looking at Thelonious Monk, he said:

"There, my good man, is the guy who deserves the most credit for starting be-bop. Though he won't admit it, I think he feels he got a bum break in not getting some of the glory that went to others. Rather than go out now and have people think he's just an imitator, Thelonious is thinking up new things. I believe he hopes one day to come out with something as far ahead of bop as bop is ahead of the music that went before it."

"He's so absorbed in his task he's become almost mysterious. Maybe he's on the way to meet you. An idea comes to him. He begins to work on it. Mop! Two days go by and he's still at it. He's forgotten all about you and everything else but that idea."

While he was at it, Teddy told me about Diz, who worked in his band following Roy Eldridge. Right off, John Birks G. showed up at rehearsal and began to play in an overcoat, hat and gloves! For a while, everyone was set against this wild maniac. Teddy nicknamed him Dizzy.

Dizzy Like a Fox

"But he was Dizzy like a fox. When I took my band to Europe, some of the guys threatened not to go if the frantic one went, too. But it developed that youthful Dizzy, with all his eccentricities and practical jokes, was the most stable man of the group. He had unusually clean habits and was able to save so much money that he encouraged the others to borrow from him so that he'd have an income in case things got rough back in the states!"

Blue Note

Monk's signing with Blue Note in 1947, a result of tenor saxophonist Ike Quebec's role as A&R man, proved to be good timing, as he had been building a repertory of compositions and had fully developed his characteristic style of playing. His only previous recording date had been with the Coleman Hawkins Quartet in 1944, in which he played on four tunes.[1] Between 1947 and 1952, Monk recorded 23 of his own compositions for Blue Note, more than a quarter of his total output as a composer.[2] According to Lorraine Gordon, wife and colleague of company founder Alfred Lion, "He had so much original music built up inside of him that it just came bursting out of him."[3] Michael Cuscuna describes how the press releases accompanying the first 78s capitalized on the image that was being propagated by writers at the time: the "high priest" and "genius" labels, and the claim that Monk invented bebop, something that likely may have

1. Monk appears as pianist on four takes, recorded October 19, 1944. The only other extant recordings of Monk between the Hawkins date and the first Blue Note recording in 1947 are broadcast recordings from the Spotlite Club with Dizzy Gillespie's Big Band in 1946.
2. There has been some debate about the number of compositions attributed to Monk. Research published by Ponzio and Postif (*Blue Monk: Un portrait de Thelonious,* Paris: Actes Sud, 1995) indicates Monk wrote 81 compositions and Leslie Gourse states that 91 compositions are registered with BMI (*Straight, No Chaser: The Life and Genius of Thelonious Monk,* New York: Schirmer, 1997). In Monk's recorded work, there are about 75 titles that can be attributed to him, depending on how you count improvisations such as "Functional" and "Chordially" or explicitly stated arrangements such as "Japanese Folk Song."
3. Quoted in Michael Cuscuna, Liner notes to *The Complete Blue Note Recordings of Thelonious Monk,* Mosaic MR 4101 (1983), p. 3.

had an adverse effect in some critical circles.[4] The reviews in *Down Beat, Metronome,* and *Billboard*—reprinted here—bear this out, one reviewer even going so far as to say "Two more sides by the pianist who did NOT invent bop, and generally plays bad, though interesting, piano."[5] In hindsight, the reviews by Paul Bacon in the *Record Changer* were visionary.

6. *Early Reviews*

Reviews from The Record Changer

The *Record Changer* was a small and independent magazine owned and managed by Bill Grauer and Orrin Keepnews, former classmates at Columbia University who transformed the traditional jazz oriented publication into a progressive voice. Paul Bacon, a graphic artist who went on to become a leading book-jacket designer, wrote for the magazine during the late 1940s in addition to designing album covers for many of Monk's recordings for Riverside in the 1950s. In defiance of commonly held opinions about Monk and his music, Bacon speaks glowingly of Monk's music, illustrating his ideas with original analogies about what makes Monk's music so different.

From the *Record Changer*, Vol. 7, No. 5 (May 1948), p. 18

'Round About Midnight

Well, You Needn't

It's useless to pick out special bits of rare value in this record, and describe them at length. This is a remarkable thing.

4. Michael Cuscuna, Liner notes to *The Complete Blue Note Recordings of Thelonious Monk* (Mosaic MR 4101, 1983), p. 4. He quotes the release as saying that they "actually found the person who was responsible for this whole movement—and we have had the privilege of being the first to put his radical and unorthodox ideas on wax—is an unusual and mysterious character with the more unusual name of Thelonious Monk. Among musicians, Thelonious' name is treated with respect and awe, for he is a strange person whose pianistics continue to baffle all who hear him." The early profile pieces are reprinted beginning on p. 41.
5. Although George Hoefer's weekly column featured Monk in a favorable light prior to these reviews. See "The Hot Box: Pianist Monk Getting Long Awaited Break," *Down Beat*, February 11, 1948, p. 11.

Monk may well be the man to finally straighten people out in the matter of modern informal music, besides having had a great deal to do with its present direction. His kind of playing isn't something that occurred to him whole—beyond its undoubted originality, it has the most tremendously expressive and personal feeling I can find in any musician playing now. It has cost Monk something to play as he does—not recognition so much, because he's always had that from the people he wanted to find it in; jobs and money, certainly, although his personality has had a little to do with that (he is best described as a dour pixie); and still more: I believe his style and approach cost him 50 per cent of his technique. He relies so much on absolute musical reflex that Horowitz's skill might be unequal to the job.

That isn't to say that the music is formless. Taken as a whole, it has a very satisfying feeling of solidity. And Monk has a beat like the ocean waves—no matter how sudden, spasmodic, or obscure his little inventions, he rocks irresistibly on.

What he has done, in part, is quite simple. He hasn't invented a new scheme of things, but he has, for years, too, looked with an unjaundiced eye at music and seen a little something else. He plays riffs that are older than Bunk Johnson—but they don't sound the same; his beat is familiar but he does something strange there, too—he can make a rhythm seem almost separate, so that what he does is inside it, or outside it. He may play for a space in nothing but smooth phrases and then suddenly jump on a part and repeat it with an intensity beyond description. His left hand is not constant—it wanders shrewdly around, sometimes playing only a couple of notes, sometimes powerfully on the beat, usually increasing it in variety, and occasionally silent.

At any rate Monk is really making use of all the unused space around jazz, and he makes you feel that there are plenty of unopened doors.

As to the record, "Midnight" is a beautiful melody, played with great feeling and charm. The band is for background only, setting the stage for Monk, and the background is good. The trumpet and alto switch parts now and then for variance in sound. Dizzy recorded this tune for Dial a while ago, but there isn't much comparison.

"Well, You Needn't" is an intriguing number, with Gene Ramey on bass and Art Blakey on drums. Blakey deserves a column of his own—he can steal a record with his drumming—and if I may quote Ike Quebec, "other drummers say 'thump'—Art says 'POW.'"

From the *Record Changer,* Vol. 7, No. 11 (Nov. 1948), p. 19

Epistrophy
In Walked Bud

Although I am a firm believer in graceful writing, and in *le mot juste,* and in picturesque speech, and whatnot, a lot of rhetoric can be dispensed with by calling this record, simply, a bitch. It is, too. I'm no longer surprised by anything Monk does, because I'm just as firm a believer in him as I am in the virtues described above. However, blind faith is enhanced by an occasional miracle, as any snake-oil salesman will testify, and "Epistrophy" is that refreshing.

By some quirk, I always think of Monk as a carpenter, lustily doing everything wrong, battling his materials, and coming up with the most uniquely beautiful houses in the world. For one thing, he looks as if he were making something when he plays, sometimes scowling at the keyboard as if wondering where to drive the next nail.

The side in question has one of the most fascinating beginnings I know of—four distinct rhythms, by piano, vibraphone, bass and drums (Monk, Milt Jackson, John Simmons, and Shadow Wilson, respectively), which build up a remarkable suspense that lasts for the whole three minutes. Jackson, a highly gifted musician, plays with Monk as if he could read his mind, and they get tasty help from the others on this lilting tune, which was written some time ago by Monk and Kenny Clarke. Monk's backing of Jackson is really something to hear, and there is a richness in all the unison work.

The difference between Monk's approach and anyone else's is felt even on a band side, like "In Walked Bud," another of his piquant compositions. The sound isn't so intensely personal, of course, although Monk himself sometimes does more interesting things in his solo spots in a band than he does with a trio or quartet, but the men who play with him conspicuously avoid the bop cliches, a most fortunate condition. Art Blakey's exemplary drumming sticks out, as usual. He always provides something I've never heard before; in this case it's a piece of cymbal work at the opening of Monk's solo—sounds like it might be the doorbell to an opium rathskeller.

George Taitt plays a lyrical trumpet, with a strange tone supplemented by Edmond Gregory's bawdy alto, and the two handle the ensembles beautifully always with matchless backgrounds provided by Monk and Blakey.

I would say that anyone really curious about the new sound in music need look no farther than "Epistrophy."

From the *Record Changer,* Vol. 8, No. 4 (April 1949), p. 23

Ruby, My Dear
Evidence

"Ruby, My Dear" was written years ago, for Ruby, I guess, who is singularly honored by the gesture. It's a beautiful tonepoem, played with great feeling and color by the splendid trio of Monk, Gene Ramey and Art Blakey. Oddly enough, I can envision this played by one of the Alec Wilder groups, or even a larger lushly instrumented orchestra, although these guys do quite well enough for me.

"Evidence," with Milt Jackson, John Simmons and Shadow Wilson, is a cockeyed, delightful abstraction of "Just You, Just Me," with an irresistible beat and one of Monk's most rollicking solos. More happens on this side—musical free verse or something—with a lot of widely spaced, apparently divergent notes, a result of Monk's habit of thinking of things as a whole, instead of a bar here and a bridge there. A seemingly lost chord may hang in limbo for 12 bars, then suddenly fall into place, Chinese-lock style. I think it's the nuts.

Reviews from Down Beat

Reviewers for *Down Beat* were less understanding of Monk and questioned his piano technique and musical ideas on every count. Ironically, because of the rating system employed, the following reviews consistently rate Monk's music as "tepid," a description that seems antithetical to any feeling that Monk's music commonly evokes, whether positive or negative.

[For the *Down Beat* reviews that follow, the following legend is used:

**** Tops
*** Tasty
** Tepid
* Tedious]

From *Down Beat,* February 25, 1948, p.19

** *Thelonious*
** *Suburban Eyes*

Two sides by the piano player generally credited with having strongly influenced Gillespie and other boppers. "Thelonious" starts out as a piano sustained note with whole tone changes moving under it. Hines used to do things like this with different change patterns. On his own solo spots there seem to be points at which Monk is thinking about the stock returns or the 7th at Pimlico—anything but his piano. He also has several passages where he plays straight striding Waller piano. As a modernist, this can hardly be excused. All present-day piano players have right hands with eight fingers and a rigid claw on the left hand. "Eyes" presents an alto in clusters at an up tempo. From the Monk, we expect better.

From *Down Beat*, April 21, 1948, p. 19

** *Well, You Needn't*

** *'Round About Midnight*

The Monk is undoubtedly a man of considerable ability both technically and harmonically but his abstractions on these sides are just too too—and I played them early in the morning and late at night. "Needn't" doesn't require a Juilliard diploma to understand, but "Midnight" is for the super hip alone. Why they list the personnel on a side where the whole band plays like a vibratoless organ under the piano solo is a mystery.

From *Down Beat*, August 25, 1948, p. 13

** *Off Minor*

*** *Evonce*

The Monk alone with but rhythm tends to make the mind wander with his superprogress even though he does prove on the medium-tempoed "Minor" that he plays with a beat. "Evonce" adds the other three members of the sextet and is pretty choice bop with a groovy collection of ensemble riffs and well-done alto and trumpet choruses by Danny West and Idrees Sulieman.

From *Down Beat*, October 20, 1948, p. 13

** *Epistrophy*

*** *In Walked Bud*

"Epistrophy" (which Funk and Wagnalls spell with an "e" on the end) is a form of repetition in which phrases always end with the same word. Where they get the derivation however, is a mystery since, outside of the repetitive triplet figure that opens it up, there are no two companion notes alike in the whole side.

We have less and less patience with the far-fetched type of composition and inventiveness which are displayed by the much publicized Monk for a very simple reason. Nothing happens. "Bud" by the quintet is more of a straight bop riffer which attempts to make something happen, but the solos and arrangement are weak. "Epistrophy" is a quartet side with vibes and piano.

From *Down Beat*, March 25, 1949, p. 14

** *Evidence*

** *Ruby, My Dear*

"Evidence" is a quartet side wherein Monk shares the grooves with Milt Jackson's vibes. Neither solo is either interesting or exciting to us, though the Monk's whole-tone harmonies and off-cadence rhythm doubtless will appeal to the more atonally minded of the jazz gentry.

One thing you gotta admit—these boys are master mathematicians. How do they ever locate the beat after two or three out of the four are wandering off into their own rhythmic transgressions? "Ruby" is a trio side—all piano and all abstract.

From *Down Beat*, June 17, 1949, p. 14

* *Misterioso*

** *Humph*

Two more sides by the pianist who did NOT invent bop, and generally plays bad, though interesting, piano. "Misterioso" is built on the sort of ascending and descending seconds Ellington used to use all the time. Milt Jackson plays a good vibe solo, while Monk fingers around trying to get over the technical inadequacies of his own playing, plus getting lost in one arpeggio cliché variation on the old boogie seventh that takes him 15 seconds to get out of. Record closes with a double time statement of the original piano phrase while Monk punctuates it with single note drum riffs.[1] This is veritably faking a rather large order, and only Jackson and John Simmons' bassing [*sic*] redeem it. "Humph" has added alto, tenor, and trumpet, cannot be ruled among the more tremendous sides.

1. The melody is actually a sequence of sixths, although, as the sixths move in parallel through seconds, if you were focusing on the bottom or top line it might sound like seconds. The phrase about the double-time statement is also confusing, because there is no double-time playing on the recording. *Ed.*

Metronome *Review*

As with *Down Beat*, the reviewer for *Metronome* berates Monk's piano technique. It is worth mentioning that this is the only review of the Blue Note releases that Metronome published, perhaps indicating that they did not even consider him a significant artist.

From *Metronome*, April 1948, pp. 45–46.

Thelonious C

Suburban Eyes C+

"Thelonious," as the title might imply, is virtually all Thelonious. Parts of it are a perfect example of an ancient piano style which sounds like the forerunner of Fats Waller. Art Blakey's cymbal drumming is tasty. On "Eyes," a fast, clean, bop affair, the ball is carried to advantage by Idrees Sulieman's trumpet, Danny Quebec West's alto and Billy Smith's tenor. Monk's piano nullifies this capable trio's efforts. Ramey's bass and Blakey's drums are impressive.

Billboard *Reviews*

The *Billboard* one-liners are less critical and more humorous than *Down Beat* and *Metronome*. *Billboard* placed the reviews of Monk's recordings in the category "Hot Jazz," with other categories including "International," "Classical," and "Religious." Though Monk's recordings did not garner high marks, they were not far below any of the marks awarded to the other jazz recordings. There is a sense of respecting Monk, perhaps because of his history at Minton's, yet the tone is one of amusement.

[For the *Billboard* reviews, the ratings are an average of operator, dealer, and disc jockey ratings, with 90–100 as "tops," 80–89 as "excellent," 70–79 as "good," 40–69 as "satisfactory," and 0–39 as "poor."]

February 21, 1948, p.117

Thelonious (68)

Granddaddy of the beboppers, pianist Monk turns out a controversial jazz disking [*sic*] worked out on a one note riff.

Suburban Eyes (67)

More on the beaten bop track than the flip: a moving opus with alto, trumpet and Monk as solos.

April 3, 1948, p. 124

Well, You Needn't (56)

Interesting bop stuff by the granddaddy of the bopsters.

'Round About Midnight (61)

Pretty Monk work which may have come off better if the tootlers [*sic*] worked together.

August 14, 1948, p. 121

Off Minor (73)

Ingenious Monk solo with rhythm backing spins a series of imaginative variations on "Merry-Go-Round-Broke-Down" theme, with interest building in the second chorus.

Evonce (68)

Art Blakey swings Monk's fanciful left-wing bop creation, weaving mediocre solos into unified whole.

September 25, 1948, p. 129

In Walked Bud (74)

Melodic and purist bop based on "Blue Skies": good beat, good trumpet and good Thelonious.

Epistrophy (65)

Monk's purist bop betrays no swiped chordal structures; the beret-goatee cult will wear this side down to the turntable.

February 26, 1949, p. 119

Ruby, My Dear (58)

Monk performs one of his originals with his trio. His unusual chord structures and odd sound and phrasing on the keyboard confine this wax to collectors' values.

Evidence (64)

There's a little more commercial meat in this quartet opus in bop. Milt Jackson on vibes and pianist Monk make this rather intriguing bit of bop chamber music.

June 18, 1949, p. 124

Humph (70)

Up-tempo bopper with weird ensemble theme and good alto, trumpet and tenor solos plus good beat.

Misterioso (61)

Boppers conception of an after hours blues spots effective Milt Jackson vibes and neurotic Monk piano.

7. *Mosaic Survey*

The Blue Note sides have remained more or less in print for over 50 years, a testimony to the fact that they arguably represent Monk's best work. When Blue Note finally moved from 78s to the new 12" LP format, all of the Monk sides (but not the alternate takes, of which there were many) were issued in 1956 on two records as *Genius of Modern Music* (Blue Note BLP 1510-1511), with liner notes by Ira Gitler. A few alternate takes were added with the double LP set *The Complete Genius* (1976), but it was not until 1983 that Mosaic records, a mail-order company that leases masters from record companies to produce limited edition box sets with extensive documentation, released all of the takes. The later reissues of Monk's Blue Note recordings, by both Mosaic (1983) and Blue Note (1994), have attracted considerable new interest in his music. As an example of the wealth of criticism they have generated in the last decade, English critic Max Harrison's incisive postmortem analysis of the Blue Note recordings as issued in the Mosaic box set reiterates the by now commonly held opinion that Monk's Blue Note recordings are jazz at its most pure. And with the newly issued alternate takes, he notes that Monk's approach to the performance of a piece, rather than a variation or exploration of the harmonic implications of the chord structure, is more akin to the striving toward an ideal—in the Platonic sense—version of the piece. Harrison has written extensively on jazz, including several critical guides to recordings and the main entry on jazz in the *New Grove Dictionary of Music and Musicians.*

This article originally appeared as "Mosaic Survey, Part I," by Max Harrison in *Jazz Forum*, Vol. 96 (1985), pp. 35–38. Used by permission of Max Harrison and *Jazz Forum.*

A sizeable book alone would provide space for an adequate account of this music, and only a few aspects can be dealt with here. Instead of the usual kind of session-by-session commentary, an attempt will be made, firstly, to isolate some of its characteristic procedures. Monk was always aware of precisely what he was up to in his best work, and much of its impact derives from specific compositional devices and the ways he employed them. Indeed, it has been suggested that the manner in which he used them is more important than the procedures themselves.[1]

That in Cootie Williams's 1942 recording "Epistrophy," retitled "Fly Right," sounds so much like a typical big band riff piece indicates how firmly grounded are Monk's ideas in basic jazz conventions. Thus he was fond of redeploying old blues devices in his own way, this in fact being a key to his harmony (another large subject). A good example is "Straight, No Chaser" (a blues in B-flat, not in F as the booklet accompanying these Mosaic reissues says). Thematically, this piece is "about" the alternation of major and minor thirds, and the flat third is first used unobtrusively as a passing note on the weak second beat of the first complete bar, then the listener is made more aware of it through its being placed on the first (strongest) beat of the next bar. In such details—and there is a myriad of them, of course, in each of his best performances—one discovers how *exactly* this great musician focused on what he was doing, and how false is the notion that "there is only one way to look (and listen) to Monk, and that is as a good joke."[2]

The short 78 rpm "form" of these Blue Notes suited Monk, or at least concentrated his mind, and the best of them have the same kind of rigor and consis-

1. Lawrence Koch, "Thelonious Monk: Compositional Techniques," *Annual Review of Jazz Studies* 2, 1983, pp. 67–80.
2. Sinclair Traill, *Jazz Journal*, January 1981, p. 39.

tency as his themes. It can, as a generalization, be said that his subsequent work for other companies became progressively (or regressively) more diffuse. On those later recordings he appears as a combo leader who wrote exceptionally good themes, whereas on Blue Note (and in only a few other places) he is one of that rare breed, a jazz composer. Perhaps more to the point, Monk's jazz was during these few years at its most pure.

Though he was in Coleman Hawkins' 1944 52nd Street group with Benny Harris and Byas, in Gillespie's 1943 combo at the Onyx with, initially, Lester Young, Pettiford and Roach, and was recorded at Minton's still earlier, Monk was never a bopper, had little to do with bop orthodoxy, and, rightly, was on none of the classic bop recordings dates led by Parker or Gillespie. There is nothing in bop, Parker included, astringent as, say, the piano solos on either of the 1948 "Mysterioso's" still less anything so sophisticated compositionally as the superimposition of thematic ideas here and in "Evidence."

Such a procedure, which loses some of its point in the more relaxed atmosphere of Monk's later sessions, is particularly appropriate to his highly concentrated music-making for Blue Note, as is his practice of sometimes squeezing a phrase or motive into a smaller space than it occupied on its first appearance. (Whether Monk knew it or not, this is an adaptation of diminution, a procedure familiar in classical contrapuntal writing.) It is also characteristic of his work at its best that "Straight, No Chaser" should expand from a single phrase, with four figures to each four-bar section. Also to be noted are single-phrase pieces like "Bemsha Swing," first recorded in 1952, for Prestige, where the thematic idea is transposed to the subdominant for the bridge. Usually, however, Monk preferred something more complicated, and liked to base his bridge passages on a development or alteration of part of the main phrase. "I Mean You" illustrates the simplest sort of case, where the notes C, D, F from bars 7–8 of the main idea are used to lead into the bridge. "Ruby, My Dear" uses a variant of the main melody to start the bridge, different harmony being used in each situation, of course, which further alters the effect of the phrase. Often several procedures come together, as in "Well, You Needn't," which has diminution, bridge development—as it might be termed, and octave displacement.

Chromaticism is naturally a constant feature of this music. Note the chromatic movement of the melody in bars 3–4 of "I Mean You." In "Ruby, My Dear" we find a series of II^7–V^7–I chords in different keys connected by characteristic Monk chromatic runs, while "Ask Me Now" is based on chromatic secondary II^7–V^7 progressions with the melody derived from the chords. Some of the melodies in fact derive very clearly from the chords, and "In Walked Bud" has the first note of each bar stating the most important note of each new chord change. But sometimes it is the other way round. Bar 3 of the "'Round About Midnight" melody outlines the E-flat seventh to A-flat harmony, with the D-flat resolving to C—Monk's favorite seventh-to-third. At other points the melody moves against the harmony, as in bars 22–23 of "I Mean You," which relate to the opening bridge motive, not to the harmony.

The central importance of rhythm in this music is presumably obvious, and only one point will be made here, concerning the way Monk shifts a motive about in relation to the beat. The main idea of "Straight, No Chaser"—to return to our initial example—begins on the second half of beat 4, moves to the second half of beat 3 and is used also on the second halves of beats 2 and 1. The phrase used as introduction and coda to "I Mean You" has this same type of shift; and the bridge of "In Walked Bud" should also be studied in this regard.

Such comments relate to Monk's improvising as well as to his composing, and it is instructive to compare these versions of "Off Minor" and "Nice Work" with those done by Bud Powell in the same year. The latter emerges as the archetypal virtuoso improviser whereas Monk plays "composer's piano," dealing in highly specific ideas. The instrument seems almost incidental, although some of its capabilities are used with brilliant insight; Monk was perfectly capable, in Koch's term, of "orchestralising" the piano. It was, of course, bop's emphasis on virtuosity that led to Monk erroneously being thought of as a theoretician at first—by many musicians as well as by writers.

Some knowing self-quotations can be found among these Blue Notes. For example, a reference to "Misterioso's" walking sixths closes the "Straight, No Chaser" piano solo, and the main phrase of "I Mean You" (which he had not yet recorded) appears in Monk's solo on "Who Knows?," the alternative take of which also alludes to "Well, You Needn't." And Dorham quotes "Well, You Needn't" in "Sixteen." These and other instances may suggest a disconcerting interchangeability among Monk's pieces, yet he always insisted that his sidemen should improvise on the theme not just on the chords. As Michael Cuscuna says in one of his two excellent essays in the booklet, Monk always "sought and valued musicians with the talent, intelligence and willingness to get inside his music simply because the realization of his music required it."[3] Not that he ever found many. Jackson and above all Blakey are the main ones here, although Thompson does very well on the final Blue Note session. This

3. Michael Cuscuna, liner notes to *The Complete Blue Note Recordings of Thelonious Monk*, Mosaic MR 4101. *Ed.*

is confirmed by the hitherto unissued "Sixteen," especially the second take, and it is a pity that Monk never used him again.

It is relevant to say here that the many alternative takes now made available for the first time offer quite different revelations from those made by, say, Parker's Dials and Savoys. Bird as he goes from one take to another travels deeper into the potentialities of the chord sequence: a fresh discovery which changes everything, because it alters the internal relationships of the entire solo, is always possible and sometimes occurs. But Monk seems to be traveling towards an ideal, as it were Platonic, version of the piece. That the ideal is almost never reached is due to the music's difficulty, not least for its composer. Notice how on the alternative, and later, version of "Criss Cross" he makes a greater use of the theme in his solo, while the later version of "Skippy" has a piano solo making a fuller use of the outline of the theme while at the same time being more varied in its contents. Again, the 1957 account of "Reflections" with Rollins included here is more searching than the 1952 Prestige trio. In each case we observe Monk drawing closer to his "ideal" performance. It is probably significant that this is not true of his recompositions—as they often deserve to be called—of music by others. The initial "Nice Work" for instance, is more adventurous than the one chosen for 78 rpm issue. "Carolina Moon," done in 6/4, may be considered, incidentally, as Monk's finest recomposition—unless you want to count "Skippy" as a version of "Tea for Two." That may sound farfetched but Youmans's banal little song (from *No, No, Nannette*) is at the root of Monk's tritone-intoxicated piece, just as "Blue Skies" is buried under "In Walked Bud" and "Just You, Just Me" is the unlikely origin of "Evidence." This partly contradicts Monk's early statement to George Simon that "I make up my own chords and melodies."[4]

"Humph" and "Thelonious" from the first session, five days after his thirtieth birthday, show, not surprisingly, that by then Monk had a mature style. They are on a quite different level from, say, Ike Quebec's "Suburban Eyes" (alias "All God's Chillun Got Rhythm"), as is obvious from the fact that the horns are more comfortable with this latter. Yet commentators have rather too often lately said that Monk had his style completely cut and dried by then, if not earlier. For his last Blue Note date he reverted to the same instrumentation as on this first session, but what a difference there is in the way he uses it! And wonderful though, for example, "Misterioso" or "Off Minor" are, "Criss Cross" shows real advances in terms of melodic and rhythmic subtlety and the use of the ensemble. Advances sometimes occur in unexpected

4. Simon's article is reprinted on p. 53. *Ed.*

places, however, and "Well, You Needn't" from the second date is the first recorded Monk masterpiece—but which version? The boiling previously unissued take has added syncopations, grace notes, and a different use of space. Both performances swing mightily, as do slow pieces like the sad "Monk's Mood." In fact, as I have said elsewhere, the most incomprehensible adverse comment on early modern jazz was that it failed to swing.

Little has been written about the rich vein of musical humor in Monk's output, but "Ask Me Now" should be noted as a satirical commentary on a certain kind of indulgently romantic piano playing. This links, of course, with the subversive goings-on behind Hagood's absurd, and again romantic, singing on two of the 1948 items. These should not be too lightly dismissed, however, because the interplay between Jackson and Monk leads us to their more acid work in the last chorus of "Evidence."

From the many earlier reviews I have read of this magnificent reissue the strangest remark was that the sound is faithful to the original 78s. As one who first heard Monk in the summer of 1949, when I bought the noisy-surfaced Blue Note 78s of "'Round about Midnight/Well, You Needn't" and "In Walked Bud/Epistrophy," I can say that Mosaic's sound is, of course, vastly better. This in turn leads to the thought that it has taken 28 years (since Monk's last session in 1957) to get all his work for Blue Note together in a satisfactory way. But in the perspective of musical history that is rather quick.

Early Profiles

The mythology spawned by Monk's tenure at Minton's began to take shape in print with the first published articles featuring him. They are all reproduced here and combine interview material, discussions of his recordings and highlights of his peculiar image and lifestyle. Time and time again, commentators have quoted statements from these early pieces. The writers represented here all share a sense of having to explain and promote Monk, in reaction against the indifferent and sometimes even hostile reviews of his recordings and the fact that Monk simply did not fit into anybody's mold, musical or behavioral.

8. *The Piano Man Who Dug Be-bop*

When Monk's first recordings for Blue Note were released in 1947, Lorraine Gordon, who was looking for ways to promote the records, convinced the editor at the New York daily *PM* to do an article on Monk.[1] Staff writer Ira Peck created a profile of Monk, taking

1. *PM* was a left-leaning, liberal-minded daily newspaper published, without advertising revenue, between 1940–1948. Several well-known writers, including I. F. Stone, Max Lerner, Ben Hecht, and John S. Wilson, wrote for the paper. Saul Steinberg and Theodor Geisel (Dr. Seuss) were featured as cartoonists.

as a departure point a hyperbolic press release from Blue Note and focusing on his peculiar habits. Peck obviously could not get Monk to say very much and had to resort to interviewing Teddy Hill as well. The descriptions of Monk's apartment include the oft-repeated observation that he had a picture of Billie Holiday stuck to the ceiling so he could look at it while lying down. The accompanying photo by Irving Hoberman (not reproduced here) shows Monk sitting on the floor next to his piano, staring at a letter-size photo of Billie Holiday crudely taped to the ceiling at a diagonal angle to the wall. The wall behind the piano has the signed photo of Gillespie. The article is a sympathetic portrait of someone who at the time must have induced bewilderment in anyone who met him. After working for *PM*, Ira Peck pursued a career as a successful editor and author of juvenile literature.

This article originally appeared as "The Piano Man Who Dug Be-Bop," by Ira Peck, in *PM*'s *Sunday Picture News (Magazine Section)*, February 22, 1948, p. M7. Used by permission of Ira Peck.

Out-of-tune pianos disturb Thelonious Monk but the controversial surrealist jazz he started is music to his ears and to a growing new cult.

The newest cult in jazz today, and the one that is being debated most hotly by people who take their jazz seriously, is be-bop. It is difficult to define be-bop adequately, for the simple reason that it is like no other jazz. Jazz critics have called it kind of "surrealist" jazz and have drawn analogies between it and the works of Picasso and Dali. Musically it has been likened to the works of Stravinsky whom most be-bop musicians are known to admire. It is a dissonant, staccato-like jazz, usually played at a breakneck pace. Technically, it is characterized by the accenting of passing notes, especially flatted fifths and flatted ninths.

Few musicians are moderate in their opinion of be-bop. Either they like it enormously or they won't have anything to do with it. Eddie Condon, who adheres to the old-time Dixieland school of jazz had this to say about it:

"I can't stand it. I can't understand it and I can't see how those guys who play it can either. That type of music—that weird, try-to-figure-it-out, serenade-to-a-toilet-in-mid-ocean stuff seems to me as musical as tonsillitis."

Young, Wonderful Minds

Duke Ellington, on the other hand, is sympathetic to be-bop. "Why be surprised that be-bop is ridiculed," he said. "Jazz and swing got the same treatment in their early days, too. Anything that's alive must progress and music is alive. This is 1948 and there are young minds, wonderful minds working on fresh musical ideas. Those ideas have spread and some part of them will certainly survive and become incorporated into the music of tomorrow."

Eugene List, classical pianist, is another admirer of be-bop. "Be-bop is to jazz," he said, "as atonality is to classical music. It uses the enlarged harmony structure of jazz but is more cerebral than emotional. I like it. Any intellectual exercise in music is fun if you want to take your mind off anything. I wish I could play first-rate be-bop."

Dizzy Gillespie, the best known exponent of be-bop, was on a European tour and unavailable for comment when this was written.

In a communiqué last week Blue Note records announced it had "actually found the one person who was responsible for this whole new trend in music. The genius behind the whole movement—and we have had the privilege of being the first to put his radical and unorthodox ideas on wax—is an unusual and mysterious character with the more unusual name of Thelonious Monk. Among musicians, Thelonious' name is treated with respect and awe, for he is a strange person whose pianistics continue to baffle all who hear him."

Down Beat, a jazz trade publication, confirmed these claims about Monk. In fact, one of their own reporters, Bill Gottlieb, had managed to corral Monk once very briefly last fall and regarded this as such an achievement that he began his story in this manner:

Mother's Favorite

"I have interviewed Thelonious Monk. It's not like having seen Pinetop spit blood or delivering the message to Garcia. But on the other hand, it's at least equal to a scoop on the true identity of Bunny Benzedrine or on who killed Cock Robin."[2]

Before interviewing Monk, I was warned that he was an "enigma" and was volunteered the following information about him:

Monk is about 29 and has lived all his life with his family in one apartment on 63d Street between 11th Avenue and the West Side Drive.[3] Besides Monk, the present occupants of the apartment are his mother (his father died a few years ago), a sister, brother-in-law, and nephew. An older brother, who had once been a prizefighter, lives in a neighboring house. The youngest of the

2. Gottlieb's article is reprinted on p. 22. *Ed.*
3. Monk was 30 at the time of the interview. *Ed.*

Monk children, Thelonious is also his mother's favorite. He depends on her for a great many favors. "He frequently says, 'My mother will take care of that for me' or 'Leave the message with my mother'."

Monk's room is his "inner sanctum," and he seldom leaves it to mingle with the rest of the family. On the other hand, he has been known to jam as many as 10 people in it when he has entertained on the piano.

Monk holds jobs only infrequently, and it is doubtful whether he could get by financially if he did not live at home. He has turned down work for a variety of reasons. For one thing, he does not like to play "commercial" jazz. He has also refused to play at clubs simply because he felt the piano was out of tune.

"Once," one of my informants said, "right in the middle of a number he stopped, got up from the piano and walked away." "The B note rings," he said. "It disturbs me."

Monk's eating habits are equally erratic. On waking up he usually plays the piano for a couple of hours, then has a couple of beers, and later on, when he gets hungry, a sandwich. He eats a meal only when he feels like it.

"I honestly don't believe," a friend of his told me later, "that food means a thing to him."

Monk seldom sleeps more than five hours a day and has occasionally gone as long as three days without any sleep at all. During that time he wanders around from one friend's house to another, working out his ideas on the piano. Apparently, nobody says no to him.

"He'll go to Mary Lou Williams' house at four o'clock in the morning and she'll just say, 'Come in, there's the piano, go ahead' and then go right back to sleep."

At the end of one of these periods, Monk is so exhausted that he is likely to sleep straight through three days. Then he sleeps so deeply that it is almost impossible to wake him.

Monk listens to records almost as much as he plays the piano and is extremely uncomfortable unless there is a phonograph or a piano wherever he is.

Women Are a 'Heckle'

Monk seems to care very little for girls, although he is occasionally seen in their company and is admired by many. One girl who lives in the same apartment building drops in frequently to clean his room and wash his dishes.

"The girl idolizes him. He sits there and she puts cigarettes in his mouth and lights them for him. Yet he hardly speaks to her. He tells me that women are a 'heckle' sometimes. He doesn't want to be tied down to anything except his music."

Armed with this fill-in, I visited Thelonious' home next day. It was a typical tenement flat—dark, tiny, and dilapidated. The central room was the kitchen in which an old cot had been placed to provide extra sleeping quarters. A tin ceiling, walls darkened by stove soot, linoleum worn through to the floor boards in places contrasted incongruously with a large, new shiny white refrigerator and next to the cot, an expensive-looking console model radio and phonograph.

There were two bedrooms off the kitchen and from one of these Monk emerged to greet me. He was a tall, well-built, gentle-mannered chap, unusual-looking only in that he wore green-tinted, horn-and-gold rimmed glasses and a small goatee. These, I learned later, are standard equipment among be-bop musicians.

Monk invited me into his room. It was just large enough to accommodate a small upright piano, a cot, a dresser, and a chair. There was only one window, which, because it faced an alley, admitted very little light. A feeble lamp on Monk's dresser provided most of the light in the room. There were several pictures around the room. One, of Billie Holiday, was pasted on the ceiling next to a red bulb. Monk said he liked to lie back on his cot and gaze at it. On the wall near his cot was a picture of Sarah Vaughan and, above the piano, one of Dizzy Gillespie. This was inscribed, *To Monk, my first inspiration. Stay with it. Your boy, Dizzy Gillespie.*

I found out soon enough why Monk had been called an enigma. Although polite, he maintained a stonewall reserve throughout the interview. To most of my questions about himself, his answer was "I don't know." He seldom spoke two consecutive sentences. About his music he was almost as uncommunicative. He defined be-bop only as "modern swing music" but would not elaborate.

I was able to gather, however, that he first began experimenting with be-bop about six or seven years ago while working with a quartet at Minton's Playhouse, a Harlem nightclub on West 118th Street. He and the other musicians, Kenny Clarke, drummer, Nick Fenton, bass fiddler, and Joe Guy, trombonist, "started making up melodies. In order to play we had to make up our own tunes. Just like Duke Ellington had to make up his own music and sounds to express himself."

"Be-bop," he said, "just happened. I just felt it . . . it came to me. Something was being created without my trying to."

The kind of be-bop being played today by Dizzy Gillespie and Charlie Parker, he said, is not the same he originally worked out at Minton's. He felt that Gillespie, who used to engage in after-hours jam sessions with him, improvised on the original and then turned out his own version of be-bop.

Monk went into the kitchen and put on a recording of one of his piano solos. It was more subdued and slower than most be-bop I've heard, but the principles were the same: there was no melody pattern—one never knew where the music was going next—a lot of unharmonious chords, and a steady, insistent rhythm. It was imaginative, interesting music and it was plain that Monk was striving for something different.

Underground in Be-bop

Monk felt that one of the reasons he has not achieved the fame and commercial success of Gillespie and Parker is his reticence.

"I don't get around as much," he said. "People don't see me as much. I'm sort of underground in be-bop."

Another reason, he felt, is that most musicians have difficulty playing with him. The exceptions are drummers and bass fiddlers "because they have more beat."

Most people, I mentioned, have found be-bop pretty weird.

"They don't know what it's all about. They don't understand the music and in most cases have never heard it. Weird means something you never heard before. It's weird until people get around to it. Then it ceases to be weird."

That was all I could get from Monk. But still curious about him I called that evening on Teddy Hill, the former bandleader who is now part owner of Minton's. Hill, I was told, probably knew more about Monk than anyone around.

I found him in his office at the club, a short chunky man with small eyes set closely together in a wide face. When I told him of the difficulty I had had with Monk he nodded.

"Monk is definitely a character," he said. "He's the type of fellow who thinks an awful lot but doesn't have much to say. Yeah, I've known a lot of musicians who were characters, but none just like him."

Absorbed in Music

"Monk," Hill said, "is so absorbed in his music he appears to have lost touch with everything else."

"He just doesn't seem to be present unless he's actually talking to you and then sometimes all of a sudden in the middle of a conversation his mind is somewhere else. He may still be talking to you, but he's thinking about something else."

"Some nights I've seen him in here with a girl. She's sitting back there and he'll get into a conversation with someone else, forget she's there, and the next thing you know he might get up, get his coat, and start walking out until somebody reminds him that his girl is there. She looks like a very nice girl but I wonder what the guy ever talks about. I've hardly ever seen him say two words to her."

Monk's preoccupation with his music, Hill said, makes him equally erratic when he is working.

"When I had him here, the band used to come to work at ten. He'd come in at nine but at ten you couldn't find him. Maybe an hour later you'd find him sitting off by himself in the kitchen somewhere writing and the band playing didn't make any difference to him. He'd say, 'I didn't hear it'."

"I always used to be so disgusted with him and yet you never saw such a likeable guy. Plenty of times I'd have been happy to hire the guy as piano player in my band but I couldn't depend on him. Everybody liked the guy. Dizzy and Kenny Clarke once said they'd assume responsibility for getting him there on time if I'd hire him, they liked him that much. Everybody wanted him but everybody was afraid of him. He was too undependable. He'd just rather mess around at home."

As the leader of a cult, Monk is much sought-after, but he chooses his friends carefully.

"He doesn't run around with just any guy who falls over him. If a guy doesn't dig him, he doesn't waste any time with him."

Hill reached for a cigar and lit up.

"Tell you something else peculiar about Monk," he said after he cleared away some of the smoke. "I've never seen him have any emotion. I've never heard him in an argument seriously with anybody yet. He'd much rather take the worst of it than to argue too much about anything. I've never seen him excited except when he's playing. It only comes out in one place and that's when he sits down at the piano."

"He'll come in here anytime and play for hours with only a dim light and the funny thing is he'll never play a complete tune. You never know what he's playing. Many times he's gone on so long I've had to come back and plead with him to quit playin' the piano so I could close up the place 'cause it was against the law to keep it open any longer."

I asked Hill about the roles of Monk and Gillespie in the creation of bebop.

Monk was actually "the guy who dug the stuff out," Hill said. Gillespie had packaged the goods and delivered it to the consumers.

"Monk seemed more like the guy who manufactured the product rather than commercialized it. Dizzy has gotten all the exploitation because Dizzy branched out and got started. Monk stayed right in the same groove."

Front and Back

"Of course, what Dizzy is playing today is not altogether what Monk had in mind. But the fundamentals are the same. Dizzy just twisted it a little bit. He decided instead of starting at the front to start at the back. But the stuff is essentially what Monk worked out."

The reason Monk had not obtained recognition, Hill felt, was not that he was lacking ability. It was his undependability.

"One reason for it, I guess, is that he was living at home with his own people. Maybe if the guy had to stand on his own two feet it might have been different. But knowing that he had a place to eat and sleep, that might have had a lot to do with it. Dizzy had to be on time to keep the landlady from saying 'You don't live here any more.' Monk never had that worry."

"I think Monk has possibilities of becoming outstanding in his field—provided he ever finds himself personally and makes a stand on his own instead of just being pushed and shoved all the time. He waits and sits until everybody does everything for him. I don't think Monk would ever get a job if other people didn't ask for him."

Hill wouldn't make any predictions as to the future of be-bop generally. We gathered it had plenty of obstacles to overcome.

"It's difficult stuff to play," Hill said. "Right now you have good musicians trying to play it and they sound horrible. The stuff played improperly can be offensive—it hurts your ears. You never hear a big band except Dizzy play it. You may hear a few guys take a riff or so but that's about all. And who's gonna write it—all those chords clashin' and everything. A lot of guys don't think it's worthwhile to invest their time in it."

An Original Talent

It was after ten o'clock when I walked out of Hill's office and I could hear the almost hysterically fast strains of a small jazz band coming from the clubroom. Unlike most nightclubs it was a bright, cheerful, gaily decorated place and the customers seemed to be enjoying themselves. Many of them were visibly stimulated by the music but only a few made any attempt to dance to it.

I saw Monk, looking as withdrawn as he had earlier in the day, with a group of friends who were urging him to play for them. When the band took a break Monk walked up to the piano and began testing it. Satisfied that it was in tune, he sat down and began playing. At first he played fairly conventional, recognizable tunes to which he gave his own twist but as he progressed he played more and more of his own music.

People shook their heads and marveled at his playing. Most of them agreed that Monk has an original talent.

"His chords, his way of thinking, his beat—they're absolutely unique," one listener said. "He's just enough off the norm to be a genius."

I spoke to Monk again a little later and asked him whether he thought bebop would catch on.

"It has to," he said. "It's the modern music of today. It makes other musicians think—just like Picasso. It has to catch on."

9. *Thelonious*

Orrin Keepnews, who in the late 1950s launched Monk's career with the Riverside recordings, first met Monk in 1948 while working on an article for *The Record Changer.* In a 1982 tribute to Monk, Keepnews recounts the circumstances in which he wrote his article:

> I had just accepted the spare-time, non-paying job of managing editor of an extremely little magazine called *The Record Changer.* Formerly a totally traditional-jazz publication, it had just been taken over by Bill Grauer (who was to be my partner when Riverside was formed a few years later); and Alfred Lion, the owner of Blue Note, felt we might possibly be open to some more adventurous music. So we all came together in the living room of Lion's Greenwich Village home: I was almost totally uninformed about both Monk and bebop, but in the test pressings of a tune named "Thelonious" and a few others I heard something that reached me, and with the arrogance of ignorance I proceeded on the spot to interview this already legendary, laconic eccentric.[1]

1. Orrin Keepnews, "Thelonious Monk: A Remembrance," *Keyboard* (July 1982), p. 18. A selection from this article is reprinted on p. 230.

But, as he goes on to say, his "lack of background was an asset, and so was the fact that as a hide-bound traditional jazz fan, I had not yet heard anything attractive in the early bop records of Dizzy and Bird."[2] This is remarkable in light of the fact that most critics and listeners were praising Charlie Parker and Dizzy Gillespie long before they accepted Monk. Significantly, Keepnews latches on to the idea of placing Monk in a lineage of original pianists and composers, like Jelly Roll Morton and Duke Ellington, who developed their own styles and applied them to a specific group of musicians, producing what he calls "unified small band jazz." He also emphasizes Monk's role as a modernist, but clearly juxtaposes his music with bebop.

This article appeared originally as "Thelonious: Monk's Music May Be First Sign of Bebop's Legitimacy" in *The Record Changer*, Vol. 7, No. 4, 1948, pp. 5, 20. It was reprinted in *The View from Within* (New York: Oxford) in 1988. Used by permission of Orrin Keepnews.

Modern music has been rolling along these past few years, converting a number of young jazz men and often making for them a good bit of money. Sometimes it seems like a very sincere, if immature and frenetic, jazz form; sometimes it gives off strong hints of un-artistic neurosis, commercial power-politics, and childish clowning. I have always been ready to concede, without too much enthusiasm, that bebop might well have a bright future, but until recently had found nothing in it capable of commanding interest or respect.

Very recently, however, what looks very much like the first ray of light has broken through the clouds. A thirty-year-old New York pianist named Thelonious Monk has cut several band records (only four sides have been released as yet) containing music that is more interesting and worthy of far more serious listening than anything else that has yet been produced by a modernist. Monk, who has been a legendary and little-known figure in bebop circles, plays in a style that bears a strong superficial resemblance to standard bop. But there are indications that his music may represent a huge forward step towards discipline and coherence in this newest form of jazz.

Comparison with past jazz greats is probably pointless; the various "schools" of jazz may go through similar periods of development, but each has its own peculiarities. However, it may serve to clarify Monk's relative position along the main stream of modern music to point out that he is engaged in de-

2. Ibid.

veloping an essentially original piano style, as men like Pinetop Smith and Cow Cow Davenport did for an earlier style. In his current record he has created a band style molded around his own ideas and shaped to his own manner of playing, much as Jelly Roll Morton and Duke Ellington did before him.

Monk was unquestionably one of the very first to play in the modern style that came to be known as bebop. In 1940, while playing in a quartet at Minton's, in Harlem, he and drummer Kenny Clarke began "thinking" in that vein, and even before that Monk had been picking up a meager living by playing around town in his natural style—a strange style that most musicians found incomprehensible.

For reasons to be touched on later, Monk's conception of jazz has developed along somewhat different lines than his Harlem contemporaries—stronger and more mature lines, in our opinion. Possibly because Thelonious is the first pianist with his own set of ideas to come along in a type of jazz thus far dominated by horn men like Parker and Gillespie, his recent sides are the first "modern" records in which the piano and the rhythm section play important roles. Monk himself complains that bebop pianists have a habit of trying to imitate Dizzy's trumpet or Bird's alto; a piano that fulfills a piano's function in the band is a rare thing, but Monk's strongly rhythmic style is pure piano, beautifully integrated into a unit with his bassist (Gene Ramey on some sides, Bob Paige on others), and with a powerful, steady and complex drummer named Art Blakey.

A great weakness peculiar to recorded jazz, and a weakness common to all schools, is the haphazard and casual business of bringing together men relatively unfamiliar with each other's styles in a hastily arranged pick-up session. Sometimes this produces great jazz; more often the product is rather disorganized music. Even if it includes great solo work, it still sounds like what it really is—a group of individuals playing in the same room, but *not* a band. On the occasions when units composed of men who understand each other's styles and ideas and peculiarities are able to get together, the results are likely to be superior, even if the individuals involved are not "all-stars." New Orleans jazz has many examples of this; the Ellington band is another case in point. Modern music thus far has been largely pick-up; the fact that Thelonious chose the men he wanted to work with, and rehearsed carefully with them, may be a major reason why his current records are an outstanding example of unified small band jazz, and sound purposeful and coordinated instead of like a cutting duel between comparative strangers.

Unfortunately, it seems to have been easier for Thelonious to find rhythm men able to adapt themselves to his style than to find suitable horns. Trumpet and tenor sax on his current sides are played by men who seem too steeped in standard bebop; their solos sometimes fail to follow the complex pattern being established by the rhythm unit, and the ensembles tend, on occasion, to fall into standard bop clichés. But one man, a seventeen-year-old alto player named Danny Quebec West (nephew of Ike Quebec), does some remarkable work. He has a firm, clear, driving style, and, apparently because he is young enough not to have fallen into current stylization, he is able to coordinate with the line along which Monk's playing moves.

Whether Monk is to become a "great," and whether his music is really as far from the beaten path of bebop as I believe it is, are things that only time and continued playing can prove. But, as of this moment, considering only the present batch of far-from-perfect records turned out by this still-young jazz man, these points stand out:

Thelonious is a talented musician, with a fertile imagination and a firm rhythmic sense; his band jazz has a feeling of unity, warmth, and purpose that contrasts sharply with the emotionless, jittered-up pyrotechnics of Fifty-second Street "modernism." And—although this is a point that cannot be proved in writing but only heard in the music—he is capable of a sly, wry, satiric humor that has a rare maturity. Monk's playing may be considered as "neurotic" as the rest of the jazz produced in the '40s, but it at least serves to indicate that the music of a neurotic era does not necessarily have to be a collection of cold, rhythmless and pointless sounds.

One of the principal reasons for Monk's "differentness," aside from the man's own probable genius, can be found in the way that choice and necessity have combined to keep him on the fringes of the bebop movement. Raised in the semi-isolated San Juan Hill district near the Hudson River in New York's West Sixties, he has lived there, away from Harlem, ever since. He started taking piano lessons at eleven, and two years later was playing solo dates at local parties and speakeasies. From the first, Monk says, "no written music sounded right" to him, although he obviously listened intently to the Ellington band of that day. His unconventional style and his unwillingness to play standard orchestra piano kept him from band jobs and led him to develop his style his own way. Those early years were undoubtedly not pleasant ones; Thelonious is a quiet, self-contained, and soft-spoken man, who doesn't seem too anxious to recall those first jobs in "juice joints," where he made $17 a week, and where people kept wanting him to "play straight."

"There are a lot of things you can't remember—except the heckling," he says.

Finally, in 1940, he went into trumpeter Joe Guy's quartet at Minton's. In those days, when "everybody was sounding like Roy Eldridge," he and Kenny

Clarke began "thinking out" the style that was to be promoted into a big thing called bebop. ("Thinking" is a word Monk uses a lot in talking about his music, and to me the word seems fitting.) A great many men drifted into Minton's and into that style in those days: Charlie Christian, Coleman Hawkins, Dizzy Gillespie (whom Monk remembers as having been there only "very rarely"), Charlie Parker.

In 1944 Thelonious recorded an album with Hawkins, on the Joe Davis label. It's interesting to note that, although the balance and the arrangements on those sides were set up to feature only Hawk, what can be heard of Monk's playing is in the same vein as it is today. Not as sure or as forceful, perhaps, but clearly along the same lines. Then came two years with Hawkins' band, in Chicago and on the West Coast, which meant that he was not on hand during the period when "bebop" (which incidentally is a term he dislikes) was first being stylized and strongly plugged.

Then he returned to New York and comparative obscurity. Always appreciated by fellow musicians (like Mary Lou Williams, Ellington, Nat Cole—who says he sat "spellbound" the first time he heard Thelonious), but never quite in harmony with the kind of jazz that was being sold, he was completely without the qualities of showmanship and self-promotion in which so many others abound. A careful craftsman and an artist, he is obviously not a man who would be at his best in a quick recording session or be happy playing chords on a six-night-a-week job with an outfit that considered the piano a half-necessary background for some free-wheeling horn men.

His current sides, on which his particular variation of modern music is played with varying degrees of success, but with not-infrequent greatness, may or may not move him from obscurity to a position as a big name and big influence in modern jazz. But they do show that at least one modernist is capable of a maturity and soundness and brilliance that leaves room for much optimism for the future of jazz.

10. *Bop's Dixie to Monk*

The piece included here by George Simon strangely enough was reprinted in one of his books on big bands, *Simon Says: The Sights and Sounds of the Swing Era 1935–1955*. In introducing the piece, he recalls a moment during the interview where Monk had left the room, leaving Monk's manager to ask him what he thought: "Monk's multi-pause style had confused me and I told him so. 'Man,' he [the manager] said, 'that's just it. It's not so much the notes he plays as the ones he leaves out that mean so much.' "[1] In contrast to the other profiles of the late 1940s, Monk deliberately sets himself apart musically from bebop and is clearly agitated by the manner in which the style has been adopted by other players. Simon began his musical career as a drummer with Glenn Miller and was editor-in-chief and feature writer for *Metronome* in the 1940s and 1950s. Most of his writing has been on the big band era, with several books published.

This article originally appeared as "Bop's Dixie to Monk," by George Simon in *Metronome*, April 1948, pp. 20, 34–35, and was reprinted in *Simon Says: The Sights and Sounds of the Swing Era, 1935–1955* (New Rochelle, N.Y.: Arlington House) in 1971.

Thelonious, responsible for much of modern jazz, isn't satisfied with all that's happening to it

Bebop should be planned and organized and then blown. Otherwise, according to Monk, "it turns out to be like Dixieland, with everybody blowing for themselves." And the trouble with most bop as it's blown today, again according to Monk, is that "too many guys don't know what they're doin'!"

Who's Monk and what's *he* doin'? Monk is Monk, first name Thelonious, if you want to get technical. He has been credited by several leading boppists, including Charlie Parker, with having started this altered chord style of playing jazz during the nights in the early forties when he played piano at Minton's in Harlem. Monk himself doesn't think he actually plays bop, at least not the way it's being played today. "Mine is more original," he says. "They think differently, harmonically. They play mostly stuff that's based on the chords of other things, like the blues and 'I Got Rhythm.' I like the whole song, melody and chord structure, to be different. I make up my own chords and melodies."

Monk has been playing his own chords for years. He's a New Yorker, born there in 1917, the only musical member of a family that, so far as he knows, is unmusical.[2] "I never studied. I just experimented arranging. You learn most

1. George Simon, *Simon Says: The Sights and Sounds of the Swing Era, 1935–1955* (New Rochelle, N.Y.: Arlington House, [1971]), p. 413. It is not clear who Monk's manager was at that time.
2. Peter Keepnews has concluded that Monk's father played piano in the home. See the article by Keepnews reprinted on p. 4. *Ed.*

harmonics by experience. You fool around and listen. Most chord structure is practically arithmetic, anyway. You just have to use common sense."

He first started experimenting with chords and rhythmic effects in a four-piece group with which he used to gig. That was in 1939. Jimmy Wright played tenor, Keg Purnell was the drummer and the bassist was named Mas-apequha. He could have gone with big bands, but "bands never did knock me out. I wanted to play my own chords. I wanted to create and invent on little jobs." So little jobs he played.

Then he landed at Minton's, a Harlem spot run by former bandleader Teddy Hill, who says, "Monk would fall asleep [at the piano] all the time. He'd stay there hours after the place closed, or get there hours before we opened. Sometimes the musicians would appeal to me to see if I could wake him up. Suddenly he might wake up and go into some intricate, tricky little passage, with Kenny Clarke playing those funny, off-beat effects on the drums."[3]

Clarke was one of the four regulars at Minton's. Joe Guy played trumpet and Nick Fenton was on bass. A lot of musicians used to hang out up there, Diz and Bird, Charlie Christian, Kermit Scott, Ike Quebec, Ben Webster, King Cole, Mary Lou Williams, Max Roach, Art Blakey, whom Monk considers the best of the modern drummers, and Denzil Best, known to most boppists as a drummer, but who, according to Monk, "was one of the best trumpets I ever heard. He'd outblow everybody in the place, but he had to quit because of his health."

The fact that Best recuperated and then came back in the role of a drummer should be an object lesson to a lot of musicians, feels Monk. "He didn't blow his top because he was frustrated. To me, a true musician is a guy who never gives up, even though he feels like it sometimes." Monk is not in favor of the undisciplined ways of too many modern musicians and can't sympathize with them because they blow their tops when they aren't appreciated. Though many feel that Monk hasn't received the recognition that's due him, he doesn't resent anything. "My time for fame will come." The many sides he recently cut for Blue Note Records should bring that time much nearer, he feels.

He's not too anxious to be associated with most of the bop that's being blown nowadays. Besides accusing some musicians of turning bop into something akin to Dixieland, he also upbraids them with phrases like, "they molest," "they magnify," "they exaggerate." "They don't pay any attention to

3. Quoted from Leonard Feather, "Bebop??!!—Man, We Called It Kloop-mop!!" *Metronome*, April 1947, p. 45. The article was subtitled "Teddy Hill, who was there, tells about the early days of Dizzy and how the kloop-moppers started bebopping at Minton's." *Ed.*

swing, and that goes both for the horns and the rhythm sections. They don't know where to put those bops. When the horns say *bloop*, the drummer shouldn't say *bloop, bloop, bloop* with them. You should throw in your rhythmic bops when a guy's taking a breath.

"Another thing is the chords. I can tell right off when a guy knows what he's doing. Diz and Bird, they know their chords. But too many horns use the flatted fifth where it sounds absurd, instead of where it should sound beautiful. They should try to keep their music melodious; when it becomes unmelodious, then it sounds like Dixieland."

Monk's philosophy also holds for big bands. "Kenton tries too hard for effects, though some of them are good. Actually, the only good-sounding band I've heard in years is Claude Thornhill's. I'd like Diz's band if they played the music right."

Monk has written for Dizzy. "Dizzy Atmosphere" has his chords. The melody is by Joe Guy. It came from Minton's. "Fifty-Second Street Theme" in Victor's *Fifty-Second Street* album is also Monk's. He wrote it about eight years ago, "same time I wrote "'Round About Midnight," which Cootie plays but for which Monk doesn't get credit. Monk also wrote Cootie's theme, "Epistrophy," which is a botanical term that means "the reversion of the abnormal to the normal."

Music hasn't reverted enough to suit Monk; it's still too abnormal for him. It'll sound more normal when enough of the newer musicians start playing with a beat and when fewer of them blow just for effect instead of making real, melodious music. Until that time he doesn't care too much how much credit he is given for having started bop. What he hears these days doesn't make him too proud of his child. He hopes his new records will help a lot of young, modern musicians hear the light. Till then he'd rather not be too closely associated with something that to him is getting to sound much too much like Dixieland.

11. *The High Priest of Be-bop*

After more than 50 years, Paul Bacon's thoughtful essay still contains some of the best-published insights into Monk and his music. He originally wrote the article included here for *Jazz Hot*, as the

Blue Note recordings were attracting attention in France, and later published it in *The Record Changer.* Bacon focuses attention on Monk's personality and how it relates to hearing his music, comparing Monk to a self-absorbed child who by virtue of his naiveté is able to create something original. It is an argument that has been repeated often in assessments of Monk.[1] As evidence of Monk's genuine oblivious state of mind, Bacon recounts a scene where Monk, bothered by the pedal of a piano he is sitting at in a club, reaches down and rips the whole unit out. The most striking paragraph in Bacon's article delivers an analogy to drawing, obviously a point of reference for Bacon, who was a designer/illustrator: he likens Monk to being someone "listening to himself, playing variations on what he hears . . . it's a little like watching an essentially right-handed but ambidextrous man draw with both hands at once . . . the right hand's effort is calculated and familiar, but the left hand's, though it almost follows suit, has a weird distortion."

This article originally appeared as "The High Priest of Bebop: The Inimitable Mr. Monk," by Paul Bacon in *The Record Changer* in November 1949, Vol. 8, No. 11, pp. 9–11, 26. Used by permission of Paul Bacon.

Even the worst enemies of the man known as the "High Priest of Bebop" are forced to admit that he is, after all, a remarkable fellow. It has become fashionable to think him a greatly overrated musician, something of a charlatan, a mystic whose very mysticism is calculated to conceal a rather prosaic flaw: poor musicianship. That is utter nonsense.

There is no doubt that Monk is a man without conventional scope, without the sense of the opportune, devoid entirely of the deft imagination which Dizzy Gillespie turned into an even more valuable property than his talent, by capitalizing on the physical oddities of the bop school, with great good will and ingratiating theatrics. Lack of that perception, and elan, is serious in the music business. It leads to other lacks which, though they aren't aesthetically noticeable, are not conducive to health and happiness: lack of things like money.

I don't pretend to hold any brief for the things Thelonious has done to, and for, himself, nor do I intend to demonstrate that he is in reality a mild, virtuous and misunderstood man. People have knocked themselves out in his

1. See the article by Gerald Early, reprinted on p. 235, for a critique of this idea.

behalf, time and again, without producing any permanent good, not because of any maliciousness on Monk's part, but because the chasm separating their senses of value from his is too great. It is better to be an amateur admirer than a promoter, in Monk's case.

I have a choice here between writing about Monk as he is, or as he seems to be, and is generally thought to be. There isn't any great difficulty about it, because both sides are fertile ground; the stories merely differ in plausibility. The trick to making a genuine legend out of an artist is quite simple—you need only to describe him in comparison with so-called "normal" people, if he is slightly eccentric, and, if he is not, describe his remarkable normality in comparison with the weird behavior of other artists. Thus, in Thelonious' case, staying up for 72 hours at a stretch and then sleeping for 48 may well be considered unusual (if he did it continually, which he doesn't, he could rest on those laurels alone), like many other things he does, unless you remember that he is a musician, that his personal life is that of a musician and not a bank clerk.

Nonetheless, there are aspects of Monk's personality which no amount of logic can solve. He is undoubtedly a very selfish man (this quality, too, is not at all unique among artists), and the business of having the world revolve around him has caused him to see things in a remarkably direct fashion—very much in the manner of a child. The process of becoming mature requires a hell of a lot of concessions, usually called "adjustments," and he has never made many. In this way, the formality of wearing clothes is inexplicable to a child, just as the formality of musical structure is inexplicable to Monk. I think that some subtle facet of his mind realizes that he has this quality, and that he cherishes it.

A self-absorption as profound as Thelonious' produces some wonderful anecdotes, many of which have been printed over and over; my favorite is an incident I was spectator to, and which has never been recounted, as far as I know.

There is, in Harlem, a monstrous barn of a dance-hall called the "Golden Gate"; quite a number of affairs are produced there every year, and the usual system is to have two alternating bands working—in the last few years the two bands have been one bop group and one Calypso band. (There are a couple of remarkable Calypso bands in New York, playing a real powerhouse music which is closer to Harlem in 1928 than Trinidad in any year.) The occasion I'm thinking of took place there in 1947, almost exactly two years ago. Macbeth's calypso contingent shared the stand with a bop sextet fronted by Monk; the boppers were second in line, so, after a long set by Macbeth, Monk's band wandered desultorily to the stand.

Monk fussed with the piano, discovering that it was a pretty venerable instrument (when he sits at a piano there is a dead key on it—no matter how recently the thing was in perfect condition. He accepts this as one of the penalties of genius) and making faces at it as he sounded notes at the other musicians' request. Close examination showed him that the pedal post was shakily attached; he jiggled the whole piano apprehensively, then shrugged his shoulders and concentrated on some music left behind by Macbeth's pianist.

A little later, I became aware that Thelonious was doing something extraordinary—tying his shoe or waving to somebody under the piano; as I watched, mesmerized, I saw that he was yanking at the pedal post with all his might (first he kept up with the band by reaching up with his right hand to strike an occasional chord, but he had to apply himself to the attack on the post with both hands, and get his back into it, too). There was a slight crack, a ripping sound, and off came the whole works, to be flung aside as Monk calmly resumed playing. He never looked at it again, but when Macbeth's man came back on the stand he stopped short, stunned. It was obvious that here was a new experience, something outside the ken of a rational man; for the rest of the evening he looked upon Thelonious with a new respect.

It is generally something much like the above bit of business which causes people to look on Monk with a new respect; nothing is quite so arresting as a man who actually doesn't give a damn, even if you think he is acting, and how do you prove that?

Take off Thelonious' famous glasses and you will look hard to find your eccentric High Priest of Bebop; they are his armor and his shield. Most people are shocked to discover that he does, after all, have eyes like their own—it's so easy to think of him as a man with a gold-plated brow and two-inch black discs for eyes. There isn't anything fragile about him, mentally or physically, as his reputation for being able to take care of himself will attest. A necessarily iron constitution is supported by a six-foot, 175-pound frame, which he drapes in double-breasted suits exclusively, most of the time with the coat unbuttoned. He moves slowly, very slowly, under any conditions; at his initial concert, in New York's Town Hall, he had to walk approximately fifty feet to the piano, after being announced; he emerged from the wings with a deliberate, measured step, taking an age to reach the Steinway.[2] Before he had completed the necessary ceremony of bench-adjusting, pedal-testing, and coattail-draping, the audience was in a state of prostration. This was not a matter of stage presence, or lack of it; only a perfect sample of the deport-

2. The concert took place on February 16, 1948. *Ed.*

ment of Thelonious Monk. As he puts it, "you have to be yourself—if you try to be different, you might miss your cues."

At any rate, this man, unmalleable, exasperating, sometimes perverse to the point of justifiable homicide, is the man who casually formed the nucleus of the group which surprised itself by changing, at least temporarily, the direction of jazz. That was ten years ago.

Minton's Playhouse, on Harlem's 118th Street, is like many another birthplace of famous people and events—it doesn't look like much. Inside, though, there is an atmosphere hard to find anyplace else in New York; an ease, a lack of the professional gimlet-eyed nightclub bandits, whose only salable commodity is an obsequiousness available to one and all, for a small consideration. There have also been, at various times, a dapper waiter named Romeo, who was as likely to dance for the customers as bring them drinks, and many young musicians working for a living; in 1939 they included Kenny Clarke and Thelonious Monk.

I might add here that Monk's part in the whole history of bebop began long before 1939. In fact, as he tells it, he was playing essentially the same way he does now in 1932, when he was fifteen years old. His conception is *not* something that grew out of what he felt was a need for something new in music—he just played that way. His ear was hearing between the lines of its own accord, and that nonconformist ego told him that what he heard was perfectly valid. Time seems to have borne him out.

Too many stories have been written about the genesis of bop at Minton's; the footprints are all obscured, and I say why not? All the recounting of who played what for whom, and who picked it up, and who sat in and said "Man, this is it!" is producing some of the asinine squabbles which are the curse of traditional jazz. It seems definite that Monk and Clarke are chiefly responsible, and Monk has the advantage, historically, because he's a pianist and Clarke is a drummer. I doubt that either of them, or anyone else, knew what they were doing, saw anything momentous on the horizon, or even cared particularly.

Monk is fundamentally a catalyst, a well-spring; he is consistently interesting whether he's playing or not. The complex personality which makes his behavior unpredictable has made his music stimulating to gifted and receptive men like Parker and Gillespie; that personality is unchangeable, the stimulus is unfading. He'll have both when he's ninety years old.

Those are the attributes he had at Minton's, and they made him a source, something fundamental, therefore priceless. Any new enterprise requires a certain personnel to be vital: several people who grasp because their sophistication tells them that here is a direction their machinery is admirably suited to travel in, and at least one who is there because he is unable to do anything else, the man with an honest germ of an idea. Monk fits neatly into the latter category; not a virtuoso, but a creator. He can't sell his product, but there are salesmen who can, and do, even, though some may not believe in it implicitly.

Well, what is his product? It is something quite fragile and intangible, like the quality in the stories of Virginia Woolf and Gertrude Stein. In fact, there have been many times when Monk has offended delicate ears with his pianistic assertion that a theme is a theme is a theme. He is perfectly aware that he has nothing new to say, no revelations to make to anyone; it is the simplest thing in the world to say "all he's done there is to play a G7th instead of, etc. . ." which is like saying that all Cezanne did is to translate nature into cones, cubes and spheres, and what's so remarkable about that?

Listen to Thelonious and you hear a man listening to himself, playing variations on what he hears, so that you never really are in contact with his immediate impressions; it's a little like watching an essentially right-handed but ambidextrous man draw with both hands at once—the right hand's effort is calculated and familiar, but the left hand's, though it almost follows suit, has a weird distortion; it's the same thing, but different, and it is likely to be more interesting.

The identity of a tune is like the identity of a word—it remains itself only as long as it is scrupulously kept in its proper place, with its proper emphasis; a great many ingredients go into recognition of either one. Everyone has had the experience of having a word suddenly become a series of foreign letters, utterly unrecognizable; in Monk's hands, a well-worn tune may dissolve into that same unreality. For instance, "Liza" is a song I've always known and liked, and however I heard it, it was always undisputably "Liza," with connotations of words, situations and sensations; but I *heard* it for the first time when Monk played it, because he is under no such hallucinations about any melody. What I have described is not the same thing as improvising: to play exhaustive variations on "How High the Moon" is not the same as to reconstruct it entirely, any more than closing your eyes makes you see as a blind man sees.

Monk's product is essentially simplicity. Because of it, he is a provocative musician, one with whom other musicians play well—sometimes better than they ever have. Recognizing that he had something beyond a reputation to offer, Blue Note Records, a firm of almost suicidal integrity, decided to take the plunge and make some records with him. The idea bore fruit in more ways than one, because they immediately discovered a whole uneaten side of the evil apple which is bebop—young musicians, without reputation, who were following the avant-garde Gillespie and Parker circles, and bringing with them something of their own. They discovered that Monk always knew of a guy "who could blow," trumpet, tenor, alto—whatever was required. Alfred and Lorraine Lion and Frank Wolff were, for a time, father, brother, moral support and employment agency for Thelonious and his crew, and there were some fantastically messed-up moments for all parties during the time the records were being cut.

The titles have the same charm as the music—"'Round About Midnight," "In Walked Bud," "Humph," "Ruby, My Dear," "Evonce," "Well, You Needn't," "Suburban Eyes," to name a few; the first one was "Thelonious," which one reviewer described as "oddly affecting," and that's pretty close.

During the time that these records were made, Monk went back to work at Minton's with a quartet which has always been one of the high spots for me in the frenetic life of bop: Edmond Gregory (Shehab, as his adopted Moslem brethren call him) on alto, Al McKibbon on bass, the amazing Art Blakey on drums, and Monk.[3] That was a perfect unit, unlike any other, before or since; they played no tunes but their own, in no way but their own; they did more rhythmically, than any musical group I ever heard anywhere; and they kept improving until the inevitable break-up came, after too short a time. That band at Minton's made an era of its own, much as Jimmy Noone's did at the Apex Club.

I'll finish by saying that in listening to Monk, the same advice applies as is given to fans of traditional jazz, on hearing bop for the first time: forget what you know, don't compare—listen. Monk is likely to be as jarring a departure from Dizzy Gillespie as Dizzy is from Louis, and yet he may hit you right away. An open ear is a wonderful thing.

3. There are no other accounts of Monk's having played at Minton's after the 1940–1941 period, or at any other club with the group he used for the Blue Note recordings in 1951. For a good summary of Monk's club engagements during the 1940s, see Michael Cuscuna's notes to *The Complete Blue Note Recordings of Thelonious Monk* (Mosaic MR401; published in 1983). *Ed.*

Prestige and Paris 1954

12. Thelonious Monk: Portrait of the Artist as an Enigma

During the years 1952–1954 Monk was under contract with Prestige records and recorded several albums under his own name and as a sideman on albums by Sonny Rollins and Miles Davis, the latter session which produced the celebrated "Bags' Groove" solo.[1] Also during this period he made his first trip to Europe, which came about as a result of the French pianist Henri Renaud's visit to him in New York. Renaud spent three months with the pianist George Wallington in New York in 1953, visiting clubs like Birdland, The Open Door, and Tony's Café, and meeting up with the likes of Bud Powell, Art Blakey, and Sonny Rollins.[2] He met Monk, who at the time was without a cabaret card and could not work in New York City, and arranged for him to appear at the Salon Internationale du Jazz in June 1954. Partly because of the fact that the local rhythm section was unfamiliar with

1. See the articles by André Hodeir and Ran Blake for further discussion of this solo, reprinted on p. 118 and p. 248.
2. Renaud gives an account of his trip in "Trois mois a New York," *Jazz Hot,* October 1954, pp. 15–16.

his music, or in part because Monk's music was so unlike the "cool" West Coast style, the concerts (he appeared twice) received little attention. The real talk of the festival was Gerry Mulligan, who met Monk backstage, gave him encouragement, and later, as a result of this meeting, recorded with him for Riverside. The French magazine *Jazz Hot* barely mentions Monk in its review, but did include him in a set of caricatures of musicians playing the festival: a piano in the shape of a sphinx, with Monk's head attached and labeled "Thelonious Monk, ou le Sphinx du Jazz."[3] However, Mike Nevard in *Melody Maker* described the opening concert:

> Between sets, we met the phenomenon known as Monk. . . . It would be easy to dismiss Monk as a musical charlatan—but you'd probably be wrong. His playing is hammy, fascinating, trite—and interesting. . . .
>
> It is sometimes startling, sometimes banal, sometimes both together. . . . His right hand stabs at the keyboard in a Chico Marx manner, apparently without flexibility. He hits with a finger and the rest of the hand arches stiffly like a fan. He hammers unrelated chords, while his feet writhe and twist on the floor. His right foot hits the pedal, misses, slips off; it poises, and bangs down sometimes on the pedal, often on the floor. His left foot drags back and forth as though tortured. An elbowed chord sounds natural in its surroundings. . . . You can't assess Monk because there are no set standards by which to judge him. By the normal criterion of jazz he is inferior . . . but there may be minds attuned to his weird, morse-like message.[4]

While in Paris, Monk recorded nine solo piano pieces for the French label Vogue,[5] and for the first time met the Baroness Nica de Koenigswarter, who later was to play a seminal role in his life.

Raymond Horricks was at the Salle Pleyel in 1954. Included here is an excerpt from a chapter on Monk in the book *These Jazzmen of Our Time,* a collection of essays edited by Horricks with contributions by

3. *Jazz Hot,* July/August 1954, p. 10.
4. "Mulligan, Monk—and then a French Surprise," *Melody Maker,* June 5, 1954, p. 9.
5. Apparently both concerts for the festival were also recorded but have not been issued to date (see Brian Priestley's notes to *The Complete Black Lion and Vogue Recordings*, Mosaic MR4-112).

Max Harrison, Nat Hentoff, Alun Morgan, and Martin Williams. As originally published, the chapter is an overview of Monk's life and music, and so duplicates much of what is included in this reader. There are nevertheless many insightful comments about Monk and his music. Toward the end of the chapter, he concludes:

> The music itself is strangely logical . . . it is hard, angular and insistent music; made with harmonic progressions in which the chords least expected suddenly appear, forcing the melodic line to climb rather than flow over them. *To Thelonious harmony is the most important musical element and rhythm, timing and accent are its allies; melody is a subordinate to be used for unusual bends and intermittent tensions rather than beauteous effect.*[6]

Horricks worked as a record producer in England for many years and wrote extensively on jazz, including books on Count Basie, Gil Evans, Stephane Grappelli, Gerry Mulligan, Dizzy Gillespie and Eric Dolphy.

This originally appeared as a chapter in *These Jazzmen of Our Time* (London: Victor Golancz) in 1959, by Raymond Horricks. It has been edited for this reprint. Used by permission of Raymond Horricks.

"ET MAINTENANT, Thelonious Monk."

A round of premature applause died away. Promoter Charles Delaunay retired from the stage. And slowly, dispassionately, the heavy green velvet curtains of the Salle Pleyel eddied back to their bases, revealing two frightened accompanying musicians and a vacant piano stool.

Some seconds elapsed before the object of the audience's skeptical handclap ambled into view. He came, half bowing, a tall Negro dressed in a loose-fitting medium blue suit, sky blue socks and shirt, taking long, seemingly tiring steps towards the microphone. He smiled inanely as he surveyed the audience: a smile conveying no meaning.

"Bonsoir tout le monde." He spoke correct, but uneasy French. "Je joue *Well, You Needn't.*"

Again the long, ponderous strides as he trekked back to the piano. He sat, fingers poised over the keys, meditating, while the French bassist and drum-

6. Horricks, "Thelonious Monk: Portrait of the Artist as an Enigma," in *These Jazzmen of Our Time*, p. 35.

mer awaited their cue. Then suddenly he arose and retraced the long journey to the microphone.

"Je joue *Off Minor*," he said in a naive voice.

There was no explanation for this change of title, not even to the supporting musicians. The audience, well known for its turbulent behavior, set off a murmuring undercurrent at this latest announcement.

He resettled at the piano and started to play the tune he'd written in the early 1940s. At last Thelonious was in action. At least, action of a kind. Fingers splayed stiffly, stabbing rather than touching the keys, legs thrashing wildly beneath the piano, searching for the pedal, missing it, banging the floor instead, body swaying, arms stretching and bending as he felt for unusual chords, grunting loudly as he found them: the fascination of it was visual rather than musical.

At the end of the second chorus he got up from the piano and pointed one large banana-like finger at Jean-Louis Viale, the young drummer. Two tense white faces showed the supporting musicians had long since abandoned hope of a logical performance, and Viale, recovering from this latest shock, began his drum solo to relieve the comedy that had taken place at the piano.

As the invention of the solo unfolded the large finger remained pointed at him, the sky blue socks and suede shoes jogged rhythmically and the heavy face, still grinning superfluously, turned to stare again at the audience, as if to question its understanding of what was going on. When Viale finally wound up his solo Monk returned to the keyboard and the playing became even more erratic; the legs thrashed more wildly, the grunting increased in volume; he struck chords with his elbow *à la* Jelly Roll Morton, and at one point stuck his fingers into the piano and flicked the hammers on to the strings. Flash bulbs were exploding around him. The lay press were especially excited by this spectacle. At length it was through and I couldn't help but breathe a sigh of relief.

Here, at the opening concert of the 1954 Paris Jazz Fair, I had been listening to one of the imported American jazzmen playing in a way which shook to the foundations my every attempt at intelligent appreciation of the music. This was something for the opponents of jazz to get their teeth into: an act in the good old vaudeville tradition, a travesty of everything supposed to be sane about modern jazz. And from a musician revered as one of the early thinkers and teachers of the modern movement, credited by the legendary Parker as being the first person to shift the emphasis in improvisation from a melodic to a harmonic source.

Tales of Thelonious the eccentric had percolated through to Europe beforehand, but this first glimpse was still quite incredible! I'd heard of his Rip Van Winkle-ish slumbers in the New York clubs, of his odd conception of time and of dress in the frantic early days of modern jazz, not least of his unconcern over critics and their criticism. (Once he remarked: "Let's not talk about music, let's play it.") But to watch him turn his own music into a parody; this was entirely unexpected.

Jazz in its short life and prolific development has owned a number of outstanding humorists—Armstrong, Waller, Shavers, Gillespie and Vic Dickenson spring to mind immediately—whose very extrovert personalities have caused a ready wit to be interpolated into their playing. Yet these I have named express humour with taste. One laughs with them—not at them.

To witness a man making a fool of himself and his music as I had just done, a man committing artistic suicide, was no such pleasant sensation. In England my record shelves held performances by Thelonious the innovator—performances by a musician creating confined but significant jazz. Now I was forced to mark him down as a kind of court jester to modern jazz.

When the concert was over and most of the musicians and journalists and listeners had retired to the smoky Salle Pleyel cabaret, there to hear jazz of a more informal nature, and to have the privilege of occupying several square inches of a floor-space highly in demand and to drink iced lager at fourteen shillings a pint, I again watched Thelonious in action.

This time he was sitting in with (and thoroughly disrupting) a session by the Gerry Mulligan Quartet, normally a piano-less group. Monk whipped out some of his contrived harmonies and upset the poise of the other musicians completely. It must have been one of the most chaotic sets ever played, and it ended as abruptly as it began when Mulligan was told by his wife that he'd been there long enough and had better pack his saxophone away and leave.[7]

By the time the sky blue socks walked off the stand I was crushed up against the bar talking with trumpeter Jonah Jones, the least temperamental jazz soloist playing at the Fair that year. Jonah chewed on his cigar stub and clutched a long lemonade and complained about his doctor taking him off whisky. ("I was a bottle-a-day man, you know, and when the doctor put his tube thing against

7. And yet this set was important in one way, in that Monk and Mulligan were left filled with curiosity about each other's music. Apparently the next day Thelonious was thoroughly depressed about the reaction to his music in Europe. "I don't think they'll listen to what I really want to play." he said at a morning reception. Gerry Mulligan overheard this and turned to the pianist. "Don't bother about them," he snapped. "I'll be listening to you. I'll be just off stage listening to you. If you turn a little that way you'll see me there." And Thelonious played his next concert like that, with his imposing figure slightly averted from the audience and turned toward the side of the stage. This marked the beginning of a musical understanding between Monk and Mulligan; an understanding that led directly to their recording together for Riverside three years later.

my chest he said I didn't have any right to be alive.") Between medicine talk he reminisced the times he'd been with Cab Calloway's band. Suddenly Monk appeared at our side with Charles Delaunay. "Hi man, you look smart!" Jonah quipped, and he elbowed room at the bar for the new arrivals. His remark was answered by the broadest of smiles but no speech. At the same time, as if he needed to verify Jonah's compliment, the pianist looked down at his suit. Then, as abruptly as he'd appeared, he moved away into the crowd.

This was the nearest I came to getting a coherent conversation out of Thelonious in Paris.

On one occasion I came across him talking quite intensely to Delaunay, but as far as I know most writers ran up against the same blank wall when they tried to talk to him. I remembered the attempt by Steve Race to interview Charlie Parker at the 1949 Paris Jazz Fair when, instead of leading a musical discussion, Parker insisted on reading aloud passages from Omar Khayyam. At least, though, Steve Race heard his quarry speak! Monk represented a study in isolation, a man oblivious to all praise or criticisms, or public relations.

(Joachim Berendt, the German writer, tracked Monk down to his hotel room the next day, only to have him discuss intelligently the so trivial things, his silk dressing gown for instance, and then answer with an evasive "it's just okay" whenever a serious subject—racial, social and so on—was broached. Berendt suggested, however, that Monk was considerably overawed by Europe—that "he felt in need of protection"—and this is interesting since it explains perhaps why the pianist drank excessively and clowned the way he did in Paris. To be overawed by Europe has been a typically American attitude even into this century; Henry James wrote repeatedly of the 'innocent' American meeting up with the 'sophisticated' European. To act the fool, of course, has been a cover-up for a feeling of insecurity in man through the ages.)

Two evenings later, though, I attended the Jazz Fair's second concert of modern jazz, this time represented by the Geo Daly Quintet, Thelonious, the Kurt Edelhagen Orchestra and the Gerry Mulligan Quartet. After an unpretentious set by Daly, Monk walked on-stage to receive a scattering of disrespectful gestures. But they were not needed. An obviously changed man, calm and subdued, he played some of the most advanced and imaginative modern jazz piano I'd heard. His touch was definitive, his spontaneous search for new harmonic structures successful, his rhythmic emphasis clear and direct and considerate to his supporting musicians; in short, a musician sure of himself and sure of his direction in jazz.

Thus the complete enigma that is Thelonious Monk, the curtain parting to reveal the other side of his nature, the Jekyll added to the Hyde existence.

Critical Recognition (1955–1961)

By signing with Riverside Records in 1955, Monk began a new phase in his career, although the New York City police department continued to withhold his cabaret card. Monk was reluctant to leave the city, so the years leading up to 1957 were lean and frustrating, even as he won acceptance from major jazz critics. Monk's wife, Nellie, whom he had married in 1947, worked as a seamstress to support the family, which by now included two children, Thelonious Jr. (b. 1951) and Barbara (b. 1954). Monk finally began to make a living as a musician in 1957 with the reinstatement of his cabaret card, and Joe Termini booked him for an indefinite period at the Five Spot Café in New York.[1] Both the long stay at the Five Spot and his recordings for Riverside generated rave reviews, and he gradually moved up in the annual *Down Beat* critic and reader polls, ending up with the most votes in the piano category of the critics poll in 1958.[2] There were many notable engage-

1. Figures for actual earnings are hard to come by. Bob Doerschuk, in his article "Thelonious Monk" (*Keyboard,* July 1982, pp. 11-16), claims Monk's earnings in 1958 were in the range of $800 per week for his band, climbing to $2,000 in 1960. Leslie Gourse, who interviewed Monk's manager Harry Colomby, cites a figure of $650 per week in 1957, leaving $250 for Monk himself after paying the sidemen and Colomby (Leslie Gourse, *Straight, No Chaser,* New York: Schirmer, 1997, p. 132).
2. Consistent poll leaders for piano during the 1950s were Art Tatum, Dave Brubeck, and Oscar Peterson, so to have someone like Monk—who at the time had a much more limited appeal—reach the top was very unusual. The voting had a lot to do with who received the most critical attention during a given year. For example, the 1958 poll had

ments during these years, a successful appearance at the second Newport Jazz Festival in 1955 with Miles Davis,[3] a television appearance in 1957, a well-publicized concert at Town Hall in 1959, and his first European Tour in 1961. In addition to the attention received from the music press, feature articles in general magazines such as *Esquire, Ebony, and Harper's* appeared, capitalizing on Monk's image as a benign, eccentric jazz musician.

Hampton Hawes and Dave Brubeck at the bottom of the list and Thelonious Monk, Erroll Garner, and Oscar Peterson at the top. Bud Powell was stuck somewhere in the middle and Bill Evans came out with the most votes under the "Piano-New Star" section.

3. Davis performed an impromptu and extremely well-received version of "'Round Midnight," which was later to become one of his signature tunes, but as he later recalls in his autobiography, Monk was not pleased with the performance. See pp. 191–192 of *Miles: The Autobiography,* by Miles Davis with Quincy Troupe (New York: Simon and Schuster, 1989).

Interviews

13. Just Call Him Thelonious

After the profile/interviews published in 1947 and 1948, it was eight years before Monk was interviewed again, this time for *Down Beat* by the renowned jazz critic Nat Hentoff, who, the following year, turned the critical tide with his five-star review of the *Brilliant Corners* album. The interview is not a literal transcription and so it reads as if Monk is thinking out loud over a series of questions, hardly a representation of a typical encounter with Monk. The piece was obviously intended to reacquaint the readers of *Down Beat* with Monk, offering a review of the years leading up to the Riverside period, with several unverified anonymous quotes, but there are nevertheless revealing statements about his own music and jazz in general. And sometimes Monk is just plain funny, as in "Do I think I'm difficult to understand? . . . Some of my pieces have melodies a nitwit can understand. Like I've written one number staying on one note. A tone-deaf person could hum it."[1] Hentoff has written extensively on jazz since the 1950s, but

1. The piece in question is "Thelonious," in which the tonic B-flat is repeated through a rhythmic figure, occasionally relieved by F. The interest of the tune lies in the juxtaposition of this simple figure and the fast moving chromatically descending dominant seventh chords, harmonized in the horns. Maybe a tone-deaf person could hum the melody, but they would need to have a very good sense of time and not be thrown off by the underlying orchestration.

he also became a novelist and award-winning commentator on politics and education.

This article originally appeared as "Just Call Him Thelonious," by Nat Hentoff in *Down Beat,* July 25, 1956, pp. 15–16. Reprinted with permission of *Down Beat.*

The most frequent word used in relation to the personality—musical and otherwise—of Thelonious Sphere Monk has been "enigmatic."

Part of the reason for this supposed opaqueness about Monk lies in the man himself, for he seldom verbalizes about his music.

His conversation on most subjects is spare enough. But with regard to his own work, his feeling appears to be that whatever communication there is in his music can be obtained only by listening and that words only obscure the issue. Monk, therefore, has written no articles about his credo and has engaged in no public debates. When he has something to say, he says it in his music.

As a result of this disinclination to talk much about his work—coupled with a cryptic sense of humor—Monk has not been an easy interviewee. Several European critics who tried to discuss music with him during his 1954 appearance at the Paris Jazz fair were baffled.

In this country, part of the fault for Monk-the-enigma is chargeable to the jazz writers. And for lack of words from the source, writing and talking about Monk by nonmusicians often has been unusually expressionistic.

There is, for example, this note on his melodies by German critic Joachim E. Berendt: "I like to think of them as 'al fresco melodies,' painted directly on 'a blank wall' with nothing under it but hard stone. You cannot take them with you as you can with paintings which are framed. You have to come back. You will if you ever get their message."

Then there is the view expressed in Chicago: "Monk's playing is like a painter who stands across the room and throws paint at a canvas. You can't object too much to the way it turns out because he has chosen such beautiful colors to throw."

Musicians who have been influenced or deeply stimulated by Monk know better. Monk's melodies can be taken with you, and his harmonic colorations are hardly conceived in a Jackson Pollock manner. Monk knows what he's doing. Yet here again, because of his own disinterest in self-exposition, there is no detailed analysis available of Monk's harmonic system.

Also to be mentioned are those listeners, critics, and some musicians who put him down as an eccentric, deliberate or otherwise, who has made peripheral contributions to modern jazz but is far from a key figure in its development. This writer disagrees with this latter view.

In any case, Thelonious Sphere Monk, named after his father, was born in North Carolina, not in New York, as the reference books say. Monk's answer concerning his birth date is: "When shall I be born? I'm just playing a game like everybody else." Leonard Feather gives his birth date as Oct. 10, 1920.[2]

His mother was Barbara Monk. He went to Public School 141 in New York City, where the family moved when Monk was 4. He attended Stuyvesant High School, where sources other than Monk say he excelled in math, physics, and music and was expert in basketball.

The rest of his story, in what, as far as I know, is the first interview with Monk to have been written in many years, is told by the pianist with occasional comments from other sources.

"It's hard to go back. Like what happened 82 bars ago. At least it's hard to go back earlier than 10 years ago. I remember fooling around a piano when I was 5 or 6 years old, picking out melodies."

"No, my parents weren't musical. I did have a few lessons when I was pretty young, around 10 or 11, but what I've learned since I've mostly taught myself. I never picked no special musicians to follow. I've liked something about nearly every musician I heard, but I never patterned myself after any particular one. Of course, you have to go through certain stages to learn how to play the piano, but that doesn't necessarily mean you're copying somebody's style. I've learned from numerous pianists."[3]

"I had decided to go into music full time 'way back, when I first took lessons. While still in my teens, I went on the road with a group that played church music for an evangelist. Rock and roll or rhythm and blues. That's what we were doing. Only now they put different words to it. She preached and healed and we played."

"We had trumpet, saxophone, piano, and drums. And then the congregation would sing. We would play in some of the biggest churches in the towns we went through. We traveled around the country for about two years." . . .

"Back in New York, I tried to find jobs. I worked all over town. Nonunion jobs, $20 a week, seven nights a week, and then the man might fire you anytime and you never got your money. I've been on millions of those kinds of jobs. I've been on every kind of job you can think of all over New York. I really found out how to get around this city. Dance halls. Every place. How long did this scuffling go on? It hasn't stopped."

2. Monk's birth date was October 10, 1917.

3. For a different account on Monk's early influences, see the article by Peter Keepnews, reprinted on p. 4. *Ed.*

"As for my style, I've always been told way back that I was unique, but I never lost a job on account of that. I first met Dizzy when I was in my early 20s. There were a lot of places all over Harlem that had three or four pieces, and there the musicians felt like blowing. Charlie Parker? I met him in Vic Dickenson's room where he was visiting one day. Charlie wasn't well known uptown around this time."

"Really, I don't remember all these details. I met a whole gang of musicians, and I wasn't paying anything that much attention. I was playing a gig, tryin' to play music. While I was at Minton's, anybody sat in who would come up there if he could play. I never bothered anybody. It was just a job. I had no particular feeling that anything new was being built. It's true modern jazz probably began to get popular there. But as for me, my mind was like it was before I worked in Minton's."

"Some of those histories and articles put what happened in 10 years in one year. They put people all together in one time in this place. Over a period of time, I've seen practically everybody at Minton's, but they were just in there playing. They weren't giving any lectures. It got a little glamorous maybe on Monday nights when Teddy Hill, the manager, would invite the guys who were at the Apollo that week. As a result, all the different bands that played at the Apollo got to hear the original music, and it got around and talk started going about the fellows at Minton's."

"Another story about that time is that Dizzy began to write down what Bird was doing. Why should Bird get Dizzy to write something down? He could write it down himself. I can't answer for what Bird thought of me, by the way, but I always went for his playing."

"Bud Powell? He wasn't on the scene at first. Nobody knew about Bud until I brought him along. I met him in a juice joint uptown. At first at Minton's, Kenny Clarke didn't want Bud to sit in at the piano. The way I would put those years at Minton's and other places uptown was that we were just fellows working, and all the musicians would come by and jam."

(Other musicians have declared that matters were not entirely so unplanned at Minton's. Gillespie and Clarke agree that there were often afternoon sessions and also caucuses on the job when Monk, Dizzy, Clarke, and Joe Guy would work out new chord progressions both to discourage incompetent sitters-in that night and also because they became more and more intrigued with the possibilities of these changing approaches to jazz.)

Feather's *Encyclopedia of Jazz* states accurately that, except for a brief date with Lucky Millinder's band in 1942—"a week or so at the Savoy," Monk remembers—and a 1944 engagement with Coleman Hawkins on 52nd St.,

Monk has always worked on his own in recent years heading a small combo.

"The first records I ever made," Monk said, "were with Coleman Hawkins." (These were in 1944.) "Hawkins can play, as far as I'm concerned. Nobody can pick up a tenor without playing some of him. He's the first one who started playing tenor. He created a very good job for the tenor players."

In 1954, Monk made his European debut at the Paris Jazz fair. His playing, according to most observers, could be characterized as inconsistent at the least. Monk's recollection: "I enjoyed the visit very much. The only drag was I didn't have my own band with me. I couldn't find anybody to play with me that could make it. All the good jazz seems to be in the United States. But I'd like to go back over with my own group."[4]

Monk, talking with characteristic slowness and long pauses between carefully phrased statements, covered several areas concerned with Monk-the-legend as opposed to Monk-seen-by Monk:

"Do I think I'm difficult to understand? Well, like what? Tell me a particular number. Some of my pieces have melodies a nitwit can understand. Like I've written one number staying on one note. A tone-deaf person could hum it."

"My system of composing? I compose as it comes, as I hear it. I have no formula for composing. For people who've never heard any of my work before, and would like to know where to start, I'd say just listen to the music in the order that I've recorded it. Get the records, sit down, and dig."

"Am I planning any long works? I'm not planning anything. I write as the idea hits me. What's supposed to happen will happen, so I've heard. As for writing for full orchestra, I've done that years back for all kinds of pieces. I haven't been doing it because I'm not the kind of person who likes to arrange, and they don't pay enough for arrangements anyway."

"I'd like to talk about the lies that have been told about me that I'm undependable on jobs and the like. I don't know how that kind of legend got around. Some fools talk a big lie, that's all. Those lies get started, and you just can't stop them. Without even investigating, people go for them, and the lies get to the booking agencies. They believe it, too, so fast and condemn you before investigating. I think the booking agents and the public should investigate if rumors are true about people before they believe them."

"I have never messed up; I have never goofed a job in my life. Sometimes my *name* has been used in places that I knew nothing about, and the promoters never tried to get in touch with me. So when the public comes and I

4. See the section *Prestige and Paris 1954* for more description. *Ed.*

haven't shown up, the promoter blames me when he explains it to them. But I *do* have a sense of responsibility about work."[5]

(A reliable Chicago observer notes that during Monk's last date there some months ago, "he wasn't elusive or unco-operative . . . On his two nights off, he played a veteran's hospital benefit one night and a college concert-jam session the next. He did well at the Beehive and was held over. Actually, the owner had an odd number of days left before the next booking, and Monk happened to be available, but this particular owner never would have kept Monk on unless Monk was doing good business for the place.")

Monk's comments on the present scene: "I keep up. I know what's going on. I've heard some so-called progressive music that sounded weird intentionally. Some people have the idea that if it sounds real weird, it's modern progressive. When you sit there and the music comes out weird, that's different. You can tell the difference when something is composed weird intentionally and when it just flows out weird. I don't like the word 'weird' anyway, but people got accustomed to it."

"About young musicians: I haven't heard anything new in so long. I mean something that is really original, distinctive, an original style. They sound like they're copying from somebody. I do like though the tenor I worked with in Chicago, John Griffin. He's one of the best. Also the bass player I worked with there, Wilbur Ware."

"I hear some of my things once in a while in the work of a gang of piano players. I don't mean all the way through. I don't want to sound conceited. I mean the way they attack a note or make a riff . . . I don't teach. Quite a few pianists have come by the house. But it's not a formal thing. I couldn't find a system probably . . .What do I do between club dates? I try to find something for the wife and kids to eat and me, too. I have a girl who is 2 and a boy who is 6. The boy likes music. How would I feel if the boy became a full-time musician? The important thing is how *he* feels. How I feel don't mean nothing. He'll be the way he wants to be, the way he's supposed to be."

Monk is assembling a quartet with which he'll travel. After rehearsals and before the first date, plans call for a "first-night" audition for the quartet for critics, magazine writers, and perhaps club owners.

5. Monk is probably referring to a concert held in October 1954 at Town Hall, the "Great Moderns of Jazz," which included Parker, Rollins, and supposedly Monk. But the promotion was erroneous, as Monk was not hired for the occasion. So when Monk did not show up, the rumors about his unreliability, already in circulation because of his habit of showing up late, began to escalate. The poster advertising the concert has been reprinted in Jacques Ponzio and Francis Postif, *Blue Monk: Portrait de Thelonious* (Paris: Actes Sud, 1995), p. 145. *Ed.*

"About original writing in jazz today," Monk added, "what I've heard hasn't sounded too original. It all sounds the same almost. The same chords. The melody might change a little, but there's been nothing really original in the last six or seven years. What is an original? If it sounds original. The construction; the melody. It has to have its own sound."

"Some people say I haven't enough technique. Everybody has his own opinion. There is always something I can't express that I want to. It's always been that way and maybe always will be. I haven't reached perfection. Maybe those people with those opinions have reached perfection. I went through a whole gang of scales like other piano players did."

14. *Ira Gitler Interviews Thelonious Monk*

Gitler's frequently-cited interview with Monk is presented as a literal transcription with descriptive information, a kind of report demonstrating how difficult it can be to interview Monk. He is careful to show that he did everything to make the interview as comfortable as possible for Monk, but in the end gets little or no information from him. Monk is unyielding in his dismissal of specific questions about his music, the exception being when he describes the bridge of a tune as being the "inside," a very revealing comment on how he thinks about the structure of a tune. At one point, Monk, satisfied that the interview has lasted long enough, announces, "Well you've got about everything you want to know right now, don't you?" If it were not for the presence of Monk's manager Harry Colomby at the interview, Gitler may have gotten even less out of him.[1] Ira Gitler was an associate editor for *Down Beat*, has contributed numerous liner notes, several for Monk's albums, and has written a number of books on jazz, including *Swing to Bop: An Oral History of the Transition in Jazz in the 1940s.*

This article originally appeared as "Ira Gitler Interviews Monk," by Ira Gitler in *Metronome*, March 1957, pp. 19–20, 30, 37.

1. In another interview by Frank London Brown, done around the same time, Monk answers the question "Where is jazz going today?" with "I don't know where it's going. Maybe it's going to hell." Whereupon Nellie begins to prod the reluctant Monk, whose mumbling then prompts her to say, "Thelonious, you can open your mouth when you speak" (Frank London Brown, "More Man than Myth, Monk has Emerged from the Shadows," *Down Beat*, October 30, 1958, pp. 14–16, 45–46).

I have written several sets of album notes for the music of Thelonious Monk. I have supervised two of his recording sessions and come in contact with him numerous times at other sessions and clubs where he was playing. From experience, I knew he was not a verbose person by any means, especially when it came to talking about music (he is reputed to have once said, "Let's not talk about it, let's play it"), and when I invited him to my house for the purpose of interviewing him, I knew beforehand that it would be a difficult task to try and pry more than intermittent, short phrases from him. His manager, Harry Colomby, a high school English teacher and amateur actor, accompanied him and I planned to make it a pleasant conversational evening rather than a rapid fire interrogation from a list of many prepared questions.

The two arrived before the appointed time (actually, a time area between 8 and 9 p.m., rather than an exact time, had been set) which was a pleasant surprise. I immediately ushered them into my music room. Monk was very nattily attired in a pepper and salt overcoat, grey felt hat and sun glasses. On removal of the outer garments, he revealed a Glen-plaid suit and, unlike his usual sport shirt, a white shirt and tie. He showed no ill effects from his recent automobile accident and, in fact, looked very imposing. If you have ever seen Monk, you know that by his very size, bearing and mien he cuts an imposing figure whether his dress is formal or informal.

After the salutations and some beer by way of hospitality we settled down into some halting conversation. I turned the tape recorder on after a while without a decrease (or increase) in the rate of words emanating from Monk. I had been making general conversation in order to lead towards the subject of music gradually. Colomby mentioned making a tape with his brother Jules (president of Signal Records) and Monk where they enacted a fictitious play about prize fighting, satirizing American prize fight movies. This led me to remember and say: "The only prize fight I've attended in ten years, I ran into Monk. Remember that . . . the Patterson-Jackson fight?" (Floyd Patterson, current World's heavyweight champion.)

Monk: "Oh yeah, that's right. I could dig him being champion when he first started. I predicted practically all the champs when they first started."

Colomby: "We wanted to watch 'Sugar' Hart fight tonight on television. He's supposed to be another Ray Robinson."

Gitler (to Monk): "Is boxing your favorite sport?"

Monk: "One of them."

Gitler: "What others do you like?"

Monk: "I like basketball. . . baseball is too slow. I like tennis, something like that. In baseball, you can stand out there and don't move all day long."

Gitler: "But it has an inner drama that builds up."

Monk: "It's the only game slow enough for the people to dig."

Gitler: "I enjoy ice hockey too."

Monk (still on baseball): "That's what I think. It's slow enough for the public. Tennis is too fast for them."

Gitler: "Well, tennis does have a smaller following in the United States than baseball."

Colomby: "You said you played basketball. Were you a center?"

Monk: "Any position."

Colomby: "Were you a defensive player?"

Monk: "Always offensive."

Gitler: "Where did you play . . . in high school?"

Monk: "Everywhere."

Gitler: "What high school did you go to in New York?"

Monk: "Stuyvesant" (Peter Stuyvesant).

(Colomby told me later of how Monk excelled in mathematics and physics in school. This is an indication of the type of mind he has and perhaps why the chords and "time" in his music are expert and ingenious).

At this point, Monk, who knew he was being interviewed for publication on the Continent, looked at the microphone as if he were broadcasting, at that very moment, to the capitals of Europe and spoke pointedly, in a jovial tone but with serious intent—

Monk: "What's going to happen with this music? When am I going to take my band to Paris and Stockholm?"

Gitler: "Well, with the release of some of your recent LPs you have been raising a lot of comment. You're being 'rediscovered.' I know some of your Prestige recordings have been released overseas and I believe some of the Riverside sessions too."

"Since you went with Riverside, you have recorded one LP of Ellington tunes and another of 'standards.' I enjoyed them very much, but I prefer to hear you play your own music because so few other people play it. A lot of musicians play ' 'Round about Midnight' but things like 'Well, You Needn't' and 'Off Minor,' things like that . . . Miles plays 'Well, You Needn't' . . . But not enough musicians pick up on them. I was discussing this recently with a musician, one who does play your works, and he felt that it was because they can't play it or they don't want to take the time to really work on it. How did you feel about doing the two Riverside albums?"

Monk: "I wanted to do it. I felt like playing it, that's all. I know that Duke started playing some of his numbers more than he had as I recall."

Colomby: "Some critics said it was Riverside's idea."

Gitler: "I remember that. Knowing Monk, I know he wouldn't do anything he didn't want to do."

Colomby: "But that's true. Every time he receives a tune, other people start recording it. 'Sweet and Lovely' got a big boost."

Monk: "Gerry Mulligan plays it all the time."

Gitler: "One thing I felt happy about . . . remember when you wanted to record 'Bemsha Swing' (a Monk-Denzil Best collaboration) and Bob Weinstock wasn't too keen on it and I called him up from the recording studio and talked him into it. So you did it on that trio date and later on. Miles Davis did it with you on piano."

Monk: "And I did it again on Riverside with five pieces."

Gitler: "What do you think about that statement I made before about musicians not playing your work because it's too hard or they don't want to apply themselves?"

Monk: "It's not hard. Ask Hall Overton, he'll tell you. It's not hard to play but I know it, that's all, maybe." (Several years ago, I asked Monk why Lou Donaldson hadn't soloed on a certain number of a Monk Blue Note Recording date and Monk told me that Lou couldn't make the changes.)

Gitler: "I don't think that everyone can play it. If he is a good musician he should be able to."

Here a phone call interrupted the proceedings. When I returned to the room we became involved in a discussion about Monk's writing. He stressed the "inside" as he likes to refer to the bridge and went on to say that if you didn't have a good "inside" one that related to the rest of the composition, then you had nothing. I started the tape going again as he was mentioning 'Bernie's Tune.'

Monk: " . . . you notice that? You dig the bridge to it? It don't even fit. (chuckling) I don't write no songs like that. My 'inside' is going to fit."

Gitler: "'Bernie's Tune' reminds me of Mulligan which reminds me . . . did you ever hear his tune called 'Motel?' To me, it's a steal from 'I Mean You' (a Monk tune recorded in the late 'forties) . . . did you ever hear it?"

Monk: "No."

Colomby: "I Mean You?"

(Here Monk sang the melody for him.)

Colomby: "I heard Herbie Nichols play that when he was at Cafe Bohemia. Do you like Herbie Nichols stuff? He plays pretty different too."

Monk: "He's all right."

I played the Mulligan record for Monk who listened reservedly and, then, chuckled philosophically: "I don't never do like that . . . steal something from somebody."

Gitler: "What do you think about the state of modern jazz today?"

Monk: "Oh, it's coming along okay now."

Gitler: "You think the people are beginning to get with it, that they're caught up to it?"

Monk: "Uh-huh."

Gitler: "Where do you think it's going?"

Monk: "I don't know and I'm not worrying about it."

Gitler: "Well, a lot of people are. They keep repeating, "Where is it going?"

Monk: "I'm just trying to play, myself."

Gitler: "I can remember the first time I heard you on record. It was with Coleman Hawkins . . . *Flying Hawk*."

Colomby: "On the Davis label."

Gitler: "Yes, Joe Davis Records. How old were you when you made that record? Was it your first?"

Monk: "I guess so. I was in my early twenties."

Gitler: "Hawk was one cat who always kept up with the times, knew what was happening."

Monk: "He was the first one that hired anybody" (meaning the moderns).

Gitler: "Yes. He did that first record date with Dizzy and Max on Apollo."

Colomby: "Thelonious has a picture of Dizzy at home which says 'to my inspiration.'"

Gitler: "Well, Monk supplied a lot of the music, the raw material for Dizzy and Bird to build on. I started going down to 52nd Street in 1945. I have always been sorry that I wasn't old enough to have been on the scene about five years earlier to see it really happen, you know, up at Minton's. Do you think too much emphasis is put on Minton's as the birthplace, Monk? Were there other places?"

Monk: "That's about true."

Gitler: "Today, it's more spread out, everyone is going in different directions. It's not like then when a group of cats got together and worked on something night after night. A lot of people today seem to be going their own way."

Monk: "I don't know. I'm trying (chuckling) . . . I'm trying to eat and sleep myself. I ain't got time to worry about all that. I've got to worry about where I'm going. I'm not worrying where everyone else is going."

Gitler: "Well, you're certainly no 'Johnny-come-lately.' You've got your music. You've been doing it a long time and you know what you want to do. What are your plans as far as groups go?"

Monk: "As soon as I can, I'm going to start working in somebody's joint . . . stay in New York as long as possible."

Gitler: "What size group do you think will be best suited to your needs?"

Monk: "Six pieces. I can get a chance to write. I can get the right amount of horns. Three horns and three rhythm."

Gitler: "Have you anyone in mind who you would like to get?"

Monk: "When I get ready to rehearse, I'll think about it . . . who's on the scene." (Harry Colomby told me later that Monk was interested in Ray Copeland on trumpet and Sahib Shihab on alto sax. He is scheduled to open at The Pad in Greenwich Village in the near future.)

Gitler: "Who do you like right now that is on the scene?"

Monk: "There's a lot of musicians I like. Everybody. There's so many people sound good to me."

Gitler: "Who are some of the people who sound good to you?"

Monk: "Everybody sounds good. Everybody that's playing sounds a 'bitch.' I hear something in everybody's playing."

Gitler: "What do you think of the 'experimental' writers like Mingus and Teddy Charles and people like that?"

Monk: "I tell you, I don't have a chance to be worrying about what I think about somebody else. I'm trying to figure something out my own self. Sounded all right to me, what I heard them play. We had a concert together at the YH (Young Men's Hebrew Association) on 92nd Street. They sound okay to me."

Gitler: "Would you call it jazz?"

Monk: "I guess . . . whatever they want to call it. (None of this was said in a derogatory manner.) How can I name his music. You can't tell people what you think."

Gitler: "Well, it's something that jazz fans are always arguing about . . . the definition of jazz."

Monk: "Let *them* argue about it. The musicians don't have time to argue about that jive. That's for the fans to do. . . well you've got about everything you want to know right now, don't you?"

Gitler: "Well, I'd like you to talk a lot more Monk. The only concrete things I've gotten from you is that you want to concentrate on playing and writing . . ."

Monk: "And make some money."

Gitler: "Well, those are three important things."

Monk: "That's all."

Gitler: "I'm still sure that your audience would like to know some of your favorites on the different instruments. You must have some you like especially well."

Monk: "Max Roach and them is playing, Sonny Rollins . . ."

Gitler: "How about Miles?"

Monk: "Miles sounds good too."

Gitler: "How about that famous session (a Davis-Monk session for Prestige in 1954 that included 'Bemsha Swing,' 'Man I Love,' etc.) . . . now I was at the session . . . well you know how rumors start flying . . . you know the record date where Miles told you to 'lay out' on certain portions of the numbers. Someone I met at a party a couple of weeks ago, as they were playing the record of the session, said to me, 'Man, Miles hit Monk at that date.' I told him that I was there and that nobody was doing any hitting. This is the way rumors get started."

Monk: "Miles'd got killed if he hit me. (chuckling) You should've told him that."

Gitler: "I don't think Miles told you to 'lay out' because he didn't dig your playing. He had done the same thing with Horace Silver on an earlier session. He just had him 'lay out' on certain parts."

Monk: "Well I 'lay out' my own self. He got that from me. He got that 'laying out' from me."

At this point Monk rose and looked behind the Venetian blinds into the courtyard below.

Monk: "You can get messed up if there'd be a fire in here. How do you get out if a fire breaks out."

Gitler: "There are no fire escapes because it's a fireproof building."

Monk: "With the 'Mad Bomber' on the scene?" (The 'Mad Bomber' is currently terrorizing New York by leaving home-made bombs in theatres and railroad stations.)

Gitler: "The 'Mad Bomber' is not going to get in here."

Monk: "Well, I'm going to go home and practice on my new Steinway."

Gitler: "When did you get it?"

Monk: "Christmas. (He moved restlessly about now.) Well, let's go. You see, being in the hospital, indoors so much, it gets on my nerves. I have to go and ride around a little while and then I'll go home and practice."

Brilliant Corners and Riverside

Monk's first album for Riverside Records, *Thelonious Monk Plays Duke Ellington* (1955), originated from Orrin Keepnews's desire for him to gain a wider audience, but in some respects the album was awkward and ill-suited to Monk. In retrospect, it is not clear whether it was to his advantage: He was already known through his Blue Note recordings—of which the critical commentary of the day continuously emphasized the virtues of his compositions over his piano playing—so by presenting him without those compositions, and in the shadow of Ellington, he may have been at a disadvantage. A *Down Beat* review went so far as to say that "it does Monk little good to force him to adapt to a program for which he has little empathy as a pianist-writer, though he may have a large liking for Ellington as a listener."[1] The second album for Riverside, *The Unique Thelonious Monk,* also did not feature Monk's compositions, and came with the qualifying statement "very personal treatments of great standards" as a subtitle on the cover. Reviews were more positive but not overwhelmingly so.

When *Brilliant Corners* was released in 1957, it was clear that Monk had crossed the threshold from being interesting and idiosyncratic to being a

1. *Down Beat,* January 25, 1956, pp. 23–24. The review also mentions that "a similar plan with Randy Weston playing Cole Porter worked because Randy is more adaptable and more of a technician than Monk, and also because Porter is less of a composer than Ellington."

force to be reckoned with, at least for the critics. Nat Hentoff gave the album a five-star review in *Down Beat,* a significant public acknowledgment of Monk's talents. The title piece, "Brilliant Corners," is dense and demanding, with its unusual 22-bar form played alternately as slow walk and double time, and, as Keepnews's comments in the liner notes reveal, the musicians were having a difficult time playing it. The theme itself is rife with rhythmic displacements and alternating fast and slow motifs. The end result after a reputed four hours of trying to get it right was a spliced version drawing on the best choruses from different takes. In the released composite take, Sonny Rollins soars over the chords with ample references to the melody, but alto saxophonist Ernie Henry seems utterly lost, not the least bit helped by the fact that Monk lays out during his solo.

Riverside, founded by Bill Grauer and Orrin Keepnews in 1953, quickly became—along with Prestige, Blue Note, Pacific Jazz, and Contemporary—one of the most important record companies to document the jazz being played in the 1950s. Besides Monk, its artists included Bill Evans, Cannonball Adderley, and Wes Montgomery. Keepnews produced the sessions, and during the period that Monk was under contract with Riverside, from 1955 to 1961, he participated in 30 recording sessions, including engagements at the Five Spot, the Blackhawk in San Francisco, and the Town Hall concert. Two concerts from the 1961 European tour were issued later as part of Monk's remaining contractual obligations before signing with Columbia.

15. Liner notes for Brilliant Corners

Keepnews wrote the liner notes to Monk's Riverside albums, including the original notes to the *Brilliant Corners* album reprinted here. The final summary of his work for Riverside is represented in an essay on Monk's Riverside years in 1986 for the LP box set *Thelonious Monk: The Complete Riverside Recordings.*[1] The box set received Grammys for Best Historical Album and Best Album Notes in 1987. Keepnews's description of the Riverside sessions is perhaps the best available documentation we have of this important era of Monk's music. In the notes below, which appeared on the cover of the original sleeve when it was released in 1957, Keepnews confesses to having deliberately

1. The box set has since been reissued in CD format as Riverside RCD-022-2.

seduced listeners with the first two Riverside albums of non-Monk material, to get them to accept Monk through the aid of familiar melodies. The description of the difficulty in playing "Brilliant Corners" omits the fact that the released version ended up being a spliced composite of several different takes, later revealed by Keepnews in the 1986 liner notes.

This originally appeared as the liner notes to *Brilliant Corners*, by Orrin Keepnews, Riverside RLP 226 in 1957. Used by permission of Orrin Keepnews.

Thelonious Monk remains among the most challenging, provocative and disturbing figures in modern music. He has consistently been described in such terms for as long as he has been on the jazz scene—which is precisely as long as there has been modern jazz, for Monk of course was one of the principal molders of the new jazz. He will very probably continue to be described this way. For Monk's music is decidedly not designed for casual listening. Everything he writes and plays is jazz into which an important creative talent has put more than a little of himself. Thus, inevitably, Monk and his music demand the most difficult thing any artist can require of his audience—attention.

Thelonious Monk's music can also be among the most rewarding in modern jazz. And it *is* that (to those who will listen) for exactly the same reasons that it challenges, disturbs and demands: because Monk is *himself*. What he offers is not smooth, public relations conscious artifice or surface skills, but merely the music that is in him and that he is impelled to bring forth. There are men who can bend and shape themselves and their work (perhaps to fit current public taste, perhaps to suit the aims of a stronger artistic personality). There are others whose natural, undiluted self expression manages to strike a responsive chord in lots of souls, or at least seems to. Finally there are those non-benders and non-conformers who don't happen to *seem* easy to understand. Among these is Monk, and for such men the basic audience can consist only of those who are willing to try a bit to grasp the stimulating, intensely rewarding message that is being sent out.

These comments are not intended as any sort of fairly clever reverse-twist psychology (you know: "only very hip people, like me and like you who are reading these notes, can really dig Thelonious"). On the contrary, we at Riverside feel very strongly that the whole emphasis on the exceedingly far-out and "mysterious" nature of Monk's music has been seriously overdone during the early years of his career, so that many who would have found themselves quite willing (and able) to listen were frightened away in advance.

This is Thelonious' third album for this label; the first two were entirely made up of standard tunes, played with trio instrumentation. This was fully deliberate, a plot to seduce non-followers of Monk into giving him a hearing. There was no musical compromise; but there was at least the handle of a familiar melody to begin with.

Those two previous albums—as reviewers, musicians and others with no special need to flatter Monk or us have noted—were outstanding, articulate efforts. But the present LP is something else again. This is Thelonious at work on matters much more difficult (and potentially even more rewarding): this is Monk writing, in his own highly personal way, for five instrumental voices. It is Monk expressing himself by means of the unorthodox construction, approach, and phrasing that is uniquely his, and that has by now matured into a style possessing great depth, wit and strength.

(The one exception here, a solo treatment of the standard "I Surrender, Dear" in a compellingly moody vein, came about because Monk felt like it and felt it was a change of pace that would fit in. It did.)

It should be noted at about this point that Monk's music is not only not the easiest listening, it is also not easy to play. Musicians could save themselves a lot of trouble by *not* recording with Monk—but it's a form of trouble that a great many of the best men have long considered a privilege (as well as an education).

Sonny Rollins is a wonderfully inventive, strong-toned artist who has already made a considerable impact on the jazz public and on fellow musicians, who is clearly going on to a position of even greater importance. Ernie Henry worked in Monk's quartet during 1956, and then took over Phil Woods' alto chair in Dizzy Gillespie's big band; he is a fluid, leaping, non-derivative stylist who has appeared on two previous Riverside LP's and whom we are betting on for near-future stardom. Oscar Pettiford and Max Roach no longer need fancy descriptive adjectives: by now surely their names alone tell the story. When Henry and Pettiford were unavailable for the final date, the replacements were of top caliber: Clark Terry (a stand out with Duke Ellington since 1951 and termed, by Leonard Feather, "one of the most original trumpet players in contemporary jazz") and Paul Chambers, currently with Miles Davis and among the very finest of the newer bassists.

These men worked hard. They struggled and concentrated and shook their heads over some passages with those half-smiles that mean: "Hard? this is *impossible*!" For the original compositions on this date represent Monk at his most inventive and therefore (to repeat myself) at his most challenging. "Brilliant Corners," with its uneven meter and its tempo changes, is undoubtedly the real back-breaker, but this doesn't mean that the others are simple: "Pannonica," which I'd describe as a near-ballad with guts; the blues, which has lots of extended blowing room (and don't neglect to dig the several things Monk is doing behind the horns): and "Bemsha Swing," only one of the four originals not specifically prepared for this record date—Thelonious wrote it several years ago, with drummer Denzil Best, and has recorded it twice previously, but comparison will show that it hasn't remained static during that time.

(A note on the odd title of the blues: it is merely an attempt to set down phonetically the pronunciation Monk insisted on as most fitting for what might most simply be called "Blue Bolivar Blues.")

These musicians worked hard, also, because Monk's creativity never stands still: during a preliminary run through of a number, between "takes" or even during one, changes of phrasing or of detail will evolve, as a constant fusion of arrangement and improvisation keeps taking place. Sometimes even instrumentation gets altered a bit. Thelonious came across a celeste in the studio, decided it would go well in "Pannonica," and so set it up at right angles to the piano to be able to play celeste with the right hand, piano with the left, during part of this number. Similarly, it was an impromptu bit of experimentation that resulted in Max Roach's "doubling" on tympani and drums through "Bemsha Swing," in most unorthodox and effective fashion.

And Monk is a hard task-master at a recording session, a perfectionist ("I've never been satisfied with one of my records yet," he says, and means it) who knows just how he wants each note bent and phrased and who drives the others as hard as he drives himself—which, in an abstract sense, is possibly a little unfair of him.

In the end, it wasn't "impossible"—merely far from easy, and in the end everyone else was satisfied and Monk probably almost satisfied. And the final results are obviously very much worth having accomplished and (to return to the first theme of these comments) worth paying attention to.

16. Down Beat *Review*

After the lukewarm receptions of the first two Riverside albums, Nat Hentoff's review of the *Brilliant Corners* album in *Down Beat* set the precedent for a subsequent series of high critical appraisals of Monk's music. The following year, 1958, Monk headed the top place for pianists in *Down Beat*'s International Jazz Critics Poll.

This article originally appeared in *Down Beat*, June 13, 1957, pp. 28–29. Reprinted with permission of *Down Beat*.

Rating: *****

This is *really* a mood album, the kind of mood that envelops corners that can be called brilliant but are more inimitable than that increasingly indiscriminate adjective might connote. Monk is an instantly identifiable individual in a music world that recently has been more marked by the ubiquitousness of its mirrors than by its one-of-a-kind landmarks.

Because Monk is wholly himself, the corners of his musical imagination yield continually unexpected, freshly personal thoughts, and these in turn are linked in consistency once the overall shape of Monk's message is absorbed and reflected upon.

He does, then, create and deepen throughout this album a mood caused by the irresistible immediacy and originality of his stories and of the language in which they are spoken by him and his colleagues.

The notes underline the fact that Monk is writing here for five instrumental voices as contrasted with two previous sets without horns for the label. Frankly, I am less impressed with the actual writing for the five, particularly that for ensemble, than I am by the beginning impetus he gives each piece by his Monk-idiomatic melodic twists and pragmatic, this-is-how-I-hear-it chord structure.

The Monk musical personality thus having been set, he is able to dominate by the force of his personality the resultant scene so that the soloists, while they retain their individuality, nonetheless fit their improvisations into Monk's perspective. There is a commanding gestalt operative in a Monk performance for no matter how many instruments, and when he has men who are willing to work with him, as here, the impact of that gestalt is all the more memorable—and influential on other musicians.

Monk remains the most formidable player of Monk, but he gets excellent co-operation here from Roach, Pettiford, and Rollins (dig Sonny on Track 2 [Ba-lue Bolivar Ba-lues-are]). [Ernie] Henry is forceful and in context but is not yet as authoritative a voice as Sonny. (It's not paradoxical to point out that Monk is heard to best advantage with strong individual personalities.) Terry and Chambers make it in their one track. And Monk by himself translating "I Surrender, Dear" into his weltanschauung is one of the listening balls of the year, any year. This is Riverside's most important modern jazz LP to date.

17. Metronome *Review*

The reviewer for *Metronome* was also positive, albeit with more reservation and ambiguity. Nevertheless, there is a recognition that the album was a significant work.

This article originally appeared in *The Metronome*, June 1957, Vol. 74, No. 7, pp. 25–26.

The strange, sometimes outlandish, complex-simplicity of the music of Thelonious Monk comes across here with the three new compositions (first three tracks), a standard played in unaccompanied solo form and "Bemsha" which has been recorded before.

Of the complex-simplicity no facetiousness is meant, only throughout all the music of Monk there are contrasting feelings and techniques that although seemingly simple grow complex as they portray Monk. The simplicities would seem to be roots from which Monk works, often deep scarlet in color and purposely indecisive in feeling. They grow into strange distortions and pieces of morbidity. "Corners" has this pervading blue-ish morbidity as does "Bolivar." The ballad "Pannonica" uses a beautiful line that near its final statement gets slightly salty. Monk's use of celeste is effective and totally in character. "Bemsha" has an odd instrumentation to it too, with Max Roach playing figures in tympani against the cymbal beat. It's on this last, "Bemsha" that the front line of Clark Terry and Sonny Rollins seems best to be able to dig in, on the others Sonny and Ernie Henry seem a bit non-plussed by Monk's conception.

This is real Monk; full of all the sometimes incongruous and often primitiveness that is so distinctly his own.

Reports from Selected Venues

18. Heard in Person: Thelonious Monk Quartet

Monk's engagement at the Five Spot marked his return to the New York jazz scene. The reinstatement of his cabaret card in 1957 allowed him to work again in establishments selling alcoholic beverages, and during his two-year stay at the Five Spot he worked with some of the best jazz musicians in New York City—Johnny Griffin, Roy Haynes, Wilbur Ware, Shadow Wilson, and John Coltrane, the latter who at that time was receiving considerable attention for his work with Miles Davis. The Five Spot played a significant role in the promotion of new jazz in the late 1950s, with lengthy and much-discussed engagements by Cecil Taylor, Charles Mingus, Ornette Coleman, and Eric Dolphy. It was the summer of 1957, when Coltrane played with Monk's group, that the popularity of the club began to take off, prompting owner Joe Termini to say "Well, we're in show business now."[1]

Unfortunately, the Coltrane/Monk collaboration went largely unrecorded, save for a few takes made in the studio with Orrin Keepnews

1. Quoted in Martin Williams, *Where's the Melody: A Listener's Introduction to Jazz* (New York: Pantheon, 1969), p. 102.

in 1957, including a moving rendition of "Ruby, My Dear" and the fiendishly difficult "Trinkle, Tinkle."[2] Coltrane was under contract with Prestige, but Monk, not feeling well-disposed toward his former record label, was unwilling to record for Prestige.[3] In 1993, however, Monk's son, T. S. Monk, who had just signed on with Blue Note, handed Michael Cuscuna a 40-minute tape of Coltrane and Monk, recorded by Coltrane's first wife, Naima. Initially, it was touted as the long-lost collaboration everybody had raved about and nobody seemed to have recorded on location, but it subsequently turned out that the recording was made on September 11, 1958, long after Coltrane's engagement had ended, and when he was substituting for an absent Johnny Griffin.[4]

Dom Cerulli's article for *Down Beat* was part of a regular feature he wrote for the magazine during the 1950s and 1960s, in which the components "musical evaluation," "audience reaction," and "attitude of performers" are separated out in an attempt to be as descriptive as possible, relaying a kind of objective report. In the case of Monk's performance, the overall impression is clearly positive.

This article originally appeared as "Heard in Person: Thelonious Monk Quartet," by Dom Cerulli in *Down Beat,* September 5, 1957, p. 33. Reprinted with permission of *Down Beat.*

Personnel: Monk, piano and leader; John Coltrane, tenor; Wilbur Ware, bass; Shadow Wilson, drums.

Reviewed: Two sets during second week of an indefinite stay at the Five Spot, New York.

2. Monk recorded "Ruby, My Dear" a month earlier (June 1957) with Coleman Hawkins during a session that also included Coltrane on the other takes. The difference in approach is striking, and even though Monk and Hawkins had worked together more than a decade before, it is with Coltrane that Monk fuses.
3. According to Joe Goldberg, Monk refused to appear as Coltrane's sideman on a Prestige recording, the only condition on which Bob Weinstock, producer at Prestige, would agree to (Joe Goldberg, *Jazz Masters of the Fifties,* New York: Macmillan, 1965, p. 36).
4. Originally, the tape was released as *Thelonious Monk: Live at the Five Spot—Discovery!* (Blue Note 077799786225), with the claim that it was recorded during Coltrane's initial six-month engagement with Monk. With the release of the *Complete Blue Note Recordings,* the historical record was set straight and the order of the tunes was reinstated to reflect the actual performance (Bob Blumenthal, liner notes to *Thelonious Monk: The Complete Blue Note Recordings,* Blue Note CDP 7243830363, released in 1994, p. 33).

Musical Evaluation: If there are any doubts about Monk's musical abilities, attendance at a couple of sets in the Five Spot should dispel them. Thelonious, working his first New York club date in more than five years, is a vital force at the keyboard and a conscientious leader. His ideas at times are astounding. He is never obvious. And there are times, too, when he is so wrapped up in what Coltrane or Ware are doing in solos, that he stands out front and digs them every bit as much as the patrons.

This is a group of which Monk is apparently quite proud. And well he should be. Coltrane is a forceful voice on tenor. On the sets caught, he blew longish lines with a fierceness that didn't impede his flow. He is achieving a distinctive sound on tenor, one with enormous vitality.

Ware is a surprising soloist. On "Hackensack," for instance, he built a throbbing and quite humorous solo based almost wholly on quarter notes, breaking their steady jab with climactic phrases. Later, on a riffish original, he picked up Monk's final figure and ballooned it into a great solo. On this one, he built patterns of broken rhythms and used the steady 4/4 to telling effect as a climactic device.

Monk was constantly inventive harmonically and rhythmically. At times, he seemed to be playing spurts of melody; at other times he worked on complex figures with Coltrane; on slower tunes, he was almost episodic in his treatment.

Wilson was generally good but often somewhat obvious. His over-all texture (he worked with two cymbals, a snare, and the bass drum) mixed well with the group's often spare sound.

Audience Reaction: Attentive, and generous in response to the soloists. In this pleasant, new room, much attention has been given by owner Joe Termini to creating an informal atmosphere. The over-all effect has been to relax the performers and to make the patrons comfortable.

Attitude of Performers: Thelonious was quite excited about his group. In fact, he was out front leading or spurring the soloists fully as often as he was at the keyboard. On Ware's solos, when everyone laid out, their attention was focused on the bassist. They appear to be digging each other, and to be quite intent on building something with the group.

Commercial Potential: Monk's music has vitality all its own. With Coltrane blowing this powerfully, it takes on an added vigor. There is no doubt that it will be an important recorded group. They can stay at the Five Spot, said Termini, as long as they wish to.

Summary: In surroundings as low-pressure on the musicians as those at the Five Spot, and with understanding such as Termini's, the group is working hard, and being appreciated fully. It has built a loyal following at the spot in two weeks and shows promise of building even more. Weekends, since the group arrived, have been turnaways.

19. *Thelonious Monk at Town Hall*

Monk's engagement at Town Hall on February 28, 1959 was the first time his music had been scored for a small orchestra (or big band), with the help of the sympathetic and talented orchestrator/composer Hall Overton. According to Orrin Keepnews, the concert came about through Monk's friend, Jules Colomby, who suggested using Overton and who also assembled the musicians.[1] Monk's "tunes," whether played on piano or with horns and a rhythm section, are never just melodies with chord changes, but are always played with characteristic and consistently applied accompanying bass lines, fills, riffs, or countermelodies. Monk oversaw the scoring and Overton incorporated plenty of Monkian musical figures and gestures. Martin Williams, in the program notes to the concert, bluntly stated that "Unlike several others who have worked both in jazz and 'classical' music, Overton makes a careful distinction between the resources and intentions of the two idioms and is not committed to the position that they are gradually merging or that they should merge."[2] It was a much-anticipated and well-attended event, but, perhaps because of everyone's high expectations, the reviews were unfavorable. John S. Wilson reported in the *New York Times* that "The arrangements smoothed out the characteristically Monkian humps and bumps, diluted his tartness and robbed the works of their zest."[3] And Whitney Balliett commented that "although they [the arrangements] had the virtue of furnishing showcases for Monk's compositions, they were, with one exception, pale, conventional small-band scoring—unison passages sprinkled

1. Orrin Keepnews, liner notes to *The Thelonious Monk Orchestra at Town Hall,* Riverside RLP 12-300, released in 1959.
2. Williams is indirectly criticizing "third-stream" jazz, a short-lived style of the late 1950s promoted by Gunther Schuller and others, which attempted to blend elements of Western art music and jazz.
3. John S. Wilson, "Thelonious Monk Plays His Own Works," *New York Times,* March 2, 1959, p. 30.

with mild counterpoint—in which almost no effort was made to strengthen the various competent but second-rate soloists, who needed it."[4]

Gunther Schuller's review of the concert also was subdued and critical, lamenting, like the others, that the arrangements lacked the characteristic Monkian edges. But Monk was apparently pleased. Schuller has been active as performer, composer, musicologist, administrator, and conductor for more than 50 years, having penned, among other things, two respected tomes on jazz history, *Early Jazz* and *The Swing Era*. He wrote many significant articles for the short-lived but influential *Jazz Review* during the period 1958–1960.

This article originally appeared as "Thelonious Monk at Town Hall," by Gunther Schuller in *The Jazz Review*, Vol. 2, No. 5, pp. 7–8, in 1959. Used by permission of Gunther Schuller.

At a time when the average jazz concert seeks to overwhelm with an "all-star cast," a circus-like variety and overlong programs, a concert devoted to the jazz compositions(!) of a *single* composer must be considered an unusual—and very welcome—event. That such a concert should be devoted to the music of Thelonious Sphere Monk was perhaps inevitable. The increased though rather belated recognition accorded him by fellow musicians as well as the more aware segment of the jazz-conscious public, and the aura of off-beat controversiality still surrounding Monk would almost seem to guarantee the success of such an undertaking. Indeed, the fact that a near-capacity audience attended the concert is cause for optimism. It may be that we have matured to the point where, along with the usual entertainment "jamborees" that try to be "all things to all people," we can count upon an *occasional* concert with a point of view, a profile and a well-planned format. Maybe!

The music on this occasion was performed by two groups, a quartet led by Monk, featuring his regular saxophonist Charlie Rouse, and an enlarged ten-piece ensemble playing orchestrations by Hall Overton (supervised by Monk himself). Of the two, the latter, of course, aroused the greater interest, and it is disappointing, therefore, to report that they did not come up to the announced

4. Whitney Balliett, "Jazz Concerts: A Celebration for Monk," *New Yorker*, March 7, 1959, p. 147. And further on: "The exception occurred in the last couple of choruses of 'Little Rootie Tootie,' when the whole group admirably executed a stunningly worked out transcription of Monk's solo part in his first recording of the tune."

expectations. Perhaps it was unrealistic to expect these ensemble performances to be—in the words of Martin Williams, who commented eruditely on the proceedings— "an extension of Monk." I say unrealistic because in all the history of jazz, there has only been one successful example of this sort of musical extension, and that, of course, was the Duke Ellington orchestra. This was achieved, needless to say, through *years* of experimentation with a very special personnel. It would have been a minor miracle if the musicians involved in this concert could have achieved similar results with only four rehearsals.

In contrast to Monk's own solo work—he was in fine form all evening—these arranged ensembles (with one exception) remained bland and thoroughly conventional. Though competently written and well played, they failed to achieve the earthy richness and propulsive swing of Monk at his best. Nor did they in any way go beyond previous experiments with this kind of instrumental group, such as the Miles Davis Nonet, Mulligan's and Brubeck's short-lived ensembles or Hodeir's Jazz Groupe de Paris. The one exception alluded to was an ensemble chorus in "Little Rootie Tootie," which was a literal transcription for the seven "horns" of Monk's improvisation on the original 1952 recording. This certainly was *not* conventional orchestration. In fact it called upon considerable instrumental ingenuity from Hall Overton, a task he fulfilled rather brilliantly. The players, too, rose to the extraordinary demands of this passage. But the idea, it seems to me, was wrong in its basic concept.

In the first place, many of us have admired Monk for years because, among other things, he seemed to write for the instruments not as an arranger but as a composer. The instrumental parts of many of his compositions of the late forties seemed to be part and parcel of the original inspiration; they were truly independent yet integrated parts of the composition, and well suited to the character of the instruments chosen. (This despite the fact that, because Monk's music is difficult in some ways, the actual performances were often rough and insecure.) Secondly, Monk, as is well known, plays with an unorthodox piano technique. This has led him to create many unusual solos, which are more "orchestral" than pianistic in concept. By that I do not mean that they are *unpianistic*. Rather they attempt to go beyond the ordinary limits of the piano in the sense that the late Beethoven sonatas are no longer merely "piano music," or in the sense that the piano writing of Brahms is more orchestral than, let us say, Chopin's.

If we accept these two premises, it seems to me quite an error of judgment (the decision was Monk's—not Overton's) to write out an instrumental chorus which, in the first place, does not have the validity of being originally conceived in Monk's mind for those instruments, and which, in the second place, happens to be one of Monk's most "pianistic" choruses! It is filled with typical pianisms that are virtually impossible to orchestrate. Certainly many moments in music belong to the special domain of the piano. Transcribing them for instruments will always be a second-best choice. In this case, too, the resultant trumpet parts were not really trumpet parts, and the saxophone parts were unsaxophonistic, and so on. This had its peculiar fascination, but at best it was an ingenious tour de force. It would have been more interesting, I think, to hear the group in a piece *written* (not arranged) for this concert and *this* instrumentation. This would also have given us a chance perhaps to hear a new Monk composition.

I have been told on good authority that Monk was very pleased with these ensemble performances, because they were clean and well balanced, even mellow. This is one of those strange paradoxes which we encounter so often in artistic personalities. Frustrated for years by inadequately prepared performances and recordings, Monk undoubtedly admired the comparative precision of this ensemble. But the pleasure he derived from this also blinded him to the fact that the players failed to get as much "Monk" out of his music as the earlier rougher performances did. Similarly Duke Ellington has for many years now proclaimed that he prefers his present band to the original band of the thirties and early forties, because his present men can read better, play more accurately and have a greater instrumental versatility. And Charlie Parker loved the lush, stereotyped string writing which accompanied him on the famous Norgran dates, while Miles Davis loves his Ahmad Jamal. Perhaps in all creative personalities there is this enigmatic other side. At any rate, the rough-hewn (not to be confused with rough), direct quality—the very antithesis of slickness—which we have come to admire in Monk, was demonstrated in every note of his own piano playing. The contrast between it and the ensemble work was therefore all the more telling.

One of the problems with the instrumentation was that it was too bottom-heavy for most of the pieces, especially in "Rootie Tootie" and "Friday the Thirteenth." Actually the only instrument with a practical high register was the trumpet, which put a considerable burden on Donald Byrd, who under the circumstances did a remarkable job. I felt, too, that the voicings could have been used with greater variety and individuality. This kind of non-contrapuntal block writing, if unrelieved, can get very tedious after a while.

To compensate for the debatable merits of the ensemble sections, there were many fine Monk solos. He demonstrated once more his unique ability to create arresting solos, which, though seemingly consisting of mere musical fragments, in retrospect always show that a fine musical mind has been at work linking these fragments into a unified entity. His improvisations are like little compositions in themselves. Monk's extraordinary sense of time—and timing—enables him to relate one passage to the next in such a way that it may surprise you at first but then, after the fact, seems to have been quite inevitable. His sense of formal structure was again very much in evidence. It betrays an orderly, disciplined mind that belies the legend of the disorganized eccentric people have been led to see in Monk. His unostentatious, sober approach (dare I use the word "serious"?) must have been a disappointment to those in the audience who look to Monk for comedy, as well as to the "Monk-debunkers."

Of course, I don't think Monk can play without swinging. And he certainly outswung everybody else on the concert. Not that he swings in any conventionally "hip" or "funky" way. But everything he played had that exciting drive, perfect timing (notably in his free-tempo playing!) and rich, unsentimental expressiveness we have learned to expect from Monk.

Martin Williams at one point repeated a remark Monk had made during rehearsals to the effect that "If you know the melody, you can improvise better." Although this seems like the most obvious kind of truism, the fact is that, some notable exceptions notwithstanding, jazz improvisation is almost exclusively based on the chords and not the melody of a tune. In any case, I wish some of the musicians involved had taken Monk's advice more to heart.

The four soloists—Charlie Rouse, Donald Byrd, Phil Woods and Pepper Adams—played the kind of solos which make the critic's task difficult and unpleasant. They were competent, certainly not *unmusical*, solos; but nothing special happened to make you sit up and compel you to listen. They were fair to good solos that were quite interchangeable with any other fair to good solos. (In reviewing this kind of solo, the critic faces a real dilemma. If he wishes to be kind and say that the solos were good, the musician will think: "Man, what a jerk; he can't even tell when I ain't sayin' nothin'." If, on the other hand, the critic says that the solos were poor, the musician says; "Man, what a jerk; he expects us to play a great solo every time. What does he know about music anyway?" Or words to that effect.)

At any rate, in the first half of the program Rouse had severe problems with intonation (for the record, he played sharp), which made him feel rather uncomfortable. After intermission, playing closer to pitch, he was able to relax and play more cohesively. Donald Byrd, a sensitive musician, was at his best when Art Taylor led him into double-time choruses. It was also interesting to note how the riff-like theme of "Friday the Thirteenth"—which Donald had to repeat endlessly in that number—kept cropping up during the succeeding piece, "Little Rootie Tootie." Phil Woods was disappointing this time. His playing was too tense and disjointed. Once or twice the opening notes of a solo would promise much, but before long he would retire to the safety of commonplace clichés. Pepper Adams played in his usual manner, again competent, with good control, making all the right changes, but rhythmically too unvaried to hold one's interest very long.

I should add that all the players more or less came into their own in the repeat performance of "Rootie Tootie" at the end of the program. Perhaps up to that moment the hour was just too early; perhaps they would have fared better 'round about midnight. But more likely it was simply the fact that all the players seemed caught in a trap which this kind of concert presents and which perhaps only the Parkers and Rollinses could survive. This dilemma is that the players are asked at one and the same time to be great individual soloists and yet fit into the style and musical concept of the composer whose music they're playing. The Parkers and Rollinses would perhaps not solve the problem; they would simply be themselves, but at least you'd have Parker or Rollins. In this concert the musicians, it seemed to me, dared not be either fish or fowl; they were caught somewhere in between. Dominated by Monk's presence, they dared not really be themselves, yet on only four rehearsals, to return to my original point, could not be the "extension" of Monk they were expected to be.

The same lack of real affinity characterized the playing of Art Taylor who, I thought, was not a good choice for Monk. Aside from rushing tempos, his playing (except for the effectively "busy" opening of "Rootie Tootie") was rather hard and inflexible. Sam Jones is a fine player using the full long notes derived from Blanton and Ray Brown that all young bass players have adopted by now. I found his intonation at times questionable, but I was primarily unhappy that Jones was not audible enough. Monk's pieces need strong bass lines.

This was Monk's concert, then, in more than one sense. On "In Walked Bud" he showed all who cared to listen how a chorus can be built economically out of simple ideas with a great formal clarity. In "Blue Monk" he demonstrated the use of thematic material while backing Rouse's tenor and then, in his own solo, effectively contrasted melodic (linear) and harmonic (vertical) improvisation. "Friday the Thirteenth" is a piece based on a passacaglia-like repetition of a two-bar chord progression, which presents serious problems for the unaware improviser. Unless he is careful, it leads him into an endless chain of short two-bar phrases which, over a period of a chorus or two, can become deadly boring. Monk, unlike Rouse for instance, skillfully avoided such straightjacketing. His free and forceful solo, in fact, made one forget the repetitiousness of the chord changes. In "Straight, No Chaser" he took what was no more than a little background idea and built it logically into a compelling solo, full of surprises. In "rubato" or free-tempo Monk was just as intriguing, lingering over phrases with tantalizing delays and time-suspensions. Such moments were too numerous to mention separately, but outstanding among these was the way Monk let that wonderful discord in the fourth bar of "Crepuscule with Nellie" ring just the right amount of time. Monk does all these things without any intellectuality. They derive naturally from the forcefulness and originality of his character—qualities which cannot be *learned*, which are inextricably a part of the man.

The concert proved, among other things, that Monk, the erstwhile iconoclast, has suddenly become "acceptable." This may explain why one bewildered listener, not to be cheated of his anticipated "revolutionary" atmosphere, upon noting the heavy representation of beards in the audience, wondered whether he had strayed into a Fidel Castro stronghold.

Who's next? Cecil Taylor?

20. *I Wanted to Make It Better: Monk at the Blackhawk*

Monk's first stay at San Francisco's Blackhawk restaurant, a two-week engagement in October 1959, inspired writer Grover Sales to write the article reprinted here. His exemplary behavior on this occasion defied all rumors of his unreliability, so much so that it was worth reporting on in *Down Beat:*

> For his two weeks at the Blackhawk in October, Monk made every set, was on time every night, signed autographs, submitted to interviews, and played his heart out. . . . "Mr. Monk can play in my club anytime," said Guido Caccienti, owner of the Blackhawk. "He's a gentleman." . . . Nightly, Monk stood on the sidewalk looking at his watch and waiting for his sidemen when time to go back on drew near. Frequently he was early for the night's performances and even

played the matinees. "I don't know what they're talking about," Caccienti said. "This guy was straight with me."[1]

Just prior to the Blackhawk engagement, Monk had made a disastrous appearance at the Hollywood Bowl, as part of the first Hollywood jazz festival.[2] Orrin Keepnews managed to get Monk in the studio for a solo session, but it was not until the following year, during a return engagement at the Blackhawk, that a live recording was made, released on Riverside as *Thelonious Monk Quartet Plus Two at the Blackhawk.*

Grover Sales alternates direct quotes by Monk—from an interview he conducted—with his own engaging observations about the club appearance. From the description, it is clear that Monk's West Coast appearance was an exciting and important event, with many curious onlookers attending. Sales is a critic, photographer and instructor at the University of California, where he teaches American music history.

This article originally appeared as "I Wanted to Make It Better: Monk at the Black Hawk [sic]," by Grover Sales, in *Jazz: A Quarterly of American Music,* Vol. 5, pp. 31–41. Used by permission of Grove Sales.

The crowd that awaited the coming of Thelonious Sphere Monk at the Blackhawk was uncomfortably, but understandably, sparse. Considering it was his first night club engagement in San Francisco, and that West Coast fans had, for over fifteen years, been teased and titillated by the jazz press and underworld telegraph of semi-literate hippies about Monk the Mystic Recluse, Monk the Enigmatic, Monk the Capriciously Bizarre, one might have anticipated an opening night *te deum*. But there had been all those odd reports of monumental goofings, climaxed, just a few weeks previously, by the distressing account of his mercurial fumblings at the Hollywood Bowl festival, and those who ordinarily would not think of missing the Bay Area premiere of a jazz artist of Monk's stature decided the gig was an elaborate con. Monk had

1. *Down Beat,* December 10, 1959, p. 13.
2. "Monk fumbled confusedly through "Misterioso," in the course of which he abruptly slammed his entire forearm across the keys . . . As the applause faded at the close of the number, Monk suddenly rose and faced the audience. Then he lurched, staggered to regain his equilibrium and sat down again without saying a word" (John Tyman, "The Bowl Fest," *Down Beat,* November 12, 1959, p. 18).

assumed the trappings of Elijah the Prophet, the invited—but not expected—guest at every Seder supper which marks the Jewish Passover, for whom all doors are ajar and a cup of sacramental wine is set. For a fortnight the audience had been ready, but in the words of at least one local columnist, "How can I give a big write-up to some cat, you don't know he's gonna show?"

Who really expects a saint or a prophet to show? And if Monk was neither saint nor prophet, he had, in the minds of most jazz enthusiasts, some of the unreal appurtenances of both. "Monk—High Priest of Bop" had become a virulent folk-saga, encouraged and perpetuated not only by the press, but also by Monk's peers. "Deep," said Dizzy Gillespie, "The Monk is deep." "Thelonious," intoned Milton Jackson, "is a *very strange person*."

By five minutes to show time, even club owner Guido Cacianti began to sniff out a threatening fiasco. A genial, imperturbable syntax-mangler, Guido has run a successful modern jazz club for ten years on the astonishing dictum of leaving the musicians strictly alone. Four years ago, he had disdained the suggestion of booking Monk into the Blackhawk: "Listen, I heard about this Felonious guy—he's some kinda nut. He'll come into the club and stare at a wall. What I mean is, he's not like Peterson or Garner, for Chrissake—he can't sit down and play you a regular show! Besides which, I hear he never gets outa New Jersey somewheres."

What had happened to change Guido's mind, between the announcement of this interdict and the Blackhawk Seder supper, of course, was that Monk, after years of almost metaphysical obscurity, had become marketable: his compositions were recorded and publicly performed by Miles Davis, Jay Jay Johnson, the Modern Jazz Quartet, Sonny Rollins and Julian "Cannonball" Adderley; André Hodeir and Gunther Schuller wrote critical dithyrambs; the early Blue Notes and Prestiges were reissued; he won the *Down Beat* Critics Poll in 1958–59; his Town Hall concert was a sellout and unanimous critical triumph; most important of all, Orrin Keepnews issued a series of Riverside LP's that helped dissolve the persistent image of Monk as a gifted, but eccentric, noodler.

So by October 20, 1959—at 9:14, to be precise—the Jazz Center of the West was finally ready for a saleable Monk, but it remained to be seen whether Monk was ready for the Blackhawk. For a while there was some doubt. Guido was getting a quick rundown from Max Weiss of Fantasy Records on what musicians could be phoned in a hurry to fill in.

Suddenly there was Monk at the bar, stalking and lurching restlessly like the Lion of Judah. Unaware that these leonine tactics were part of the customary Monk stance away from the piano, Guido interpreted the intense pacings as anxiety over the unexplained absence of all three sidemen. For, all forebodings to the contrary, the single member of the Thelonious Monk Quartet to show—and show on time—was the leader.

> *"They're always putting me down for blowing the gig. I never do that.* I'm *here—it's them* musicians *who ain't here!"*

After many frantic phone calls, Monk began his first set at 10:15 in uneasy alliance with Brew Moore, San Francisco tenor sax veteran, Willie Bobo, drummer with Cal Tjader, and Dean Riley, bass. None, except Moore, had ever played with him before, and since Monk often goes an entire evening without playing a composition other than his own, the unlikely group hastily settled on the classic "'Round About Midnight" and some rather nervous blues.

It was an unforgettable set. To hear Brew Moore's moving, uncomplicated Lester Young-style superimposed on Monk's compelling and audacious harmonies and precipitous rhythmic stabbings was to recall André Hodeir's observation that "If Johann Sebastian Bach had been a jazzman, he undoubtedly would have a hard time getting along with Schoenberg at the piano and Bartók on drums![3] The obvious incongruities of the Monk-Moore confederation dramatically showed—more strikingly than Monk's regular group could ever show—how he had taken the blues and altered them, transmogrified them and bestowed upon them brazenly new harmonic and rhythmic dimensions.

With the arrival of the tardy musicians later that evening, Monk was heard to better, if less startling, advantage. Tenorman Charlie Rouse is one of the handful of "horn players" capable of working with Monk, since he has mastered the imposing repertoire of intricate and cliché-free compositions. Invariably, each number begins and ends with piano and tenor unison statement of the theme, much in the manner established by the Parker-Gillespie combo. Given Monk's tunes and his thoroughly individual method of phrasing, such unison work is hazardous going. Frank Butler, the brilliant drummer from Los Angeles, functioned as Monk's third hand. When he took over from Willie Bobo—himself a far from unexciting drummer—the group attained a cohesiveness and unity that emphasized Monk's abilities as a composer, in addition to his already amply evident gifts as a pianist; Butler later proved one of the few drummers in the history of jazz capable of imparting structure and listenability to a ten-minute drum solo. (George Morrow, unable to make the engagement, was replaced by San Franciscan Eddie Kahn on bass.)

3. André Hodeir, *Jazz: Its Evolution and Essence* (New York: Grove Press, 1956), p. 221.

The effect of Monk on the audience was staggering. "I did not believe," said a classical pianist with a wide jazz background, "that such sounds could come out of a piano." Those who knew and admired his work on records learned, from the first night, that the phonograph can reveal only a fragmentary knowledge of this unbelievably endowed artist. No one was prepared for what was heard: the raw, slashing power, the truly incredible swing, the gutty ecstasy of his blues, the eerie loveliness of his exquisite ballads, the harmonic daring of his massive chords and the wholly unique fusion of emotionalism and unalterable logic that pervades everything he writes and plays. Those in the audience who knew Monk primarily as a Character, and who came to see if he would really show up, wore expressions of perpetual surprise and bewildered awe.

> *"Crowds don't bother me. I can always get them quiet. Seems to me people always dug my music and applauded—anything to the contrary is just gossip in the papers. And the musicians—they always dug me!"*

The word "always," appearing as a *leitmotif* in his laconic and infrequent conversations, is a reminder of the long years of neglect, public indifference and unemployment. "You know," said Charlie Rouse, "he didn't work hardly at all for all of ten years. Man, they were *mean* to him! I mean he couldn't *find* work! But through it all, he always kept his own style."

The origins of this "style" are fascinating to explore. A persistent aura of confusion, and legerdemain enshrouds his formative years, and Monk, being somewhat less verbal than the least verbal jazz musician, does little to help. Born and reared in New York City (notwithstanding his blurred accents, sorghum-thick with resonances of the piney woods), he began formal study of the piano at seven.

> *"Didn't have to study hard—used to amaze all the teachers! No one had to make me study. I was gifted, you know—music. Learned to read notes before I took lessons. My older sister took—the girls always took in those days—and I learned to read by looking over her shoulder. Got interested in jazz right from the start. Fats Waller, Duke, Louis, Earl Hines—I dug all kinds of music—liked everybody. Art Tatum? Well, he was the greatest piano player I ever heard! Lester Young? He was good, had a new style, but it all come from Coleman Hawkins—all those tenor players had to do something he did!*
>
> *My first jobs I got in house parties; used to hear all my favorites at those parties. Copy anybody? No, I never copied—never had what you might call a major influence."*

On this point, Charlie Rouse is adamant: "Monk, he never in his whole life copied anyone—ever. He always played just like himself." One hesitates to use an overworked word like "unique," but to whom would it apply more than Monk? Louis had his King Oliver, Fats his James P. Johnson and Lester Young confessed his idolatry of Frankie Trumbauer. In at least one sense, Monk is unique because he seems influenced by everyone in general and no one in particular. By 1942 he had assimilated all valid and lasting developments of jazz, stripped them of frills and embellishments he considered unessential, imposed upon them his pungent harmonies and startling rhythms and hit the big Fifty Second Street scene as an Influence.

> *"I started composing around 1942 when I was at Minton's. Parker, Dizzy, they all come in to hear me. Bird never excited me like he did the others. 'Bird is a god,' they said. He wasn't to me! No, and no one else was, either!*
>
> *Dizzy, he was playing like Roy Eldridge. He* changed *when he hear me. When he went with Lucky Millinder (1942), he got me hired on piano so's he could be around me . . .*
>
> *I told Miles, I said, 'You better stop playing like Diz, you want to get somewhere,' but all you read about today is how Miles followed Diz, Parker, Fats Navarro around like a puppy—everybody but me. Read everything but the truth. Charlie Christian, he used to drop in Minton's every night to sit in with me after he finish with Goodman. Used to tell me, 'Man, Benny is a drag—he don't swing!' Goodman never knew that—he always thought he was knocking Charlie out!*
>
> *Who do I think is playing something new today? I've heard nothing new in so long! Ahmad Jamal? Yes, I like him, but then I like so many piano players—like Elmo Hope. I enjoy each one of the Modern Jazz Quartet personally—know them all, but haven't heard them together in a long time. John Lewis has been influenced by my playing."*

Part of the extensive mythology about Monk, given credence by more than one pre-eminent critic, is that his playing is "technically limited." A similar observation has often been made about Picasso by those hostile to modern art who are also unfamiliar with the painter's early representational works. With Monk, like Picasso, the break with traditional forms was conscious and deliberate, involving no imaginary technical shortcomings. He can stride like Waller and make right hand Tatum runs, but does so with sardonic intent, usually for the sake of parody. Even if he could play like Bud Powell—and who can?—it would not suit him to join the seemingly endless cortege of

Powell imitators; the crowded cult devoted to blinding up-tempo right hand bedazzlement simply holds no allure for him.

> *"Bud Powell? I'm the only one he really digs."*[4]

Before his discovery of Monk, André Hodeir commented that "jazz musicians, with a few rare exceptions, do not have strict enough standards of harmonic beauty to know how to avoid certain chords or progressions."[5] That no one is more the "rare exception" than Monk was obvious on hearing the few pop tunes he slipped in during each evening, such as "Memories of You" or "Just a Gigolo," which, like "Body and Soul" after Hawkins was done with it, will never sound the same again. His best known work, "'Round About Midnight," is featured once every working night and sounds utterly unlike the more familiar interpretations of this especially haunting song. As is the case with all of Monk's compositions, its tempo is radically altered each time it reappears. The real *tour de force*, however, is his wildly imaginative reorganization of "Tea for Two." Nearly unrecognizable for the first chorus, the "melody" is stripped down to its bare bones, appearing only as isolated shattered fragments, and the audience visibly tenses for what begins as the most austere and forbidding composition to which most of them have been exposed. Imperceptibly, with all the sly humor at Monk's command, the familiar outlines of the tune emerge—half a dozen musicians in the crowd set up a delighted giggle. By the second chorus, half the audience catches on, and with the conclusion, everyone explodes into mingled laughter and applause.

> *"Anything that's very good will make you laugh in admiration, so it must be humor to make you laugh—or maybe it makes you laugh in surprise because it knocks you out."*

To watch Monk at the piano is to grasp Charlie Rouse's comment that "Monk thinks only of music." Gingerly mounting the bandstand, he suddenly wheels around to face the crowd as if startled in a private rumination. His approach to the instrument is that of a clever child encountering a piano for the first time—("I wonder what would happen if I played *this*—and *this*; sounds pretty good!

4. Monk's influence on Powell is evident in the latter's recent Blue Note LP *Time Waits*, particularly on the track named "Monopoly" [recorded on May 24, 1958 and originally released as Blue Note 1598, *Ed.*]
5. Hodeir, op. cit. , p. 141.

Now what about *that* on top of it!") The tentative probing gains momentum and the halting chords take on disciplined mastery. Nodding the torpedo-like head atop an awesome, hulking frame, he weaves and keens over the keyboard like a medieval alchemist over a bubbling flask; the huge spatula-straight fingers slap the keys awkwardly like a toddler flattening out a mud pie. When a snarling rumble in the bass appears hopelessly involved, the right *elbow* suddenly smashes out treble tone clusters that are stringently correct, and once more the transfixed audience relaxes into laughter.

By the second week, the Blackhawk was swollen with music majors and piano students who had turned out to hear Monk. "What he needs," said a music professor at San Francisco State, "is a piano with quarter tones—you can bet he'd use them!" During intermission, a dreadfully earnest Ph.D. cornered Monk with intense queries regarding 12-tone rows and Webern. Was there, asked the doctor, any special musical theory to which Monk subscribed?

> *"Music theory? Well, when I was a kid, I only knew I wanted to make it better."*

The conversations of Monk, like the letters of Arnold Schoenberg, reflect the towering pride of an innovator long denied his due.

> *"Oscar Peterson never gives me any credit.*
>
> *George Shearing copies so much jive from me; he names everybody but who he really digs. I don't care who I mention 'cause I don't envy anybody—it seems they go out of their way not to mention who they dig.*
>
> *I brought Bud Powell around when he first started—that's never been in print. Doesn't worry me—truth got to come out some time. Why do people take such pains to hide the truth? They lose.*
>
> *When Miles asked me to lay out during his solo on that record, I never thought nothing of it— Roy Eldridge had his piano lay out years ago.*[6]
>
> *Miles has got troubles in jazz—I don't. Miles never yet mentioned how much he learned from me, sitting up on the bandstand with me.*
>
> *I never lie—it's too hard. Have to spend too much time thinking, 'now what's that lie I told?'—then you have to tell still another lie."*

Erroll Garner, in town for a Sol Hurok concert, dropped in closing night. "Monk is right about Miles; he was taught by us all—including me. I feel there's a good chance that what happened to my song 'Misty' will happen to

6. "Bags Groove," December 24, 1954, Prestige LP 7109.

Monk's tunes—somebody will put words to all those lovely ballads of his, and they'll get to be hits! He's playing beautifully now—he must feel like playing—not like that Hollywood Bowl gig. I asked him, 'Monk, what happened at that Hollywood Bowl? What I hear, you really blew it!'—and he gives me that sly little sheepish smile of his and says, 'I guess maybe I ought not to have *done* that,' and I say 'No, Monk, I guess maybe you ought not!' I've heard him play four complete sets now and every time I get up to go he comes out from somewhere and yells, 'Is my boy still out there?' and I answer, 'Yes, Monk, I'm still here!' and sit back down again!"

Those who play with Monk accord him the kind of respect and devotion usually reserved for such canonized figures as Casals or Toscanini. Frank Butler said, "I'm in school right now. With Monk, you never know what will happen musically. I was with Duke Ellington in 1954—Monk doesn't tie me down the way Duke did—Duke even asked me to use two bass drums like Louis Bellson; Monk only asks me to swing. Monk grows all the time—Duke is stagnant." Graciously and gently, the mentor chastened his pupil:

> *"No, he isn't—Duke is still distinctive. I know you must be kidding, or not listening. You mean Duke's band sound the same now that it did ten years ago? It don't."*

Charlie Rouse, a serious and reflective musician, is highly articulate about Monk the theorist and Monk the person. His feelings about both border on veneration. "Everything about his music is correct and makes perfect sense. Take 'Monk's Mood'—the reason it sounds so different and intriguing is that it has an unusual five-beat count. We all work very hard to learn his tunes; not much written music is used in rehearsals—Monk plays new things for us and then we play it with him. It's a happy group—Monk doesn't hire anyone he doesn't like. Playing the Town Hall concert with him was a wonderful experience; Monk was trying to have ten men get a big band sound, but still play loose like a small combo—a little like Miles Davis's Nonet."[7]

> *"What really knocked me out about the Town Hall gig was the full house."*

For young Eddie Kahn, the bass assignment with Monk was an unexpected break, and he was both elated and terrified. "Monk is a genius—I never heard anything like him! We never even had a rehearsal together, and the first few

7. See Gunther Schuller's review of the Town Hall concert, reprinted here on p. 94.

nights were plenty rough. I was scared, and Monk was putting me down all the time, so I go to the Jazz Workshop to talk to 'Cannonball' Adderley and his bass player, Sam Jones, who used to be with Monk. Cannonball told me, 'Man, you got to stand *up* to Monk! You got to say to him, 'Look, man, if you don't think I can play your shit, you go get somebody you think *can*!' That's just what I did and Monk, he backs down right away. After those first few nights, everything was beautiful."

Monk had been happy at the Blackhawk and closing night found him benign and euphoric. The management had left him at peace and the customers had been attentive and quiet. In fact, they had observed *concert hall* quiet most of the time; heretofore, only the Modern Jazz Quartet had been extended this courtesy by a Blackhawk audience. Monk was deeply affected by this treatment and his attitude and demeanor had noticeably changed. The stiff hauteur and "above the battle" mannerisms which had shielded him during the long decade of public rejection began to dissolve, and by the closing set of his engagement, Monk was signing autographs, answering requests to play "Ask Me Now," "Straight No Chaser," "Reflections," and had even managed the suggestion of a smile and a curt bow toward his paying audience. For two weeks Monk had shown himself to be a consistently disciplined musician and an impassioned artist who could, beyond question, "sit down and play you a regular show."

> *"They were always telling me for years to play commercial, be commercial. I'm not commercial. I say, play your own way. Don't play what the public want—you play what you want and let the public pick up on what you doing—even if it does take them fifteen, twenty years."*

The Nonmusic Press

By the late 1950s, just about anyone who was interested in jazz had heard about Monk, and feature articles on him began to appear in leading general magazines of the day, including *Esquire, Ebony, Harpers,* and smaller ones such as *The New Leader* and *The Nugget*. These pieces relied for the most part on previously published material—the interviews and early profiles—with some interpolation of new statements extracted from Monk or whoever happened to be available for comment. The mythology surrounding Monk continued to develop as writers like Charles Edward Smith, a notable writer and New Orleans jazz specialist, wrote a piece for *The Nugget* entitled "The Mad Monk: Madness Turned Out to Be Musicianship." Smith quotes the program notes for a concert that read "Rarely seen, Monk is the Greta Garbo of jazz, and his appearance at any piano is regarded as a major event by serious followers of jazz."[1] Frank London Brown wrote a piece for *Ebony,* the leading publication of African-American culture at the time, with the subtitle "Thelonious Monk started out as church organist, is now often hailed as genius who originated modern jazz."[2] The article ran with a

1. Charles E. Smith, "The Mad Monk," *The Nugget,* October 1958, p. 68.
2. Frank London Brown, "The Magnificent Monk of Music," *Ebony,* May 1959, pp. 120–122, 124–126. A year earlier, Brown published a lengthy interview with Monk in *Down Beat* ("More Man than Myth, Monk Has Emerged from the Shadows," *Down Beat,* October 30, 1958, pp. 13–16; 45–46).

picture showing Monk's silhouette against the Manhattan skyline, taken in the Baroness Nica de Koenigswarter's New Jersey home. And in 1960 Nat Hentoff wrote a lengthy profile of Monk in *Esquire,* opening with, "It has become inescapably hip in the past year to accept Thelonious Sphere Monk as one of the reigning council—and perhaps *the* lama—of modern jazz."[3]

21. *Man, You Gotta Dig That Cat, Thelonious, the Thinker, the Skull, the Long Medulla*

Although not typical of the writing about Monk, and perhaps a bit outlandish in substance and tone, Albert Goldman's piece has been included here because of the humorously simulated bebop lingo and opinionated statements about the music. What is interesting is that the mocking tone of the piece is not that different from the bewildered statements of the early profiles that were published in the late 1940s, more than a decade earlier. "The long medulla," or medulla oblongata, as it is known in the medical community, is a metonym for the brain, and Goldman makes a point out of casting Monk as an original thinker: "Sometimes he's thinking so hard, he doesn't even bother to get a sound." He admits though, that Monk's strength is that "he never loses a strong racial sound . . . like some old oil well that keeps on pumping up the good black stuff when all the new rigs have gone dry," a somewhat crass but engaging analogy. For several years Goldman wrote a music column for *The New Leader,* a left-leaning journal of labor politics. He later became known as an author of several infamous biographies on subjects such as John Lennon and Elvis Presley, always full of colorful, stimulating language and—unfortunately—unsubstantiated facts.

This article originally appeared as "Man, You Gotta Dig That Cat, Thelonious, the Thinker, the Skull, the Long Medulla," by Albert Goldman in *The New Leader,* October 19, 1959, p. 27. Reprinted with permission of *The New Leader.*

3. Nat Hentoff, "The Private World of Thelonious Monk," *Esquire,* April 1960, p. 133. The article is available in an expanded form in Hentoff's *The Jazz Life* (New York: Dial Press, 1961).

Thelonious Monk is a hard man to place. When you mention Monk to somebody who knows the jazz scene, they always give you the same bit: "He's the guy who started Bop." Well, we all know that, but still you can't dig Monk as a Bopper—he's too individual for that tag. Then, there are the cats who go into a thing about "Monk, the Genius of Jazz," the man who plays and writes and arranges, and does everything, the end. Well, I wouldn't call what he does playing the piano, and you never hear those pieces of his played the same way twice.

No, man, you gotta dig Thelonious as the thinker, the skull, the, long medulla. Just watch how he sits there on the stand. He don't hump over the keys like them studs who just wanna rave on all night. Maybe he's got one leg over the other, sitting sidewise with his elbow on the rack while he flaps the keys with one hand. You dig right away the cat is thinking. He don't wanna play for anybody, he just needs an audience so's he can be alone and work things out for himself. Sometimes he gets so frustrated trying to get something down, he just gives up and lets the other boys rave on without him. Sometimes he's thinking so hard, he don't even bother to get a sound.

Monk's solos are the craziest things because every two bars he's off on a new idea. He'll start in with some weird little blip he just picked up from outer space, and then, just when you're sure he's gonna make it, he gives the dial a twist, and his rig starts bringing in the funny old sound of some Harlem piano player, *circa* 1925. Two bars of that jazz and the set suddenly jams on an African time-signal—one swinging note struck over and over again until you're ready to flip! You see now what it is when a guy is always thinking—he can't get himself together so's he can play.

Monk's ideas are mostly things he does with tonality and rhythm. He'll set his bass player going in one key, then he'll come on strong in another key. Or, maybe he'll make two different rhythms fight it out, drums against piano. That left hand of his is always feeling around, grabbing chords nobody else would think to play. Every time he lays a strange chord down, the music tilts to a different angle. Sometimes he tilts it so sudden and so sharp, like, the cat who's taking the solo comes tumbling down like a bottle off an upturned table.

Monk's right hand isn't worth much. He has a hard time playing what he hears in his head. Compared to a great piano man like Bud Powell, Monk sounds like a cat who needs lessons. That's why you always wanna catch Monk inside a combo where he don't have to do the big solo bit.

The cats who play with Monk are the most grooved men in America. He keeps feeding them crazy ideas until they're out of their skulls. Sometimes you'll see him play something, and then look up to see whether he reached the other man. Monk's always sending messages like that and trying to turn the other boys on. One night he got so far out he even tried to turn the audience on. He shuffled off the stand and started yelling at the people to dance! Now, there's a scene for you—imagine all those cool cats lobbed out in their seats getting up and firking around to that insane beat!

I guess what gasses musicians the most about Monk is this—no matter how gone he gets with his atonal jazz, he never loses a strong racial sound. You see, most of the modern cats are pretty well hung up between jazz and the classical stuff. They all took a little vacation up at Juilliard after the war, and before they got away they were hooked on Bach and Debussy. Now, a man like Monk is good for these cats. He's like some old oil well that keeps pumping up the good black stuff when all the new rigs have gone dry.

Even the Modern Jazz Quartet has picked up on Monk. Milt Jackson, their vibes man, used to play with Monk years ago. I guess some of those rough chips must have stuck in his brain, 'cause every so often I hear a nutty sound in his playing, and I say to myself, "Now, there's a man that digs Thelonious."

22. *Monk Talk*

Robert Kotlowitz's article on Monk, based on his attending a rehearsal, was featured in his regular column "After Hours" for *Harper's Magazine*. There are some exceptional insights into Monk's music about melody and harmony that rely on metaphor and simile alone. He also touches on the issue of Monk's outlandish image and his stature, and how it has resulted in three groups of attendees: those who are attracted by the fact that Monk is considered "hip," those who are attracted by his image, and those who are attracted by his music. In reality, of course, many listeners would easily fit all three categories simultaneously, but it highlights the fact that Monk's appeal clearly crosses over into the extra-musical. Kotlowitz wrote for *The New York Times*, *Harper's*, and *Esquire* in addition to having several novels published.

Thelonious Monk—the jazz pianist who has been variously described as "an unpredictable sideshow" and "a pure, individual artist"—lives in a slum neighborhood in Manhattan bordered by the New York Central freight yards. This has been his home since 1924, when, at the age of four, he forsook his native North Carolina. One of the signs of his permanency is a metal-framed calling card on his front door; it bears the inscription "T. Monk" in turn-of-the-century type and may well be the only one of its kind in the area. Over the years, Monk has acquired a wife, now the highly competent executive of his household, and a couple of children.

He has also, and much more recently, acquired an impressive and enthusiastic following. Only the past few years have provided him with anything like steady employment, although, for as long as he can remember, he has wanted to play his special kind of music. Starting his career as a teen-age pianist in the neighborhood community center, Monk went on to work wherever he could—for saloons, depression rent parties, a traveling evangelist, and, briefly, for Lucky Millinder's band.

In the early 'forties, together with Charlie Parker, Bud Powell, and Dizzy Gillespie, among others, Monk began to join the after-hours jam sessions at Minton's Playhouse in Harlem. Critics and chroniclers, often eager to establish a firm tradition in print where one may not exist in reality, had it that Minton's produced a carefully planned school of new jazz deliberately designed to overthrow everything that preceded it. This is dramatic, sentimental, and not very truthful. If the Minton sessions were important to jazz, it was because dissatisfied musicians came together and discovered they were dissatisfied with much the same thing—in simplest terms, the old ways of jazz. There was little talk about it; to the best of Monk's recollection, "we just played."

Parker, Powell, and Gillespie, although popular artists long before Monk, shared his desire to return to impulse and instinct as the twin sources of music. Bop was wonderful to listen to, dull to talk about. It was music to be played and heard; it was not, as most of music is not, the subject for exegesis.

Since Minton's, Monk has put in two full decades of bone-wearying persistence to maintain his personal outpost in the avant-garde of jazz. The problem of where to appear still plagues him today. There are more festivals and more concert dates, but the first are generally potluck affairs, mixing a stew of ill-assorted musicians for a few performances, and the second are sporadic. There are probably more night clubs too, but Monk guesses there are four in the country in which a jazz musician can enjoy playing—two of them in New York.

"Most club owners," he has said, "think you're a traveling vaudeville routine, with a clear-cut act twenty minutes long that's ready to go on four times a night. They want every musician to get a line six blocks long outside the place every night."

Nevertheless, his records sell and his price is high for public appearances. Today, Monk appears a lonely but not separated artist to his fellow jazzmen, and a dedicated but not intransigent artist to the critics, who see in him the *sine qua non* of artistic acceptance in America: personal integrity. In recent years, he has been characterized as "one of the most unmistakably original talents on the jazz scene," by composer Gunther Schuller, and as "a major formative influence on jazzmen—not only pianists and writers, but players on all instruments," by critic Nat Hentoff. "Monk stands out," says drummer Max Roach. He is "the main reason I came to New York from Chicago," says arranger-composer George Russell, who goes on to explain that "the first time I heard Monk in the 'forties, he reached me faster and more deeply than either Gillespie or Parker."

What Monk's audience thinks of him depends on which audience is being talked about. There are three.

One is in attendance because it has gathered that it is the hip thing to do. Its unstated premise is simple: it is better to appear "in" than "out" in any context that is fashionable, even if it also turns out to be totally incomprehensible. For this audience, jazz is in and Monk is in, although what he plays makes little musical difference. Jazz offers swollen legends of narcotics, of drink, race guilt, and violence, bearing a strangely attractive aura of sadness and pain. For the "hippies," it means an evening's brush with emotional anarchy for the price of a beer.

A second audience comes because it has heard that Monk is a character. Monk *is* a character, in that his natural differences from other people are clearly defined and insisted upon. He speaks, eats, and sleeps only when he feels like it. He sometimes arrives late for performances, almost always wears a hat when playing: a goatee covers his chin; and his baritone voice, often liquid and soft in conversation, can be hoarse beyond imitation. Moreover, he is almost as big as his piano, and he tends to get up in the middle of a set and dance around the platform while the members of his group solo. For this audience, he is a spectacle; it is sheerest coincidence that a little music is thrown in.

The third audience, young, ardent, and often bearded without being beat, will come to a night club for a Monk performance, but it won't drink very much. It is loyal, intense, and responsive to the music, which is what it comes to hear.

Monk's music—"*My* music," he always calls it—is dark, like mahogany, but not gloomy, staccato but not nervous. It is old chords, new chords, and more chords, almost all mass and density exploding in chunks of sound between which carefully composed silences fall. It is vertical rather than horizontal music, it has only a tenuous line. When Monk serves up a melody, it usually stays in a corner, where he hoards it with miserly care; he gets from one corner to the next riding bizarre harmonies and thrusting rhythms, jabbing and rocking like a boxer making rights, lefts, rights, and sometimes both simultaneously, straight out and far.

In the past ten years the "sound" of Monk's music has not changed dramatically, although it has intensified, pared down of all waste motion. It cannot be imitated with any success. When another musician picks up a Monk melody, it crumbles without the Monk harmonies; on the other hand, the harmonies are so individualistic that only suggestions of them work in another's playing and even then they must be incorporated carefully. Like Debussy's work, and for the same reasons, Monk's music remains a self-sufficient island.

It is not easy for Monk's kind of music to hold the listener's attention. With only the barest linear quality, it sometimes loses suspense, and, like much other contemporary jazz, the range of its emotional variation often barely extends from thumb to forefinger, fully outstretched. What compels the listener is surprise—the next note coming where it should not, the chords, one after the other, apparently never heard before, the silences, which fill up before a vacuum can set in, and rhythmic propulsion and the beat, immediately reaching into the very center of the listener's nervous energy and taking hold. Like almost all of jazz, it is very much here-and-now music.

Although he often "re-composes" and improves on standard popular tunes, Monk usually plays his own compositions with three or four other instrumentalists.

The actual composing is done at a Steinway grand at one end of the kitchen in Monk's apartment. Since Monk is inclined to sit down at the piano at any time, day or night, the kitchen ceiling is soundproofed, while all four walls, as well as the front door which leads right into the room, are paneled in walnut. When Monk composes, he is virtually hermetically sealed from the outside world. He may work alone or with a member of his group, the noise in the rest of the apartment may exceed his piano's volume; he continues to work. "I find something almost every time I sit down at the piano," he says. "No matter what's going on around me."

With their minimal formal training, Monk's hands at work would be the despair of every good piano teacher in the land. The fingers, almost never curved, lie nearly flat on the keys, like ten miniature spatulas. The hands themselves are small for such an oversized body (Monk stands taller than six feet and, like his work, he has the mass and density to go with it). He is not noted for a fabulous technique, but he can do exactly what he needs to do.

Arpeggios and runs, for example, are managed safely enough, although they have no great speed or cleanness of line. Sometimes he gives up using his hands entirely, aiming an elbow at a tonal cluster with surprising accuracy. Monk's dazzle lies in his compositions. As a performer, he tends to treat the piano for what it is—a percussion instrument—instead of trying to disguise its limitations.

Rehearsing with a colleague, he rarely uses a score. "I've got it all written down," he says, "but we do just as well without reading notes. That way nothing distracts." A rehearsal may go on for two hours or longer. Monk feeds his tenor sax man, Charlie Rouse, a note or phrase at a time. Rouse takes it bite by bite, each note or phrase a mouthful digested to bewildered shakings of the head. It can take the entire two hours to get one full minute of music set between the two.

Monk and Rouse say their notes, as though music were the simplest, most direct language available to man, and, even more, as though B-C sharp, played on an instrument, means something as precise and unmistakable as C-A-T. Throughout the rehearsal, Monk directs with short comments. "You're not making it," he says placidly after the seventh repetition of an octave jump. "Dig it." Well into the next phrase, Monk says, "Don't touch the note, hit it. And when you hit it, augment it."

To visitors, he is as terse. "This dragging you?" he asks politely as the repetitions continue. When satisfied, Monk utters his favorite comment, the word "Solid," pronounced slowly and with geometric firmness.

Once the rehearsal is over, Monk likes to relax by listening to jazz records. He may start to dance, a glass of orange juice in his hand. "Jazz is America musically. It's all jazz, everywhere," he says, rocking loosely to the music. "When I was a kid, I felt something had to be done about all that jazz. So I've been doing it for twenty years. Maybe I've turned jazz another way. Maybe I'm a major influence. I don't know. Anyway, my music is my music, on my piano, too. That's a criterion of something. Jazz is my adventure. I'm after new chords, new ways of syncopating, new figurations, new runs. How to use notes differently. That's it. Just using notes differently." So Monk talks, creating little dances in his kitchen, swinging away under a black beanie from Chinatown, keeping a telescopic eye out for the moving frontiers of jazz.

Critics

During the 1950s, criticism of Monk's work began to focus more deeply on essential aspects of his music rather than on his behavior or idiosyncratic piano technique. Journals like *Jazz Monthly* (1955–1971), *The Jazz Review* (1958–1961), and *Jazz Journal* (1948–) were beginning to produce substantive, weighty critical appraisals of modern jazz. Writers such as Max Harrison, Gunther Schuller, Martin Williams, and the two included here, Michael James and André Hodeir, began formulating analytical and theoretical models of jazz improvisation and composition, more often than not derived from Western music theory and criticism. This stood in contrast to the practical "How to" columns in *Down Beat* and *Metronome*, where theory and analysis had more to do with practical aspects of the act of improvisation rather than theoretical abstractions about its structure and meaning. The term "serious," normally reserved for academically affiliated and endorsed art music—however absurd this may now seem—began to be applied to jazz, as its entertainment role was left behind by the bebop revolution.

23. *Monk or the Misunderstanding*

The noted French composer, critic and musicologist André Hodeir wrote extensively about jazz for the French magazine *Jazz Hot* throughout the 1940s and 1950s, some of which was translated and published in his book *Toward Jazz.* He was one of the first musicologists to systematically discuss jazz improvisation, specifically in relation to bebop, in his book *Jazz: Its Evolution and Essence.* Hodeir's ideas are sharp and often controversial, the article on Monk being no exception. According to Hodeir, what sets Monk apart from other jazz musicians is his understanding and treatment of musical form, an understandable proposition coming from a classically trained composer. Although realizing Monk's unorthodox piano technique may be unpalatable to some, he urges us to look beyond his incompleteness and see the deeper significance of his contribution to jazz history—his reinvention of traditional musical structures. Perhaps his most telling statement about Monk, at least in defending him against the naysayers, is that he is "the first jazzman who has had a feeling of specifically modern aesthetic values," forging a link with composers like Schoenberg, Stravinsky, Berg, and Webern.

This appeared in André Hodeir's *Toward Jazz* (New York: Grove Press) in 1962, pp.156–177. It is an English translation of a two-part article originally published in French in *Jazz Hot,* Nos. 142 and 143 in 1959. Translated by Noel Burch.

1

Nietzsche provided a subtitle for his book. It is: "A Book for Everyone and No-one." "For Everyone" does not, of course, mean for each one in the sense of just anybody. "For Everyone" refers to every person insofar as he is truly human and to the degree that he is reflective of the root of his being. ". . . and No-one" means not for those curiosity seekers who gather from everywhere, intoxicate themselves with isolated bits and passages taken out of context and become dizzy from the book's language, half-singing, half-shouting, sometimes thoughtful, sometimes turbulent, often lofty and occasionally flat—instead of committing themselves to the train of thought which is seeking here its verbal expression.

—Martin Heidegger

The world of jazz is a stage on which it matters less what the actors say than the way they say it. Conviction, rather than creative genius, is the key to success, whether it be the artificial—or simulated—conviction of a rock 'n' roll star, the sincere conviction of the crack rhythm and blues expert, or the absolute conviction of a musician who has only his conviction. For the crowd's need to be convinced is the nose by which it is most easily led. The millions of addlepates who cheered Hitler on the eve of the second World War were expressing and sharing an absolute conviction; many of them died before they could realize that their enthusiasm reflected nothing more than abysmal feeblemindedness.

In other words, it matters little that you have nothing to say, so long as you say it ardently and artfully. The best method of convincing an audience whose average mental age is under twelve is to comply with that norm yourself. If you happen to have the intellect and sensibility of an adult—even those of a backward adult—a shadow of a doubt, something resembling a conscience is likely to creep into your mind and that will be the end of your capacity for expression. If ever you lag behind your audience for a fraction of a second they will slip from your grasp and pass judgment on you. In that fraction of a second they will see how ridiculous you are; never again will you be able to restore the sacred ties that held them at your mercy.

Conviction, then, is essential on both sides of the footlights, as is that clear-cut propensity for intellectual vacuity which, as everyone knows, is the most obvious sign of acute musical gifts. So now the stage is set; the curtain is ready to rise on a play the plot of which must, of course, be "simple and direct." This is the magic recipe which jazz critics have been using for the past thirty years to designate, for the benefit of admiring crowds, the *ne plus ultra* in jazz. But tradition grows richer with the passing years. In highly cultured periods such as ours, new concepts may be brought to light, and indeed, today that prime aesthetic virtue, *facileness*, has found a place among the basic values. In order for music to be good it must be simple to understand; after all, is it not meant to be enjoyed by the greater number? There are, however, a few counts which still leave room for improvement. For example, judging by their audience-participation reactions, newcomers to jazz seem to be having greater and greater difficulty assimilating certain rhythmic elements;[1] the *afterbeat*, in particular, seems to constitute an insoluble problem for them. May I therefore suggest that we simplify jazz rhythms, which are definitely becoming too complicated. By doing away with the afterbeat, by rehabilitating the Sousa approach to accentuation, jazz would unquestionably win over those thousands of men and women of all ages who, like the characters in the *Grand Illusion* or Céline's Bardamu, are fascinated by military bands. Moreover, that

1. One characteristic of the fanatic is his desire to participate. In jazz, this participation takes the form of hand-clapping.

perplexity which sometimes besets the lone hand-clapper in a side balcony would give way, for the greater good of public morals, to the joys of unanimity fully achieved at last. One! Two! One! Two! What could be more simple and direct than this language, so dear to the heart of every true-blue Frenchman?

Have the pleasures of irony led me astray from reality? I wish this were so. I wish that a hideous march in the form of a blues had never been cheered by a large crowd, satisfied at last in its craving to identify, if only for a moment, its own national folklore with the highly touted music of the Negro. On the other hand, I hope that a particularly respectful salvo of applause will one day greet the presence on a Parisian stage of such a true artist as Thelonious Monk.

Now Monk is neither simple nor direct, he does not always say what he has to say as well as he might and the things he has to say are subtle, seldom easy to grasp, and not at all meant for the enjoyment of the greater number; his rhythmic notions go far beyond that afterbeat which some find so elusive, and yet, by one of those paradoxes common to jazz, if ever we are lucky enough to hear him in Paris, he will probably reap the same wild cheers that have marked recent performances given by great, not-so-great, and mediocre jazzmen alike. I'll even bet he has a good box office take.

Only yesterday Monk was a has-been, a half-forgotten page in the history of jazz. Today he is an established value, with a label and a price tag. A single article was all it took for everyone in France to grasp the significance of the new Messiah, and it wasn't even a real article, just a hasty discussion over the tape recorder of *Jazz Hot*.[2] The next day everyone swore by Monk and Monk alone. Not so long ago he couldn't even find work and now he is vying with seaside charmers and Granz's circus stand-bys for the top berths on opinion polls. The musician who once terrified us all no longer seems to disturb a soul. He has been tamed, classified, and given his niche in that eclectic Museum of Great Jazzmen which admits such a variety of species, from Fats Domino to Stan Kenton. Only a man like Miles Davis has the courage to fear Monk: "I like the way he plays, but I can't stand behind him. He doesn't give you any support."

Thelonious Monk is not a great classic, one of those musicians who, like Armstrong or Parker, attracts impressive crowds of disciples. Monk is a man alone, disturbing and incomplete. In the eyes of history he may be on the wrong track; but this, perhaps, is what most endears him to me. He is the solitary man who, when he looks back, does not see his fellow travelers—who

2. I am referring to a discussion between Michel Fano, Nat Peck, and myself which appeared in *Jazz Hot*, No. 116, 1956.

doesn't even know if he has fellow travelers. A few years ago, I thought his example would be irresistible; today I am not so sure. The enticements of facileness, the sense of security that lies in numbers, the love of success and the cult of the dollar may, in the end, prove stronger than the strange aesthetic vertigo which a few people experience on hearing some of Monk's fiery outbursts.

Monk may not have gone far enough yet. His music may not yet be sufficiently well-developed to exert any lasting influence on the majority of musicians. One wonders how much attention the young jazzmen of the forties would have paid to Charlie Parker had his music not been so thoroughly accomplished. Moreover, the desire for change is not nearly so widespread now as at the end of the war. The situation today is more like that of 1940 than of 1945. But then perhaps the contrary is true. Perhaps Monk, without even realizing it, has already gone too far on the path he has chosen; for it is a path which must inevitably lead to that complete divorce between jazz and popular music prefigured, I feel, in the shocks periodically inflicted on jazz by the few artists who have managed to divert it from its original course (and these shocks have been increasingly violent: the Bird was a less "popular" musician than Lester, Lester less than the Duke, and the Duke less than Armstrong). If this hypothesis is correct, we may expect to see any attempts to propagate Monk's conceptions thwarted by a powerful inertia on the part of both public and musicians. Monk is fashionable now; let him make the most of it! Before long he may again be as neglected as he was on his first visit to France, for there is reason to fear that his present success is based on a sad misunderstanding.

Snobbery does not in itself explain Monk's popularity, which is fairly limited in any case. True, his music probably does provide the snob with almost as good an opportunity for intellectual bullying as the Modern Jazz Quartet's. John Lewis fans like to refer to Vivaldi, Monk's may drop the name of Webern. But there undeniably exist music lovers who are sincerely fond of his work, for Monk has that power of conviction without which, as we have seen, it is impossible to crash the gates of success; his is certainly not as great as that of an Erroll Garner or even a Horace Silver, but he does have it. And even those who confess that Monk's music disagrees with them have to admit that it does not leave them indifferent. Moreover, his music may benefit by the aura of strangeness created by the scintillation of a thousand bizarre details which add color to the clear-cut structures of a basically traditional language. If Monk's music were no more than the alloy of bizarreness and security which many think it is, it would seem insignificant indeed alongside that mad, delirious tempest that the Bird, in his greatest moments, sent sweeping across the valleys of jazz. The Monk craze cannot last unless it be strengthened by the difficult exploration of the real Monk. Is such a thing conceivable? Each of us must provide his own answer to this question in the light of his personal experience. Not to mention the sense of dread that the outwardly rather monstrous appearance of Monk's world inspired in me for so long, I found that in order to begin to grasp its deeper meanings I first had to come up with solutions, and, above all, come to grips with problems similar to those suggested in his work.

For there is something else.

Monsieur Dumesnil would be very surprised to learn that a semiliterate Negro is capable of conveying, through a musical idiom which he would peremptorily regard as highly primitive, beautiful ideas that are both thoroughly musical and truly modern, ideas which his favorite composers, whose "achievements" he periodically hails with that leveling pen of his—I am referring to men like Florent Schmitt and Henri Tomasi—would be quite incapable of even conceiving.[3]

"Ideas that are *modern* and *musical*;" does this mean that Monk is not a true jazzman? After all, the true jazzman is not supposed to overstep the bounds of his art, venturing onto the arid steppes of serious music or, worse still, the glacial plains of the twelve-tone row. But here we may rest assured, for no twelve-tone sirens have lured Monk away from jazz. He probably doesn't even know that such music exists. I can safely say that the gradual development of his language has been the result of intuition and intuition alone. Those who debate as to whether or not this language is still part of jazz are simply quarreling over words, and I prefer not to join them. I feel that although Monk's sonority and his system of attacks and intensities are highly personal, they are definitely in the tradition of jazz. Even his opponents acknowledge the rhythmic precision of his playing and the great power of the swing he produces. It is rather hard to apply the word "funky" to Thelonious's music and for this reason some may deny that he is a great blues musician. I do not agree, however; I feel that on the contrary, his stroke of genius consists precisely in having applied a fresh treatment to the blues theme, making a renewal of its inner structures possible without any distortion of its style (always perfectly intact in his music).

The fact that this true jazzman and eminent blues musician, whose improvisations are free of any academic formalism, should display such overt con-

3. I am referring to René Dumesnil, the scholarly musicologist of *Le Monde* who will, I hope, forgive my using him here as a symbol of that useless criticism which has an exact counterpart in jazz.

cern with *form per se*, ought to provide the reader with food for thought. Contrary to the belief of certain naive observers who prefer to deny the existence of aesthetic problems rather than come to grips with them, jazz is not generated spontaneously. It is the work of human beings, of a special kind of human being called the artist. Now the nature of the artist, in contrast with that of the mere musician, amateur or professional, is to be dissatisfied. This feeling of dissatisfaction is a basic, permanent, and inexorable force in the artist, compelling him to upset the equilibrium achieved by his creative predecessors (and sometimes, in the case of the very great, by the artist himself). The truth of the matter, as seen by any objective historian, is that jazz, born during the decline of Western civilization, has made contact with that extraordinary concept of musical form which made it possible for Western music—or at least its masterworks—to rise above all the art forms of any known civilization. This is where one may expect the stalwart champions of "pleasurable music" to arch their backs and bare their claws. For is not this notion of form the beginning of the end? If jazz is that happy, fun-making music they love and which satisfies their appetites, then anyone who isn't satisfied is wrong. Monk is wrong. In the eyes of these people, *who do not feel that the absence of form is a deficiency*, the very idea of form is necessarily parasitic. Its entrance into the world of jazz constitutes the rift in the lute. But the worst is yet to come, since the existence of form calls for someone to organize it, someone who thinks music, in other words, that personification of evil, the composer![4]

I am not afraid of being contradicted on this point, I *know* that I will be, and loudly so. When conservative critics are out to combat a new idea they invariably find ten musicians (and not necessarily bad ones) to defend their theories. This time we may expect them to find a hundred, for the subject is an important one. I will not lose any sleep over this, however, since even a hundred musicians who are blind to the necessity of form cannot prevent the existence of a Thelonious Monk. However, in order to forestall a useless flood of well-meaning protest, I must be more explicit. When I say that the absence from jazz of a certain dimension that I call form is a deficiency, I do not mean that jazz is now entirely devoid of form, but that form does not play a vital, active role in it.[5]

4. The reader is requested to refer to Chapter 9, which contains a summary distinction between the composer, the arranger, and the tune or theme writer. [The chapter is "Freedom and Its Limitations in Improvisation and Composition," *Toward Jazz* (New York: Grove Press, 1962), reprinted by Da Capo Press. *Ed.*]

5. Certain works of Ellington are among the rare exceptions to this rule.

The pioneers of jazz borrowed from Occidental folk music a sense of symmetry and the principle of regularly recurring structures. With these ideas as a starting point, jazz, like every other form of music inspired by Occidental folklore, grew up according to a fixed, stereotyped, formal principle which stopped developing almost entirely once jazz ceased to be folk music. In the meantime, the notions of symmetry and continuity in musical discourse were being destroyed by Debussy, Schonberg, Stravinsky, and Webern, and replaced, in the works of the major contemporary composers—Barraqué, Boulez, Stockhausen—by a completely different conception. If a twelve-tone score like *Sequence* or *Le Marteau sans Maitre* bears as little resemblance to a classical symphony as a Klee abstraction does to a Corot landscape, it is because the world of music is now based on the notions of asymmetry and discontinuity. Thelonious Monk is to be hailed as the first jazzman who has had a feeling for specifically modern aesthetic values.

2

The danger threatening the author of an article like this—which is not meant to be one of those "surveys" conducted at a respectful distance but a very personal essay, an attempt at "subjective" analysis—lies in the fact that he is constantly tempted to alter the course of reality, insidiously shaping it in the image of his own wishes. I must continually guard against painting an ideal picture of Monk; it would be as unfaithful and as inadequate as the portrait for everyday use which we have already rejected. Monk constitutes a splendid promise in the world of jazz; we must not make of him a false Messiah.

Monk, as I have already said, is incomplete, and must be taken as he is. How could I seriously claim to see his work in its ultimate perfection? Do I have the right to look over his shoulders, to look into the future with his eyes—for would they even *be* his eyes? Would they not be mine, jaded by their contact with contemporary art, hampered by a cultural background which, in this particular struggle for insight, may not be the right weapon? These scruples may seem out of place, yet the reader had to be informed of them, for they constitute the very substance of the form of commitment I have chosen. If critical analysis is to be regarded as a creative act, then it must be conducted with that same rigor which characterizes, I feel, the work of art. In a field where pure speculation can so easily assume the guise of established truth, we cannot legitimately tolerate any retreat into the realm of imagination.

Monk has occasionally disappointed me. Not that I have ever regarded him as more advanced than he actually is; it's just that no one can be expected to maintain those positions of extreme tension which define the creative act. Is there any man, any artist, brave enough to hold out against the tremendous weight of the tradition from which he sprang and the pressure of the milieu to which he belongs? Then too, it is just possible that what I take for a yielding on his part is actually a sign of renewed effort. Those ballads that Monk, in the solitude of his apartment, plays over and over again may be leading him through secret channels toward some unexpected explosion. Close though he may seem to the origins of jazz—"I sound a little like James P. Johnson," he says, not without a touch of irony—we suddenly find his tremendous shadow stretching out across those ill-defined regions where the stride piano is but a memory and where the notion of steady tempo, which is at the very root of jazz, seems to have vanished.

It is not hard to see why I am so fascinated by his remarkable "I Should Care" on the record called *Thelonious Himself.*[6] It consists of a series of impulses which disregard the bar line completely, pulverize the musical tissue and yet preserve intact that "jazz feeling" which so readily evaporates in the smoke of a Tatum introduction. These elongations of musical time, presented here in a "non-tempo" context, are probably the direct descendants of those "in tempo" elongations to which his famous solo in "The Man I Love" (with Miles Davis) had already accustomed us. Is it so unreasonable to think that they exist as a function of a second, underlying tempo, imperceptible to us but which Monk *hears* in all the complexity of its relationships with the figures he is playing?

One may wonder what remains of the theme of "I Should Care" after this acid bath, and, in fact of the ballad in general, considered as an essential element of jazz sensibility. Personally, I am delighted at this transmutation, which is in keeping with the breath of fresh air brought to jazz, in my opinion, by his own original themes. Will Monk's concepts abolish at long last those "standards" with which every great jazzman since Armstrong has carried on an exhausting and, despite an occasional victory, perfectly fruitless struggle? Will he supply the Lester Youngs and Charlie Parkers of the future with new themes that will constitute a loftier challenge to their talents? Yet hardly has this hope been uttered, than Monk himself dashes it by rehashing a theme as insignificant as "Just a Gigolo" (though, again, this may not be the retreat that it seems, but simply one more assault on that fortress where great treasures lay hidden).

Are we dealing with the return of the prodigal child, exhausted by his travels, or the obstinate—though perhaps hopeless—labor of the gold digger who never says die? This is the only alternative to be deduced from Monk's

6. Recorded on April 5, 1957 and originally released as Riverside RLP 12-235. *Ed.*

constant and disconcerting seesaw motion. For it goes without saying that I refuse to accept the intermediate hypothesis, whereby a man who has upset the very fundamentals of the jazz repertory is really satisfied with these degradingly insipid popular songs. If this were true he would have followed the examples of Garner and Tatum and sought a wider choice of melodies for, as it has often been remarked, his is unprecedentedly narrow.[7] In recording sessions and public performances, as well as in his own practice periods, Monk plays the same pieces over and over again. We may find his choice of tunes surprising, not so his desire to limit himself, for it is one of the most characteristic channels of expression for his basic feeling of dissatisfaction.

It is Monk who first introduced a sense of musical time into jazz; the interest of this new dimension does not, however, lie solely in its foreshadowing the destruction of a thematic lore to which the vast majority of jazzmen—and their public, as well—still seem very much attached. Of course, this battle is worth waging—and winning. Some may miss "But Not for Me" or "April in Paris" the way others will miss "Honeysuckle Rose;" their sentimental attachment to a tradition blinds them to the fact that these very tunes are the most damning evidence against that tradition. The real problem, however, is situated on a higher plane; the repertory question is merely a necessary, though attenuated reflection of that problem, which is to determine whether or not form—I haven't lost sight of it—can become an active ingredient of the jazzman's poetic universe. Musical time is one of the two main props sustaining this notion of form; the other is musical space. And Monk has revolutionized musical space as much as musical time.

Let's look at Monk's accompanying technique. Is Miles Davis right in saying that he doesn't give the soloists any support? Would it not be more accurate to say that he gives them a new kind of support, which jars with the more traditional notions of Miles, but which might be capable of stimulating the improvisational gifts of a less self-assured soloist? Referring to his collaboration with Monk at the Five Spot, John Coltrane has said: "I learned a lot with him. . . . It's another great experience."[8] If we are to believe Bobby Jaspar, who

7. Not only do Garner and Tatum accept the legacy of ballads and "standards," they actually welcome it with open arms. Monk, on the other hand, does keep his distance, though often succumbing to the temptation of decorative arabesque in the form of awkward and conventional arpeggios. (Cf. Gunther Schuller's essay on his records, *The Jazz Review*, November, 1958.) One wonders whether these figures, practically nonexistent when he improvises on his own themes, do not indicate the inward discomfiture of the least "decorative-minded" of all jazzmen in the face of material whose very impurity cries out for decoration.

8. August Blume, "An Interview with Coltrane," *The Jazz Review*, January, 1959.

says that Monk and Coltrane "attained the highest summits of jazz expression," the two musicians must have gotten along fairly well. Personally, however, I must admit that I have never heard any soloist (except perhaps Milt Jackson) who wasn't bothered to some extent by Monk's approach; nor can I easily conceive of a soloist to whom Monk's accompaniment would be *indispensable* in the way that Roach's was to Parker.

Indeed, Monk brings to his accompaniment a concept of discontinuous musical space, which I have yet to find in the playing of either Coltrane or Rollins. Making the most of the piano's specific qualities, he has built his accompanying style on a system of isolated or contiguous note-groups which contrast with one another through sudden changes of register. The mountains he pushes up, the valleys he hollows out cannot, of course, pass unnoticed. Yet Monk is not trying to show off or create an illusion of orchestral accompaniment. Even while seeking to *free himself of the soloist*, Monk's ultimate goal is to exalt him anew by enveloping his melody with an aura of polyphony. The assistance given soloists by the discreet vigilance of the traditional accompanist, whose only concern is to clarify tricky harmonic passages, always results in a pedantic formal subservience; because of their close interrelationship, both parts are subjected to the strict rules of a hierarchical system which allows for no value inversions whatsoever. Thus, ever since the end of the New Orleans era, improvised jazz has deliberately confined itself within very narrow limits, the very limits from which even Italian opera, despite its formal poverty, managed to escape from time to time: accompanied melody considered as the only possible form of musical discourse. Monk's sudden jumps from one register to the next constitute a far more drastic attempt at transcendency than previous devices (such as that of dividing a chorus into shared four-bar sequences the way modern jazzmen do). The soloist's supremacy has been challenged at last but Monk has gone even further than that; his technique restores to jazz that polyphonic fabric that was once so important, through the new notion of discontinuity. This twofold contribution may greatly complicate the task of future soloists, but jazzmen have already shown that they were capable of rising to challenges of this sort.

Similarly, while this conception of accompaniment implies a promotion of the accompanist, it also makes great demands on the musician who accepts it. Continual changes of register do not automatically make one a genius; these changes must be the expression of an interior vision which must, in turn, derive from a keen insight into musical space and time. Ten years of mediocre row music have taught us that discontinuity can, at times, be nothing better than an alibi for incoherence. If Monk's conceptions win out, it will be much more difficult to be a good accompanist in the future. Monk himself is a great accompanist—or more precisely a *great background organizer*. He has a marvelous gift for measuring the weight of a given dissonance and the density of a given attack in order to combine and place them at that precise point in musical space where their impact will be most effective, relative to the length of time he intends to hold the note and, above all, to the length of the surrounding silences—in other words in function of a subtle space-time relationship which no jazzman before him, not even Parker, had ever experienced in all its urgent beauty.

Once this is established, it matters little that Monk is not, as some say, a great harmonist, in the usual sense. Anyone who is bent on destroying all those insipid ballads with their attractive chords must agree to abandon most of that harmonic cast-off. The pretty passing chord with its Ravel-like savor nearly killed jazz; I say let it die, and good riddance! Monk is accused of depersonalizing the chord; I say more power to him. He is also accused of establishing, in his own themes, a system of extreme dissonances, which is likely to invade jazz as a whole. This may be so, but it may also be the only condition under which he can rejuvenate the conflict of tension and repose, shifted by him from the domain of harmony to that of registers.

Though by and large Monk's solos are less daring than his accompaniments, occasionally they are far more so. The solo idiom enables him to play a dominant role in the form of the collective work, shaping it in terms of that basic choice between symmetrical and asymmetrical structures. Prior to Monk, Charlie Parker had already brought a certain melodic and rhythmic discontinuity to jazz, but in order for this idea to have germinated in his work the Bird would have had to reconsider his highly traditional approach to the set pattern. Such a reappraisal would undoubtedly have led him to a new form of structural equilibrium. Within more modest limits, Gerry Mulligan did have the courage to transgress this basic notion of the set pattern, but his innovation belongs to the composer's rather than the improviser's domain; it was probably more accidental than deliberate, and did not deeply affect the basic substance of a musical vision still governed by the notions of symmetry and continuity.

If one examines separately Parker's discontinuity and Mulligan's unorthodox patterns, Monk may seem less advanced than they, but this is a mere optical illusion. Only in Monk's music do asymmetry and discontinuity enhance one another, thereby assuming their full, symbiotic significance. This symbiosis is highlighted successively by each of the other components of a language which, though not yet thoroughly coherent, is nevertheless sufficiently well-formed to have already given us glimpses of the role that formal abstraction can play in jazz (as in the "Bags' Groove" solo).

The principle underlying Monk's chief structural contribution is one of brilliant simplicity. The incorporation of shifting, asymmetrical structures into a symmetrical type of fixed "combo" structure constitutes an obvious, though partial, solution to the problem of form in jazz—so obvious in fact that I am surprised no one ever thought of it before. Monk made no attempt to escape from the closed circle of the twelve bar chorus; he simply reorganized it along less baldly "rational" lines. In other words, he has done for jazz structures what two generations of musicians before him had done for jazz rhythms. There is a very fine analogy here between, on the one hand, the play of rhythmic tension and repose stemming from the arrangement of figures and stresses with respect to a permanent tempo, and, on the other, that formally static—or kinematic—situation resulting from the symmetrical or asymmetrical balance of a set of secondary structures within a fixed primary structure. Compared with the rhythmic concepts of Chick Webb, those of Kenny Clarke constituted a decisive step toward asymmetry and discontinuity; this forward leap created a gap which has been filled at last by Monk's comparable advance on the level of form.

True, this is only a partial solution to the problem; the structural conflict devised by Monk does not suffice to establish the over-all formal unity of a piece. Other than the style, the only unifying elements in his music are unity of tempo and key, a unified range of timbres and an over-all sequential framework;[9] these constitute a foundation that is far too weak to sustain that deep, inner life-beat which we know to be the highest and most secret form of musical expression.

The chief problem facing the creative jazzman today is, to my mind, that of *capping the piecemeal unity that has been achieved on the structural level with a true, organic unity*. There are two ways—and it would seem, only two—of reaching this still distant goal. One may be called thematic; it implies a constant effort on the part of the improviser to remain in contact with the original theme, as he infers from each new variation a whole set of fresh material intimately related to both the theme itself and the various transformations it will have undergone on the way. According to a recent essay by Gunther Schuller, Sonny Rollins has succeeded in making important progress in this field (which Monk has not disdained to prospect, either).[10]

9. By sequential I am referring to the succession of chords constituting the framework of a chorus, or of part of a chorus.

10. Gunther Schuller, "Sonny Rollins and the Challenge of Thematic Improvisation," *The Jazz Review*, November, 1958.

I must confess, however, that I cannot share this eminent critic's enthusiasm for the thematic approach as conceived by Rollins. The large proportion of his solos devoted to ad lib playing compared with the brevity of the thematically connected sections, inclines me to feel that, despite the appreciable results obtained by this outstanding saxophonist in these thematic passages, thematic improvisation is a delusion to be avoided. Several centuries ago this field was opened to the investigations of the individual composer, and I expect that it should remain his domain. The improviser is most likely wasting his time in attempting to appropriate it. A soloist with an extraordinary memory (and a thorough mastery of composition) might conceivably improvise fifteen or twenty choruses and still remain strictly thematic, in other words take account of all the various intermediary situations arising on the way. But in a less utopian perspective, I am afraid that the thematic approach can only sterilize jazzmen's sense of improvisation. If they are at all concerned with rigor they will gradually be led to "crystallize" their solos, so to speak. Many will probably regard the thematic approach as a mere recipe with which to fill the gaps in their imagination, while the others will behave like the water-carrier who, for lack of a magic rod to strike forth fresh springs along her path, must continually return to the same well.

One may wonder whether a thematic revolution in jazz would have much point today, when the thematic approach is vanishing from serious Western music. I would never claim, of course, that jazz can take a short cut to that arduous, esoteric realm from which the very notion of theme is banished. It is completely unprepared for such a jump, and I do not feel, in any case, that jazz, which is tonal and modal by nature, need seek its salvation in that direction. The search for formal concepts peculiar to jazz is a special problem for which jazzmen must find a special solution. Monk's solution, though related in some ways to the formal conceptions of serious modern music, is not indebted, for its guiding principle, to any school of music, past or present, which is foreign to jazz; this, I feel, is essential.

His solution seems to have grown out of a number of obsessions which crop up in recordings done during the fall and winter of 1954. The most famous of these–"Blue Monk" and "Bags' Groove"—have a strange kinship; it is as though the first were a prefiguration of the second. "Blue Monk" contains nearly all the structural elements which were to serve as a basis for the idiom of "Bags' Groove"; if it seems less "pure" than the later solo, this is because its structures are not correctly situated with respect to formal space and time. Monk's solo in "Bags' Groove" constitutes, to my knowledge, the first formally perfect solo in the history of jazz. With it was born the notion, to my mind primordial, that a space-time dialectic is possible in jazz, even when it is weighed down by symmetrical superstructures and their rigid, apparently ineradicable, tonal foundations. This *unique* achievement of Monk's goes to prove that, above and beyond the traditional "theme and variations" (or rather "sequential variation") a musical tissue can renew itself indefinitely as it goes along, *feeding on its own progression* as it leaps from one transformation to the next. This concept, which may be called "open form," is both thematic and "athematic;" it constitutes an unexpected illustration, through jazz, of the existentialist axiom, "existence precedes essence," and is admirably suited, by its very nature, to that "spur of the moment" art form which is musical improvisation. Moreover, I am convinced that some of the best choruses of the great improvisers of the past already contained the embryo of a notion which was left to Thelonious Monk to bring to light. The key to this emancipation seems to have lain in his earlier discovery of the catalysing effect that asymmetrical structures can have on symmetrical ones.

This contribution could not, however, lead him directly to that supreme realm of musical form where the very existence of a work of art—a collective work, in any case—is determined. Still, his contribution as a bandleader is very appreciable, if less revolutionary than some of his achievements as a soloist.

Roger Guérin has given us the following description of the formula used by Monk last summer at the Five Spot in almost all the pieces played with his quartet: after the statement of the theme, the tenor would take a great many choruses, accompanied only by bass and drums; then Monk would gradually worm his way into this trio and the increasing density of his accompaniment would rapidly lead the tenor to conclude. Monk would now go into his main solo; after a few choruses, however, his playing would tend to grow gradually sparser until it became the background for a bass solo; the piece would end with a restatement of the theme, preceded only occasionally by a solo on the drums. Compared with the usual succession of choruses, this form, which may be regarded as a jazz equivalent of the "tiling process" first used by Stravinsky in the *Rite of Spring* (the piano "covering up" the tenor only to be "covered up" by the double bass) represents an immense forward stride. The weakness of this procedure lies in its invariability, for when applied to a group of pieces it becomes a *mold* and constitutes a reversion to the aesthetic level which Monk had surpassed with such mastery in "Bags' Groove."[11] Monk's sense of form has not yet been extended to the band per se and though an ex-

11. Monk's ensemble records do not belie Roger Guerin's account, though they do not always corroborate it.

traordinary theme writer, and a unique improviser, he may simply not have the means to do so. The realization of the all-encompassing formal concept implicit in his ideas may have to await the intrusion into jazz of that foreign species, the composer.

The scope and gravity of the problems raised in this chapter, the reappraisal of jazz as a whole which they imply, plus my own awareness that I have proposed only very partial solutions to them, make it, I feel, unnecessary for me to enter as deeply as I might into the minor facets of this great musician's gifts. It is generally agreed that Monk periodically lapses into the errors of his youth, that he resorts to facile piano tricks, and is not a great keyboard technician. But then Art Tatum was a great keyboard technician, and look what he did with his virtuosity! Even that cruel, sarcastic humor of Monk's, though it has real depth, is, in the last analysis, merely an incidental aspect of his musical temperament.

I like to remember that one of the great composers of our time, a man who can hardly be accused of any indulgence for jazz, once listened to the "Bag's Groove" solo with an ear that was more than merely attentive.[12] Disregarding the tiny technical defects, he immediately grasped the meaning of the acute struggle between the disjunct phrasing and those pregnant silences, experiencing the tremendous pressure that Monk exerts on his listeners, as if actually to make them suffer. When the record was over, just one remark was enough to compensate for all the rebuffs that the mediocrities of jazz had made me suffer from his lips; it was made in connection with the F sharp that follows a series of C's and F's in Monk's first chorus, and which, for all its brevity, constitutes one of the purest moments of beauty in the history of jazz. "Shattering," was my friend's only comment.

The recorded works of Parker and even Armstrong are probably more substantial and more consistently successful than the erratic and restricted music of Monk; yet there are moments, fleeting though no doubt they are, when Monk rises to summits which neither Armstrong nor Parker, in their records at any rate, ever managed to reach. It is not unthinkable that in the eyes of posterity Monk will be THE Jazzman of our time, just as Debussy is now seen to have been THE composer of the period immediately preceding the first World War. I am not in the habit of making predictions, but I will say that I would be deeply happy if this one were to prove correct. It is always possible

12. The "Bags' Groove" solo was recorded on December 24, 1954, and released on *Miles Davis and the Modern Jazz Giants* (Prestige LP 7150). [See Ran Blake's article on p. 248 for a transcription and discussion of the solo. *Ed.*]

that Monk himself would not recognize the portrait I have drawn of him here, and that I have merely deepened the misunderstanding that I wished to dispel. Let us hope, however, that beneath an outer skin which to some seems rough and dry, and to others delightfully provocative, I have managed to reach the core of that strange fruit which is the music of Thelonious Monk.

24. *Thelonious Monk*

The English critic Michael James first published this essay in his book *Ten Modern Jazzmen,* a collection of articles on artists such as Miles Davis, Stan Getz, Dizzy Gillespie, Charlie Parker, and Bud Powell, some of which were originally written for *Jazz Monthly.* The piece on Monk is sprinkled with rich and poignant commentary on his style and significance as a composer and performer and his genuinely nonconformist approach to music and life. At the risk of oversimplifying his central argument, the theme of the essay is Monk's use of ironic humor, enabled by the "faculty of detachment required to indulge successfully in the joyful and systematic debunking of the modern *love*-song." Rather than wallow in its sentimentality, Monk assaults the popular song, and rather than discarding the melody, as so often is done in jazz improvisation, he embraces it. As with most other commentators, James is struck by Monk's highly developed sense of form, which he describes as an innate facility for musical construction with its implied opposite, demolition, or as current intellectual practice would dictate, deconstruction. In addition to writing for *Jazz Monthly,* James wrote for the *Jazz Review* and *Melody Maker.*

This appeared as "Thelonious Monk" in Michael James's *Ten Modern Jazzmen,* (London: Cassell) in 1960, pp. 81–92. It was adapted from an article in *Jazz Monthly,* Vol. 3, No. 5, July 1957. Used by permission of Leena Shaw.

With regard to an artist of Monk's unusual qualities, one can hardly expect any measure of critical unanimity during his lifetime. Baffled by the strangeness of his harmonic ideas, many observers seem to be at a loss when it comes to an evaluation of his work. No one would deny that Monk, in a way, has become a legend: his very name calls forth a crowd of rather nebulous associations, conjuring up on the one hand visions of dark glasses, beret, and goatee, and on the other the concept of a startlingly original style which has afforded inspiration to almost every post-Minton pianist. Despite, however, this undoubted influence, some enthusiasts still look upon him as an eccentric poseur, or, alternatively, as a musician richly endowed with ideas, but lacking the necessary technique to express himself to the full. Monk excites both ridicule and enthusiasm. His detractors appear suspicious of his overt disregard for orthodoxy both in musical and sartorial fields; his admirers, insisting upon his brilliant originality, are often puzzled by his persistent refusal to take anything whatsoever at face value.

This paradox seems to represent the present consensus of opinion concerning Monk's place in jazz. Yet if we are to assign any value at all to his contributions to the music, this contradiction must patently be resolved. Neither eccentricity of dress nor of mode of life has any importance, except in so far as they add to our understanding of the musician in question: to take a definite example, Percy Heath's distinction as a bassist should not be confused with his ability to fly an airplane. What is, or rather appears to be especially disconcerting in Monk's case is his penchant for remarks tending to disparage his musical ability. His reported remark when asked to explain a certain aspect of jazz evolution—'Those simple chords ain't so easy to find now'—is outstanding for its humor but not for its sobriety of outlook. Similarly, his reluctance to discuss his own problems in a sociological context, as described recently by the German critic Herr Berendt, is not calculated to reassure anyone dubious of his artistic authenticity. Yet without going any further afield than the early masters of New Orleans jazz, it is evident that artistic creation is not necessarily dependent upon the possession of a conscious aesthetic. Again, Django Reinhardt was almost illiterate, but only a simpleton would condemn his guitar playing on that score. There are many reasons for believing that Armstrong himself is unaware of his exact importance, musically speaking; and although this may explain the weaknesses of some of his records of the past decade, it in no way reflects upon the incontestable greatness of his earlier output.

There is in fact quite a strong case for supposing that the consciousness of being an artist, especially in present American society, can have disastrous effects should this consciousness once become an obsession. Monk, though, falls into neither of these categories. It is not so much that he does not appreciate his place in jazz: he would actually seem, if we are to judge from the reports of those who have tried to interview him, to be unaware of any real need to discuss his own musical activities. One might almost be forgiven for imagining that he regards them as inconsequential. Unwilling to discuss either his own music or his own peculiar social position, he might easily figure as the jazz faker *par excellence*, the pseudo-musician eager to capitalize on the public taste for the gimmick; but this, too, is an untenable viewpoint. Quite apart from the admiration of the late Charlie Parker and other prominent musicians, among whom we may number Charlie Mingus, Monk is obviously a man devoted to music. Whatever he may say to the contrary, he has made sacrifices for his art; it is at the expense of a measure of material comfort that music occupies the central position in his life. This discrepancy between his offhand behavior and the basic pattern of his existence presents an apparently insoluble problem; but his music, vibrant as it is with the full force of his personality, points unerringly to the only feasible explanation. The dominant emotion in his playing is that of irony: just as he will not accept the conventional outlook in any field, cultural or otherwise, his treatment of the most diverse tunes is invariably stamped with a dry humor which makes his expression among the most personal in the history of jazz. This refusal to conform to a generally accepted scale of values is not a mere caprice, unimportant apart from its interest as an artistic curiosity, but a perfectly valid spiritual position, as I shall presently attempt to show. For the moment I shall confine myself to an investigation of the different ways in which this emotion is conveyed by his work, for without an inquiry of this sort the listener unacquainted with Monk's art may still be tempted to dismiss him as a musical charlatan, even though he might concede the authenticity of his attitude from a theoretical standpoint.

The uses to which the fabrications of the popular songwright have been put in jazz are many and varied, and such is their scope that there is no place here for a detailed analysis, interesting as it would be. The truism that the jazzman adapts the song to his own needs is deceptively simple, since, after all, it hardly takes us any further than the rather ingenuous dictum that a melody can assume a different character in the hands of a performer other than its composer. By and large it is true that a musician's task is to cleanse the tune of the tawdriness which has accrued to it during its wide circulation—if it did not, as is so often the case, contain the seed of vulgarity in the first instance—and, at the same time, to endow it with a real meaning culled from personal experience. Many jazzmen, especially among the modernists, concerned primarily with the harmonic basis of the composition, have tended to reject the original melody, all too conscious, perhaps, of its spurious attributes: even here, though, a similarity of mood may sometimes persist, as, for example, in Parker's "Lover Man," where the purport of the lyric, a statement of isolation on a sexual plane, is expanded into the tragic declaration of a man aware not only of his separation from the mass of his fellows but of the identity of the problems he shared with them and which he felt they had to understand. The point of departure is the same in both cases. The emotional transmutation here is an extreme one, of course, but there are numberless jazz records where the impression conveyed, though generally more convincing, is not so very alien to the gist of the lyric, cleverly attuned as this always is to the character of the written melody. Monk's playing, on the other hand, is a glaring exception to this trend. This is not because he is unconcerned with the popular associations of the tune he is using, for familiarity with the composition in its pristine form is a valuable aid to appreciating his treatment of it. An intimate connection does, in fact, exist between model and improvisation; the bond, however, is not that of similarity but the far stronger one of opposition. Monk, naturally enough, is not always intent upon satirizing the vague sentimental associations of the average commercial song. Occasionally his approach is along the orthodox lines I have defined above. Such, nevertheless, is the frequency of his performances in a mocking vein and so refreshing the unconventionality of his outlook, that it is worth while examining the various devices which translate this scepticism in musical terms.

In the normal course of events Monk is not content with one weapon alone, but turns the whole weight of his armory upon the unfortunate target of his scathing humor. The most subtle of his means is the deliberate choice of a highly unsuitable tempo: "Honeysuckle Rose," recorded in 1956, is a prime instance of a tune which could be interpreted in a customary way at either slow or fast tempo, but certainly not at the middling pace it is taken at here, where it has neither romance nor gaiety.[1] The ludicrous air of the theme statement, in particular, stems from the choice of key, which conflicts alarmingly with the lilt of the melody: here again we have a favorite stratagem of Monk's. Yet more effective than any of these is his cunning use of dissonance which, despite the criticism it has often provoked, is never deployed without a valid aesthetic reason. His 1952 trio recording of "Sweet and Lovely" shows how devastating the wilful selection of the eccentric chord can be, especially when allied to a certain hesitancy of execution which serves to heighten the atmosphere of buffoonery.[2] Where other modernists have been wary of expressing themselves too freely when improvising on a popular tune, for fear of being themselves engulfed in the fog of sentimentality which it exudes, Monk overcomes dilemma by making a frontal assault upon the offending ob-

1. Originally released on Riverside RLP 12-209. *Ed.*
2. Originally released on Prestige PRLP 7027. *Ed.*

ject itself. In one sense, I suppose, this is a destructive process. Yet there is no doubt that the dogma which puts forward a partnership between man and woman as the guarantee of a blissful existence, irrespective of all other factors, is a notorious impediment to the achievement of a deeper conception of living; while the vulgarization of this credo in the hands of the commercial lyricist has repeatedly led to the most preposterous of conceits which have found acceptance only because of the sanctified hypocrisy that confuses the whole issue in the public mind. Monk's audacity in carrying the struggle into the enemy's own territory is indicative of his contempt for such false values.

The faculty of detachment required to indulge successfully in the joyful and systematic debunking of the modern *love-song* has not meant that Monk is unable to use similar material in a completely different way. In "Darn That Dream," another recent recording, he plays with poignant tenderness throughout, making the tune his own musical property from the first bar of the introduction. There is not a trace of the cutting irony he expresses elsewhere. What is particularly striking about his work in this vein is his ability to conjure up so convincing an air of sincerity without resorting to the involved melodic transformations which abound in the improvisation of Navarro or Konitz. His deviations from the song's written line are rarely pronounced, and he relies upon a highly original sense of timing and of chordal design to attain his ends. "You Are Too Beautiful," a recording from the same session as "Darn That Dream," is proof of his talent for successfully extending a tune over two choruses at slow tempo with a bare minimum of linear invention, for despite the consistency of mood this helps to create, no hint of monotony intrudes for even a moment.[3] Conceived in the same manner is his interpretation of "I Let a Song Go Out of My Heart," a 1955 performance from an album of Ellington compositions: but here the role of the rhythm section is more obvious, the atmosphere rather more carefree as Monk swings gaily through the extemporized passages set between a modestly embroidered theme statement. There is a curiously tensile air about the entire performance, springing not from the excellence of the bass playing alone, but from the impressive coordination of all three musicians.

One of the strangest features of Monk's work is the calculated change of mood which differentiates his style from that of so many of his contemporaries. Formal development is at least an aim of most musicians, even if it is not always achieved; yet the greater number are concerned with the establishment of a fixed emotional aura rather than any kind of progression in this

3. Recorded in 1956 and originally released on Riverside RLP 12-209. *Ed.*

sphere. However moving Getz's work, the content is essentially a static one; while, on the other extreme, Bud Powell's playing, with all its chaotic transpositions of mood, could hardly be regarded as a presentation, in logical sequence, of a series of attitudes. In contrast, Monk does possess this faculty of spiritual construction. I have already spoken of "Honeysuckle Rose" as a demonstration of his ironic bent; perhaps it would have been more correct to have pointed out that with the end of the first devastating chorus this quality relinquishes its dominant role. The leader hands over the melodic line to Oscar Pettiford, returning later in far less extravagant humour to build his solo upon the foundations expertly laid by the bass upon the wreckage of the melody. It is significant that the final rendering of the tune is characterized by a squareness of form which, though contrasting with the customary interpretation, is equally at variance with the blatant irony of the initial chorus. Shedding the apparel of distaste, he attains by degrees the epitome of self-expression towards which all his efforts have been directed. The metaphor of *construction* not altogether appropriate in the case of most jazzmen, is especially applicable to Monk, since his conception quite often embraces not only the building process consistent with successful jazz improvisation but the work of demolition which his own personal aesthetic sometimes demands.

It should be obvious that such an evolution within the limits of a single recording could not take place without some measure of conscious control, a discipline which in its turn supposes a highly developed faculty of dissociation. It is this power, I believe, that underlies Monk's skill in musical description; though retaining many of the hallmarks of his style, he manages to portray a set of circumstances without any of these lyric gifts unduly obtruding; occasionally, in fact, his characteristic moods add to the appeal of his creations in this vein. Such, for instance, is the case with "Little Rootie Tootie" and "Locomotive," two pieces evocative of the sound and movement of the railway engine. The first, recorded on 15th October 1952 with Art Blakey on drums and Gary Mapp on bass, is a very lighthearted affair, distilling a quaint humor summarized in the laconic repartee of the theme, where a gay single-note motif is answered by heavy chords in a manner which invokes both the quotidian and magical aspects of the *journey*, besides echoing the jarring rhythm of the machine.[4] It is fascinating to follow the train's progress, as Monk simulates acceleration, not by any increase in tempo, but by an ever-renewed attack at the start of each section of eight bars. Blakey's drums are an inestimable asset here, just as they are throughout the performance, as in turn

4. Originally released on Prestige PRLP 7027. *Ed.*

he emphasizes, complements, and underlines Monk's explorations, combining in his accompaniment the virtues of surprise and inevitability. In the same way his presence on "Locomotive," a quintet recording made on 11th May 1954, is a real inspiration to the pianist.[5] Here the portrait is filled out in more sinister hues, with implications of ruthlessness and power. The solo voices of Frank Foster and Ray Copeland, forceful as they are, add nothing to the descriptive value of the performance, but Monk in his solo seems to blend impressionism and the personal thought as he relentlessly works each variation out to its conclusion.

The pianist's work in this field, however, is not confined to the obvious type of subject characterized by its own sound, but embraces a variety of situations. Ellington's "Sophisticated Lady" takes on beneath his touch a hard yet brittle exterior: there are no explicit indications of tenderness to soften the sharp contours of the phrasing. In contrast, "Smoke Gets in Your Eyes," recorded at the same session as "Locomotive," has a lithe glamour deriving for the most part from the heraldic supporting figures voiced by the horns. Monk's own playing, too, is less metallic as he hammers out the rich chordal designs that infuse the somewhat wistful melody with new force and fire. It is interesting to compare this performance with the 1947 recording of his own composition "'Round About Midnight." The framework is identical, the execution just as forthright, yet the atmosphere quite dissimilar: the alternate stridency and flatness of the wind instrumentalists' tones, especially when their line is doubled by the piano, brings out all the menace that the leader seems to associate with the nocturnal hours. The recording of this tune made by Miles Davis and Charlie Parker, for all the insight and concentration of their playing, does not offer this picturesque appeal, and though this in no way detracts from their achievement here or elsewhere, it is undeniable that Monk has an interest in representation that is shared by neither of these two musicians. The composer's version is fraught with the nervous anticipation linked in the sensitive mind with moving shadows and sudden darkness.

This same ability to stand apart from a given composition, to interpret it rather than use it as a tool, would explain Monk's grasp of the accompanist's art; the deliberate range of his accomplishment in the roles of improviser, arranger, and composer is continued in his work behind the solo horn. It would be foolish to suggest that his accompaniment is the ideal one for every soloist: his peculiar harmonic ideas and the continual attack of his playing indicate why the musicians with whom he habitually works and records are

5. Originally released on Prestige PRLP 7053. *Ed.*

those who share some of his enthusiasm for the robust expression which is present in his work even at the most langorous of tempos. Miles Davis's reported expressions of contempt when asked to play with him on the Christmas Eve 1954 date for Prestige can be ascribed, at least in part, to the forceful angularity of his support which, over and above the harmonic conflicts involved, seems at the start of "Bemsha Swing" to be more of an obstacle than a help to the trumpeter's invention. Yet within the group of musicians whom one might with some exaggeration refer to as his own coterie, Monk fosters the impact of the instrumentalist's lines, adapting the frequency and volume of his chording to the requirements of the moment. On "The Way You Look Tonight" his work behind Rollins becomes fiercer and more insistent in the last two choruses, as the performance reaches its climax:[6] "Think of One," recorded almost a year earlier on 13th November 1953, finds him complementing the tenorist's phrases with unvaried vehemence, while his support to the less effusive french horn playing of Julius Watkins is even more insistent as he points the melodic gaps with masterly understanding, simultaneously spurring the soloist on to renewed invention.[7] His total dependence upon chords as opposed to the melodic embroidery favored by such different artists as Al Haig and Walter Bishop Junior is in a way reminiscent of the perfunctoriness of a Bud Powell, yet he is no less concerned than they with the creation of a musical entity: even in "Humph," a tune recorded as early as 1947, his work behind the horns, sparser as it is than in more recent performances, provides the exact emphasis to the improvised line.

In the face of this evidence, his accompaniment is open to criticism in one particular instance, for the vigor of his chording often seems to veil the continuity of the solo bass line. Monk is not content with a gentle implication: more often than not he comes crashing in to superimpose an extra pattern upon that woven by the bassist. Though the force of his playing probably springs in no small degree from the excitement of the moment, it may also be traced back to his conception of the trio as a musical entity. Unlike most modern jazz pianists, Monk seems very willing to give opportunities for extended improvisation to both bassist and drummer, and his own solo construction has an economy which makes full use of the rhythm section's potential.

To neglect the importance of the deliberative faculty which governs Monk's operations in the disparate spheres of irony, impressionism, and accompaniment would be to misunderstand the essence of his achievement. Of

6. Recorded in 1954 and originally released on Prestige PRLP 7075. *Ed.*

7. Originally released on Prestige PRLP 7053. *Ed.*

equal moment, however, is the corresponding ability of involvement, that is to say his unusual aptitude for temporarily shutting out all considerations foreign to the task at hand; absorbed in the process of creation, he evinces a power of concentration rivaled only by the finest of his contemporaries. Tempting as it is to equate this continuous application with the fugitive value of sincerity, it is necessary to remark that the impact very often depends upon the pianist's unorthodox harmonic practices. Monk's work has been the butt of numerous criticisms because of his divergence from the norm in this respect; and it is here, I am convinced, that the layman tends to have an advantage, surprisingly enough, over the professional musician, or the critic versed in a knowledge of musical theory. The nontechnical listener, unaware of the mechanism of invention and consequently shut off from the interest it offers, is not debarred from appreciating the patterns of sound, nor from savoring the mental reactions they provoke. There is no reason, of course, why the theoretically knowledgeable should not enjoy a performance at the same level of intensity, if not, indeed, a higher one, than their less adept counterparts; unfortunately, they often seem to miss the emotional appeal, not perhaps owing to any radical lack of sensibility, but because their thoughts are given over to the technical substructure. Those who come to music with so exclusively analytical a view are almost certain to be rebuffed by the art of a revolutionary like Monk, who does not recognize the harmonic bases which underlie the work of his contemporaries in the same field. Yet, after all, appreciation implies a measure of order, and a music devoid of form can never be a wholly satisfying one. That Monk's style is no agglomeration of esoteric mannerisms would be attested by the success of his group performances, were it not already evident from his solo playing: his chordal variations possess their own peculiar logic of development. Gunther Schuller's study in the November 1958 issue of *The Jazz Review* showed that, like any other jazz musician, he works within the references of a fairly stable code of formal values.[8] His harmonic construction is certainly very involved, but the overall effect is one of an entity that conforms to its own laws.

It is with Monk's interpretations of his own themes that all the aspects detailed above emerge in their entirety: untrammeled as he is when building upon a structure of his own making, it is in such favorable conditions that he reveals the full force of his art. One of the most baffling features of his projective power to those unfamiliar with his idiosyncracies is the constant re-

8. Schuller's essay was later reprinted in *Jazz Panorama*, edited by Martin Williams (New York: Collier Books, 1964). *Ed.*

currence of the moments of ambiguity, when the sympathetic listener is torn between the possibilities of scorn and seriousness; but even here the impact is just as strong. The answer to the dilemma of recognition must surely be traced back to the unique immediacy of his playing, an upshot of the concentration I spoke of above. For Monk is the searcher for the truth, not just one of its attractive varieties, but the whole truth, embracing as it does the most contradictory of moods. Harmonic considerations aside, it is no coincidence that his music, like so much of modern jazz, is not exemplified by a rounded, highly polished beauty of form: and if the music of his place and time has rejected the traditional criteria, his own strivings represent the acme of such a revolt. The hazards, internal and external, of the jazzman, as of any artist who is not ready to worship at the altar of commercialism, are legion; and Monk is in a better position than most to judge in what degree the tragedies he has witnessed, the addiction, the rackets, and all the base paraphernalia of exploitation are occasioned by the gullibility of a society which reveres the Presleys of this world. No sensitive person could exist for long in such an environment without yielding to revulsion and its kindred states of mind, and much of the anger, sorrow, and disgust of a whole jazz generation burns in Monk's work as he cuts his way to the very heart of each theme. On compositions as separated in time as "Well, You Needn't," "Friday the Thirteenth," and "Blue Monk," the self-same qualities are evident; but the tenacity of attack never becomes wearisome. The emphasis of his playing never degenerates into rhetoric, couched as his expression is in the least theatrical of terms.

If Monk is fully aware of the indignities attendant upon the jazzman's existence, he has never become obsessed by them: the thick thread of humor is woven through every solo, and in one or two cases is exaggerated to such lengths that one can only assume the pianist is capable of satirizing his own style. The 1954 Christmas Eve session for Prestige is a good example of this diabolical frame of mind, and it is irresistible to wonder to just what extent Monk was set upon exasperating Miles Davis. His opening choruses on "Bags' Groove" carry economy of statement to absurdity; while his solo on "The Man I Love" is downright ridiculous as he begins by groping hesitantly for the chords and then stops playing altogether.[9] If this was a manouevre to annoy the trumpeter it was a very successful one, since Davis, unable to bear any more with this farcical silence from the pianist, comes in with a lone distinctive phrase which has the immediate effect of spurring Monk into action

9. Originally released on Prestige PRLP 7109. The "Bags' Groove" solo is discussed at length in Ran Blake's article, "The Monk Piano Style," reprinted on page 248. *Ed.*

like a man possessed. Humor has never been the forte of the modernists, but there are times when Monk compensates with a display of this kind for all the straightfaced gravity of his generation.

I feel certain that it is in such a fusion of the vehement and the grotesque that the clue both to Monk's everyday pose and to the driving force behind his music may be found. Each has its roots in a deep-seated distrust of society. The apparent indifference to interest in his work is but one facet of the extensive defense mechanism he has built up over the years against any possible encroachment on his personal thoughts. In the same way, although the content of his music is not veiled over with a surface unconcern, it is colored with an irony whose bitterness is apparent only to the sympathetic mind: to the uncomprehending his witticisms are amusing but meaningless. Adequately protected from the cold stare of the inimical eye, he is unsparing in his efforts to make contact through his music with the listener unfettered by the prejudice of uncertainty or cynicism.

The atmosphere of much of his work, perhaps, is one of subterfuge; but the emotive range he commands is wider than that of any other jazz musician to emerge since the mid-'forties. Rarely approaching the intensity of Parker's offerings, his work, for all its many facets, is no academic translation of imagined states of mind; it carries the passport of authenticity, in so far as it echoes the mode of its maker's life. Without ever sinking into histrionics, Monk depicts the furtive workings of the lone mind in the face of mass suspicion and scorn; simultaneously, his knack of suffusing all his activities, musical and otherwise, with so personal a brand of ironic humor enables him to come to some kind of terms with the exterior world. His construction of such a discipline is a most adroit sleight of mind in an environment where addiction and death have too often been the upshot of the inevitable clash between two opposing sets of values, represented on the one hand by the demands of boredom and on the other by the intransigence of sensitivity.

In late years, however, Monk has not used as consistently as in the past those savage satirical powers which have always been the delight of his admirers. His music has lost none of its humorous qualities, but he seems, on record at least, to be less concerned with destroying the sentimental pretensions of the popular tune. Irony abounds, for instance, in his solos on "Brilliant Corners" and "Pannonica," recorded in December 1956, but his unaccompanied piano feature—"I Surrender Dear"—from the same session is in a rather more serious vein. His album of Ellington interpretations, done as early as July 1955, is distinguished by a similar sobriety of mood, though this may be owing to his admiration for the composer's work. It is difficult to say whether this tendency is just a mark of musical maturity, or an upshot of the attention his efforts have received since his successful appearance at the Paris Jazz Fair in 1954.[10] In any case Monk now seems content to let the mask drop a little. His has never been the tragic lyricism of a Bud Powell or the romantic detachment of an Erroll Garner, but this new direction his work appears to be taking makes more obvious than before the strong emotional roots in his playing. Fortunately enough, the increasing openness of his emotive approach has not incurred any diminution of intensity; his numerous ballad recordings of the past four years prove that a less ambiguous style is no handicap to the forcefulness of his expression, and the power of his work in this comparatively straightforward vein augurs well for his future activities, whatever form they may assume. Yet, however equivocal the atmosphere invoked, Monk has never been guilty of misrepresentation. In a social context where the creative artist is poised precariously between the lures of exile and concession, his achievement merits both our interest and respect.

10. Monk performed twice at the festival, once with disastrous effects. See Raymond Horricks's article on p. 63. *Ed.*

Mainstream Arrival and Withdrawal (1962–1981)

A title of one of Martin Williams's articles on Monk aptly describes the peculiar status Monk attained during the 1960s: "Thelonious Monk: Arrival without Departure."[1] In terms of public exposure and acceptance, the Blue Note/Prestige and Riverside years conveniently divide Monk's career into early and middle periods, and his "arrival" years with Columbia Records, from 1962–1968, are his late period. Without drawing too much on the analogy as used in standard historical-musicological practice, we can safely say that Monk's late period was his least creative but most financially rewarding.[2] The big marketing and distribution machine of Columbia Records ensured that his recordings sold well, and he made several more tours through Europe, Mexico, and Japan.[3] Monk recorded approximately two albums per year during his contract with Columbia, but he only produced 10 new compositions, or roughly one-ninth of his life's work.[4] And those compositions arguably seem less memorable than the ones composed in the 1940s and 1950s. On his last quartet album for Columbia, *Underground,* recorded in late 1967 and early 1968, he introduced his final four

1. Martin Williams, "Arrival without Departure," *Saturday Review,* April 13, 1963, pp. 32–33.
2. The use of "early," "middle," and "late" as a way of demarcating Monk's musical development is even less useful, as the majority of his compositions were composed during the early period.
3. Between 1961 and 1970, Monk toured Europe seven times, Japan three times, and Mexico once.
4. See footnote 2 on p. 26.

compositions, each still clearly recognizable as Monk, but somewhat lacking in the usual distinctive melodic inventions with close-knit and prearranged component parts.

Monk's image as an eccentric individualist reached its apex with the packaging of *Underground.* Earlier on in his career, Monk had objected to being photographed in a pulpit with a glass of Scotch, as he felt it had nothing to do with him, but he did consent to having an album cover with him sitting in a toy wagon while appearing to be composing, because this related to something he had actually done.[5] With the Underground cover photograph, a new limit was set: He was placed in what appears to be a barn hideout for members of the French Free Army during World War II, with a photograph of de Gaulle with "Vive la France" scribbled on the wall, a captured Nazi, a female resistance fighter in the background, various hand grenades and field communication devices, and Monk sitting at the piano next to a stash of dynamite and a machine gun hanging over his shoulder. What could all this mean? There is a possible reference to the Baroness Nica de Koenigswarter's past, her former marriage to a hero of the French Resistance, but other than that, it seems just another portrayal of Monk as the quintessential nonconformist crackpot, weird but lovable.[6]

Notable engagements during the period 1962–1976 included Lincoln Center (1963 and 1974, the latter with his son T. S. Monk on drums), annual appearances at Newport (including 1963, which resulted in the *Miles and Monk at Newport* album, and 1976, his last public appearance), Tokyo (1963, which resulted in the *Tokyo Concerts* album), the new Five Spot (1963), and Carnegie Hall (1966, 1975, and 1976). Until 1970, he essentially worked with two quartets, with tenor saxophonist Charlie Rouse as a constant. The 1971–1972 "Giants of Jazz" tours, with Art Blakey, Dizzy Gillespie, Al McKibbon, Sonny Stitt, and Kai Winding, were a promoter's idea, and as with most all-star configurations, the music was secondary. However, with the rhythm section of the group, Al McKibbon and Art Blakey,

5. The album in question was *Monk's Music,* originally released as Riverside RLP 12-242 and recorded June 26, 1957.
6. Though it is tempting to deconstruct the image created by the album cover, we should not forget that it appeared in 1967, a time when album covers were displaying a range of experimentation with imagery, particularly for rock music. For example, during the same year the Beatles' *Sergeant Pepper's Lonely Hearts Club Band* appeared, also a montage of historical figures.

Monk made some inspired final trio recordings for Black Lion Records in London in 1971.[7]

During the 1960s, Monk made a great deal of money—estimated at about $50,000 per year—but he continued to live in his old apartment on West 63rd Street in Manhattan, with his children at boarding school. His mental health, however, began to deteriorate. He had always suffered from bouts of withdrawal, becoming disconnected or detached, sometimes perhaps benignly interpreted as mystic or endearingly eccentric behavior (certainly in the early years, when his reputation for playing "weird" music and his unusual costume reinforced this perception). But these bouts became more frequent during the 1960s and Monk had to be hospitalized several times. T. S. Monk has described how Monk would pace for days, and how he realized that sometimes when he would look his father in the eye, he could not be sure if his father knew who he was.[8] Nellie was at his side at all times, ensuring that he got dressed, fed, and off to his engagements. And when he moved to live in the Baroness's house in 1972, across the river in New Jersey, both Nellie and the Baroness looked after him. At one point he then told the Baroness that he felt that he was very seriously ill.[9] His remaining years were spent mostly in a room in the Baroness Nica de Koenigswarter's house, from which he rarely emerged. The piano in the Baroness's house remained virtually untouched by Monk during his final years.

7. Monk toured Europe with his quartet seven times and Japan three times during the period 1961–1970. His last recordings were made during the 1972 "Giants of Jazz" tour during their stop in Switzerland.
8. Quoted from the film *Straight, No Chaser* (1988; produced by Charlotte Zwerin and Clint Eastwood; 90 mins.; Warner Bros. Videocassette.)
9. This is recounted by the Baroness in the film *Straight, No Chaser.*

The Time *Cover*

25. *The Loneliest Monk*

When *Time* magazine made Thelonious Monk the subject of its February 28, 1964, cover, it was the fourth time that a jazz musician had been so recognized, the first three being Louis Armstrong (1949), Dave Brubeck (1954), and Duke Ellington (1956). It also instigated a minor spate of public discourse about how the mainstream media had presented Monk and jazz musicians in general, and whether or not *Time*'s cover article was an honor or a patronizing profile of yet another eccentric entertainer. The sentence "Every day is a brand-new pharmaceutical event for Monk: alcohol, Dexedrine, sleeping potions, whatever is at hand, charge through his bloodstream in baffling combinations" attracted some attention and was construed as damaging to Monk and jazz musicians in general. In fact, other comments in the article about Sonny Rollins, Charles Mingus, John Coltrane, and Miles Davis cast the jazz musician in an unfavorable light. There was anger that mass media had appropriated something that really belonged to a knowing audience. But there was no denying that Monk was one of Columbia's artists, available through the Columbia Book and Record Club just like any other mainstream artist, and that he was fair game for publications like *Time*. Moreover, his peculiar lifestyle and persona made for good copy.

According to the editorial in the February 28 issue, staff writer Barry Farrell "had about 30 chats with Monk, spread over two or three months, mostly walking around outside the Five Spot, Monk's Manhattan base, or sitting in some dark bar at 2 a.m.—'just like Cosa Nostra.'"[1] It is astonishing, yet telling, that, after 30 "chats," Farrell came up with virtually no significant quotes from Monk that had not been published before, and, in fact, all of them seem to have been culled from other sources.[2] Monk either repeated the stories about himself verbatim or he offered no information at all. Nevertheless, it is a sympathetic profile with lively descriptions of Monk and his music. The cover portrait, a sideward, menacing view, was done by Boris Chaliapin, who had difficulties keeping Monk awake during the sittings, and who offered the assessment "Monk's very strange—in the best sense of the word."[3] Farrell worked as correspondent for Time and Life during the 1960s.

Everyone who came to meet his plane wore a fur hat, and the sight was too much for him to bear. "Man, we got to have those!" he told his sidemen, and for fear that the hat stores would be closed before they could get to downtown Helsinki, they fled from the welcome-to-Finland ceremonies as fast as decency permitted. And sure enough, when Thelonious Monk shambled out on the stage of the Kulttuuritalo that night to the spirited applause of 2,500 young Finns, there on his head was a splendid creation in fake lamb's-wool.

At every turn of his long life in jazz, Monk's hats have described him almost as well as the name his parents had the crystal vision to invent for him 43 years ago—Thelonious Sphere Monk. It sounds like an alchemist's formula or a yoga ritual, but during the many years when its owner merely strayed through life (absurd beneath a baseball cap), it was the perfect name for the legends dreamed up to account for his sad silence. "Thelonious Monk?

1. "A Letter from the Publisher," *Time*, February 28, 1964, p. 6.
2. In the film *Straight, No Chaser*, Harry Colomby described the first meeting of Monk and Farrell as a near disaster since it was clear to Colomby, before entering Farrell's office in Radio City, that Monk was beginning to show signs of withdrawal, or "strange behavior," which was known to happen a couple of times a year. When the meeting was over and they had left the building, Monk had completely disconnected.
3. "A Letter from the Publisher," Ibid.

He's a recluse, man." In the mid-'40s, when Monk's reputation at last took hold in the jazz underground, his name and his mystic utterances ("It's always night or we wouldn't need light") made him seem the ideal Dharma Bum to an audience of hipsters: anyone who wears a Chinese coolie hat and has a name like that *must* be cool.

High Philosophy

Now Monk has arrived at the summit of serious recognition he deserved all along, and his name is spoken with the quiet reverence that jazz itself has come to demand. His music is discussed in composition courses at Juilliard, sophisticates find in it affinities with Webern, and French critic André Hodeir hails him as the first jazzman to have "a feeling for specifically modern esthetic values."[4] The complexity jazz has lately acquired has always been present in Monk's music, and there is hardly a jazz musician playing who is not in some way indebted to him. On his tours last year he bought a silk skullcap in Tokyo and a proper chapeau at Christian Dior's in Paris; when he comes home to New York next month with his Finnish lid, he will say with inner glee, "Yeah—I got it in Helsinki."

The spectacle of Monk at large in Europe last week was cheerful evidence of his new fame—and evidence, too, of how far jazz has come from its Deep South beginnings. In Amsterdam, Monk and his men were greeted by a sell-out crowd of 2,000 in the Concertgebouw, and their Düsseldorf audience was so responsive that Monk gave the Germans his highest blessing: "These cats are with it!" The Swedes were even more hip: Monk played to a Stockholm audience that applauded some of his compositions on the first few bars, as if he were Frank Sinatra singing "Night and Day," and Swedish television broadcast the whole concert live. Such European enthusiasm for a breed of cat many Americans still consider weird, if not downright wicked, may seem something of a puzzle. But to jazzmen touring Europe, it is one more proof that the limits of the art at home are more sociological than esthetic.

Though Monk's career has been painful and often thankless, it has also been a tortoise-and-hare race with flashier, more ingratiating men—many of whom got lost in narcotic fogs, died early in squalor and disgrace or abandoned their promise, to fall silent on their horns. Monk goes on. It is his high philosophy to be different, and having steadily ignored all advice and all the fads and vogues of jazz that made lesser musicians grow rich around him, he

4. See the article by Hodeir reprinted here on p. 118. *Ed.*

now reaps the rewards of his conviction gladly but without surprise. He has a dignified, three-album-a-year contract with Columbia Records, his quartet could get bookings 52 weeks a year, and his present tour of Europe is almost a sell-out in 20 cities from Helsinki to Milan. In his first fat year, Monk earned $50,000, and on checks as well as autograph books he signs his grand name grandly, like a man drawing a bird.

Monk's lifework of 57 compositions is a diabolical and witty self-portrait, a string of stark snapshots of his life in New York.[5] Changing meters, unique harmonies and oddly voiced chords create the effect of a desperate conversation in some other language, a fit of drunken laughter, a shout from a park at night. His melodies make mocking twins of naïveté and cynicism, of ridicule and fond memory. "Ruby, My Dear" and "Nutty" are likeably simple; "Off Minor" and "Trinkle Tinkle" are so complex that among pianists only Monk and his early protégé, Bud Powell, have been able to improvise freely upon them.

Monk's inimitable piano style is such an integral part of the music he has written that few jazz pianists have much luck with even the Monk tunes that have become part of the standard jazz repertory. Monk himself plays with deliberate incaution, attacking the piano as if it were a carillon's keyboard or a finely tuned set of 88 drums. The array of sounds he divines from his Baldwin grand are beyond the reach of academic pianists; he caresses a note with the tremble of a bejeweled finger, then stomps it into its grave with a crash of elbow and forearm aimed with astonishing accuracy at a chromatic tone cluster an octave long.

Monk's best showcase has always been a café on Manhattan's Lower East Side called the Five Spot, where he ended a highly successful seven-month engagement in January. The ambiance of the Five Spot is perfect for Monk's mood—dark, a little dank, smoke-soaked and blue. Night after night, Monk would play his compositions—the same tunes over and over again, with what appeared to be continuing fascination with all that they have to say.

Then he would rise from the piano to perform his Monkish dance. It is always the same. His feet stir in a soft shuffle, spinning him slowly in small circles. His head rolls back until hat brim meets collar, while with both hands he twists his goatee into a sharp black scabbard. His eyes are hooded with an abstract sleepiness, his lips are pursed in a meditative O. His cultists may crowd the room, but when he moves among them, no one risks speaking: he is absorbed in a fragile trance, and his three sidemen play on while he dances alone in the darkness. At the last cry of the saxophone, he dashes to the piano

5. See footnote 2 on p. 26.

and his hands strike the keys in a cat's pounce. From the first startled chord, his music has the urgency of fire bells.

Pretty Butterfly

At the piano, Monk is clearly tending to business, but once he steps away from it, people begin to wonder. Aside from his hat and the incessant shuffle of his feet, he looks like a perfectly normal neurotic. "Solid!" and "All reet!" are about all he will say in the gravelly sigh that serves as his voice, but his friends attribute great spiritual strength to him. Aware of his power over people, Monk is enormously selfish in the use of it. Passive, poutish moods sweep over him as he shuffles about, looking away, a member of the race of strangers.

Every day is a brand-new pharmaceutical event for Monk: alcohol, Dexedrine, sleeping potions, whatever is at hand, charge through his bloodstream in baffling combinations. Predictably, Monk is highly unpredictable. When gay, he is gentle and blithe to such a degree that he takes to dancing on the sidewalks, buying extravagant gifts for anyone who comes to mind, playing his heart out. One day last fall he swept into his brother's apartment to dance before a full-length mirror so he could admire his collard-leaf boutonniere: he left without a word. "Hey!" he will call out, "Butterflies faster than birds? Must be, 'cause with all the birds on the scene up in my neighborhood, there's this butterfly, and he flies any way he wanna. Yeah. Black and yellow butterfly. Pretty butterfly." At such times, he seems a very happy man.

At other times he appears merely mad. He has periods of acute disconnection in which he falls totally mute. He stays up for days on end, prowling around desperately in his rooms, troubling his friends, playing the piano as if jazz were a wearying curse. In Boston Monk once wandered around the airport until the police picked him up and took him to Grafton State Hospital for a week's observation. He was quickly released without strings, and though the experience persuaded him never to go out on the road alone again, he now tells it as a certification of his sanity. "I can't be crazy," he says with conviction, "'cause they had me in one of those places and they let me go."

Much of the confusion about the state of Monk's mind is simply the effect of Monkish humor. He has a great reputation in the jazz world as a master of he "put-on," a mildly cruel art invented by hipsters as a means of toying with squares. Monk is proud of his skill. "When anybody says something that's a drag," he says, "I just say something that's a bigger drag. Ain't nobody can beat me at it either. I've had plenty of practice." Lately, though, Monk has been more mannerly and conventional. He says he hates the "mad genius" legend he has lived with for 20 years—though he's beginning to wonder politely about the "genius" part.

Monk's speculations were greatly encouraged in December, when he crowned all his recent achievements with a significant trip uptown from the Five Spot to Philharmonic Hall. There he presided over a concert by a special ten-piece ensemble and his own quartet. The music was mainly Monk's own—nine compositions from the early "I Mean You" to "Oska T.," which he wrote last summer under a title that is his own transcription of an Englishman's saying "Ask for T." ("And the T," says Thelonious, "is me.") The concert was the most successful jazz event of the season, and Monk greeted his triumph with grace and style. At the piano he turned to like a blacksmith at a cranky forge—foot flapping madly, a moan of exertion fleeing his lips. The music he made suggested that the better he is received by his audience the better he gets.

Happenings in Harlem

For Monk, the pleasure of playing in Philharmonic Hall was mainly geographical. The hall was built three blocks from the home he has occupied for nearly 40 years, and Monk serenely regards the choice of the site as a favor to him from the city fathers, a personal convenience, along with the new bank and the other refinements that urban renewal has brought to his old turf. The neighborhood, in Manhattan's West 60s, is called San Juan Hill. It is one of the oldest and most decent of the city's Negro ghettos. Monk's family settled there in 1924, coming north from Rocky Mount, N.C., where Thelonious was born.

He was a quiet, obedient, polite child, but his name very quickly set him apart. "Nobody messed with Thelonious," he recalls, "but they used to call me 'Monkey,' and you know what a drag that was." His father returned to the South alone to recover from a long illness, leaving Monk's mother, a sternly correct civil servant, to work hard to give her three children a genteel polish. At eleven, Thelonious began weekly piano lessons at 75 cents an hour.

It took Monk only a year to discover that the pianists he really admired were not in the books—such players as Duke Ellington, Fats Waller, James P. Johnson. By the time he was 14, Monk was playing jazz at hard-times "rent parties" up in Harlem. He soon began turning up every Wednesday for amateur night at the Apollo Theater, but he won so often that he was eventually barred from the show. He was playing stride piano—a single note on the first and third beats of the bar, a chord on the second and fourth. Unable to play with the rococo wizardry of Art Tatum or Teddy Wilson, though, he found a way of his own. His small hands and his unusual harmonic sense made his style unique.

Monk quit high school at 16 to go on tour with a divine healer—"we played and she healed." But within a year he was back in New York, playing the piano at Kelly's Stable on 52nd Street. The street was jumping in those days, and in advance of the vogue, Monk bought a zoot suit and grew a beard; his mood, for a change, was just right for the time. The jazz world was astir under the crushing weight of swing; the big dance bands had carried off the healthiest child of Negro music and starved it of its spirit until its parents no longer recognized it. In defiant self-defense, Negro players were developing something new—"something *they* can't play,' Monk once called it—and at 19, Monk got to the heart of things by joining the house band at Minton's.

The New Sound

All the best players of the time would drop by to sit in at Minton's. Saxophonist Charlie ("Bird") Parker, Trumpeter Dizzy Gillespie, Drummer Kenny Clarke and Guitarist Charlie Christian were all regulars and, in fitful collaboration with them, Monk presided at the birth of bop. His playing was a needling inspiration to the others. Rhythms scrambled forward at his touch; the oblique boldness of his harmonies forced the horn players into flights the likes of which had never been heard before. "The Monk runs deep," Bird would say, and with some reluctance Monk became "the High Priest of Bebop." The name of the new sound, Monk now says, was a slight misunderstanding of his invention: "I was calling it bipbop, but the others must have heard me wrong."

When bop drifted out of Harlem and into wider popularity after the war, Monk was already embarked on his long and lonely scuffle. Straight bop—which still determines the rhythm sense of most jazzmen—was only a passing phase for Monk. He was outside the mainstream, playing a lean, dissonant, unresolved jazz that most players found perilously difficult to accompany. Many musicians resented him, and he quickly lost his grip on steady jobs. Alone in his room, where he had composed his earliest music—"'Round Midnight," "Well, You Needn't," "Ruby, My Dear"—he worked or simply stared at the picture of Billie Holiday tacked to his ceiling. In 1947 he made his first recording under his own name and witnessed, to his horror, a breathless publicity campaign that sounded as if the Abominable Snowman had been caged by Blue Note Records.

The same year, Monk married a neighborhood girl named Nellie Smith, who had served a long and affectionate apprenticeship lighting his cigarettes and washing his dishes. Monk had always been unusually devoted to his mother; Nellie simply moved into his room so he could stay home with mom. Thus, to his intense satisfaction, he had two mothers. He still found jobs hard to come by, so Nellie went to work as a clerk to buy him clothes and cheer him up with pocket money.

A Drink at Least

Things were terrible until 1951, when they got worse. Monk was arrested along with Bud Powell when a packet of heroin was found in their possession. Monk had always been "clean," but he refused to let Powell take the rap alone. "Every day I would plead with him," Nellie says. "'Thelonious, get yourself out of this trouble. You didn't do anything.' But he'd just say, 'Nellie, I have to walk the streets when I get out. I can't talk.'" Monk held his silence and was given 60 days in jail.

As soon as he was released, the police canceled his "cabaret card," a document required of all entertainers who appear in New York nightclubs. Losing the card cost Monk his slender livelihood, but he had a reputation as an oddball and the police were adamant. For six years Monk could not play in New York; though he made a few records and went out on the road now and then, he was all but silenced. "Everybody was saying Thelonious was weird or locked up," Nellie recalls. " But they just talked that way because they'd never see him. He hated to be asked why he wasn't working, and he didn't want to see anybody unless he could buy them a drink at least. Besides, it hurts less to be passed over for jobs if you aren't around to hear the others' names called. It was a bad time. He even had to pay to get into Birdland."

Monk was the man who was not with it, and jazz was passing him by. Miles Davis had come on with his "impressionist" jazz style—a rubato blowing in spurts and swoons, free of any vibrato, cooler than ice. The Modern Jazz Quartet was playing a kind of introverted 17th century jazz behind inscrutable faces, and Dave Brubeck (*Time* cover, Nov. 8, 1954) introduced polished sound that came with the complete approval of Darius Milhaud. Suddenly jazz—one of the loveliest and loneliest of sounds, the creation of sad and sensitive men—was awash with rondos and fugues. The hipsters began dressing like graduate students.

Money and Medicine

Monk was sustained during much of this bleak time by his friend, mascot and champion, the Baroness Pannonica de Koenigswarter, 50. The baroness had abandoned the aseptic, punctual world of her family[6] for the formless life of New York's night people. In 1955 she acquired undeserved notoriety when Charlie Parker died in her apartment (BOP KING DIES IN HEIRESS' FLAT); she had merely made an honest stab at saving his life with gifts of money and medicine in his last few days. From then on, though, Nica cut a wide swath in the jazz world. She is, after all, not a *Count* Basie or a *Duke* Ellington, but an honest-to-God Baroness; seeing her pull up in her Bentley with a purse crammed with Chivas Regal, the musicians took enormous pride in her friendship.

Monk was her immediate fascination, and Monk, who only has eyes for Nellie, cheerfully took her on as another mother. She gave him rides, rooms to compose and play in and, in 1957, help in getting back the vital cabaret card. The baroness, along with Monk's gentle manager, a Queens high school teacher named Harry Colomby, collected medical evidence that Monk was not a junkie, along with character references by jazzmen and musical scholars. The cops gave in, and for the first time in years Monk began playing regularly in New York. The music he made at the Five Spot with Tenorman John Coltrane was the talk of jazz.

Monk was making a small but admired inroad into the "funk" and "soul" movements that had superseded the "cool." Funk was a deeper reach into Negro culture than jazz had taken before, a restatement of church music and African rhythms, but its motive was the same as bop's—finding something that white musicians had not taken over and, if possible, something they would sound wrong playing.

Then Monk lost his card again. Monk, the baroness and Monk's present saxophonist, Charlie Rouse, 39, were driving through Delaware for a week's work in Baltimore. Monk stopped at a motel for a drink of water, and when he lingered in his imposing manner, the manager called the police. Monk was back in the Bentley when the cops arrived, and he held fast to the steering wheel when they tried to pull him out—on the Monkish ground that he had done nothing to deserve their attention. Even though the baroness shrieked to watch out for his hands, the furious cops gave his knuckles such a beating that he bears the lumps to this day. The baroness took the rap for "some loose marijuana" found in the trunk, but after three years' legal maneuvering she was acquitted. No narcotics charges were placed against Monk, but because of the scandal the police again picked up his card.

6. She is the daughter of the late British banker Nathaniel Charles Rothschild and the sister of the 3rd Baron Rothschild. But she takes her title from her 20-year marriage to Baron Jules de Koenigswarter, a hero of the French Resistance who is presently French ambassador to Peru.

You Tell 'Em

Two years later, after further lobbying at Headquarters, Monk returned to the scene. Since then his luck has changed. Three years have passed without a whisper of trouble. Abroad, at least, he is approached as if he were a visiting professor. (Interview on an Amsterdam radio station last week: "Who has had the greatest influence on your playing, Mr. Monk?" "Well, me, of course.") Most pleasing of all to Monk is a new quartet led by soprano saxophonist Steve Lacy that is dedicated solely to the propagation of Monk's music. In the past Monk has been the only voice of his music; he even has trouble finding sidemen.

His present accompanists—Rouse on tenor, Butch Warren, 24, on bass, and Ben Riley, 30, on drums—have a good feeling for his music. Rouse is a hard-sound player who knows that his instrument suggests a human cry more than a bird song, and he plays as if he is speaking the truth. Warren's rich, loping bass is well suited to Monk's rhythms if not his harmonic ideals; he is like a pony in pasture who traces his mother's footsteps without stealing her grace. Riley has just joined the band, but he could be the man Monk has been looking for. A great drummer, as the nonpareil Baby Dodds once observed, "ought to make the other fellas feel like playing." Riley does exactly that, with a subtle, very musical use of the drums that forsakes thunder for thoughtfulness.

Monk's sidemen traditionally hang back, smiling and relaxed, and apart from an occasional Rouse solo, they seem content to let Monk lead. "That's right, Monk," they seem to be saying, "you tell 'em, baby." But Monk demands that musicians be themselves. "A man's a genius just for looking like himself," he will say. "Play yourself!" With such injunctions in the air, the quartet's performances are uneven. Some nights all four play as though their very lives are at stake; some nights, wanting inspiration, all four sink without a bubble. But it is part of Monk's mystique never to fire anyone. He just waits, hoping to teach, trusting that a man who cannot learn will eventually sense the master's indifference and discreetly abandon ship.

Now that Monk is being heard regularly, he seems more alone than ever. Jazz has unhappily splintered into hostile camps, musically and racially. Lyrical and polished players are accused of "playing white," which means to pursue beauty before truth. The spirit and sound of each variety of jazz is carefully analyzed, isolated and pronounced a "bag." Players in the soul bag, the African bag and the freedom bag are all after various hard, aggressive and free sounds, and there are also those engaged in "action blowing," a kind of shrieking imitation of action painting.

Within each bag, imitation of the "daddy" spreads through the ranks like summer fires. Trumpeters try to play like Miles Davis. And hold their horns like Miles. And dress like Miles. Bassists imitate Charlie Mingus or Scott La Faro; drummers, Max Roach or Elvin Jones. Sax players copy Sonny Rollins or John Coltrane, who is presently so much the vogue that the sound of his whole quartet is being echoed by half the jazz groups in the country.

Bud Powell, Red Garland, Bill Evans and Horace Silver all have had stronger influences than Monk's on jazz pianists. Monk's sound is so obviously his own that to imitate it would be as risky and embarrassing as affecting a Chinese accent when ordering chop suey. Besides, Monk is off in a bag all his own, and in the sleek, dry art that jazz threatens to become, that is the best thing about him.

A Curse in Four Beats

In the gossipy world of jazz, Monk is also less discussed than many others. Occasionally he will say some splendid thing and the story will make the rounds, but there are personalities more actively bizarre than Monk's around. Rollins is a Rosicrucian who contemplates the East River, letting his telephone ring in his ear for hours while he studies birds from his window. Mingus is so obsessed with goblins from the white world that person to person he is as perverse as a roulette wheel; his analyst wrote the notes for his last record jacket. Coltrane is a health addict—doing push-ups, scrubbing his teeth, grinding up cabbages.

And Miles Davis. Miles broods in his beautiful town house, teaching his son to box so that he won't fear white men, raging at every corner of a world that has made him wealthy, a world that is now, in Guinea and the Congo as well as in Alabama and New York, filled with proud little boys who call themselves Miles Davis. He is a man who needs to shout, but his anger is trapped in a hoarse whisper caused by an injury to his vocal cords. The frustration shows. Onstage, he storms inwardly, glaring at his audience, wincing at his trumpet, stabbing and tugging at his ear. Often his solos degenerate into a curse blown again and again through his horn in four soft beats. But Miles can break hearts. Without attempting the strident showmanship of most trumpeters, he still creates a mood of terror suppressed—a lurking and highly exciting impression that he may some day blow his brains out playing. No one, Dizzy Gillespie included, does it so well.

Racial woes are at the heart of much bad behavior in jazz, and the racial question is largely a confusion between life and art. Negroes say whites cannot play, when they mean that whites have always taken more money out of jazz than their music warranted. Whites complain of "Crow Jim" when what they mean is that work is scarcer than ever—even for them. The fact is that most of the best jazz musicians are Negroes and there is very little work to go around on either side.

At bars and back tables in the 20 or so good jazz clubs in the country, talented, frustrated musicians—many of them historic figures in jazz—hang around in the hope of hearing their names called, like longshoremen at a midnight shape-up. Junkies who were good players a year ago swoop through the clubs in search of a touch, faces faintly dusty, feet itching, nodding, scratching. The simple jazz fans in the audience sit shivering in the cold fog of hostility the players blow down from the stand. A dig-we-must panic inhibits them from displaying any enthusiasm—which only further convinces the players that their music is lost on the wind.

An Oriental Garden

Monk surveys these sad facts with some bitterness. "I don't have any musician friends," he says. "I was friends to lots of musicians, but looks like they weren't friends to me." He sometimes makes quiet and kindly gestures—such as sending some money to Bud Powell, caged in a tuberculosis sanatorium outside Paris—but his words are hard. "All you're supposed to do is lay down the sounds and let the people pick up on them," he says. "If you ain't doing that, you just ain't a musician. Nothing more to it than that."

Now that his turn has come, Monk cuts a fine figure on the scene. Nellie spends an hysterical hour every evening getting him into his ensemble, and when he steps out the door he looks faintly like an Oriental garden—subtle colors echoing back and forth, prim suits and silk shirts glimmering discreetly. He spends hours standing around with his band, talking in his unpenetrable, oracular mode. "All ways know, always night, all ways know—and dig the way I say 'all ways,'" he says, smiling mysteriously. When he is playing anywhere near New York, the baroness comes to drive him home, and they fly off in the Bentley, content in the knowledge that there is no one remotely like either one of them under the sun. They race against the lights for the hell of it, and when the car pulls up in Monk's block, he skips out and disappears into his old $39-a-month apartment. The baroness then drives home to Weehawken, where she lives in a luxurious bedroom oasis, surrounded by the reeking squalor her 32 cats have created in the other rooms.

Monk spends lazy days at home with Nellie—"layin' dead," he calls it. Their two children, Thelonious, 14, and Barbara, 10, are off in boarding schools, and Monk's slumbers go undisturbed. Nellie flies around through the narrow paths left between great piles of possessions, tending to his wants. Clothes are in the sink, boxes and packages are on the chairs; Monk's grand piano stands in the kitchen, the foundation for a tower of forgotten souvenirs, phone books, a typewriter, old magazines and groceries. From his bed Monk announces his wishes ("Nellie! Ice cream!"), and Nellie races to serve; she retaliates gently by calling him "Melodious Thunk" in quiet mutters over the sink.

Nellie and the few other people who have ever known Monk in the slightest all see a great inner logic to his life that dignifies everything he says and does. He never lies. He never shouts. He has no greed. He has no envy. His message, as Nellie interprets it to their children, is noble and strong. "Be yourself," she tells them. "Don't bother about what other people say, because you are you! The thing to be is just yourself." She also tells them that Monk is no one special, but the children have seen him asleep with his Japanese skullcap on his head or with a cabbage leaf drooping from his lapel, and they know better. "I try to tell them different," Nellie says, "but of course I can't. After all, if Thelonious isn't special, then what is?"

26. *Feather's Nest*

Leonard Feather's response to the *Time* article, written for *Down Beat* shortly after, is uncharacteristically critical of the image presented, perhaps not solely as a concern for Monk's reputation, but the reputation of jazz at large. He rightly complains about damage to the public perception of jazz in light of education and funding opportunities. Although the description of Monk's eccentricities and drug use may seem harmless and entertaining, for mainstream America it only reinforces stereotypical notions. Feather also questions why Monk was chosen over so many other deserving jazz musicians who may not have led such newsworthy lives but whose contribution to jazz was equally significant. Feather's credentials as a jazz writer and producer are extensive, including columns for *Metronome, Down Beat, Jazz Times, Esquire,* and editor of the long-standing *Encyclopedia of Jazz* series.

This article originally appeared as "Feather's Nest," by Leonard Feather in *Down Beat,* April 23, 1964, p. 39. Reprinted with permission of *Down Beat.*

Barry Farrell's *Time* cover story on Thelonious Monk was one of the best pieces of writing about a jazz personality ever printed in that publication. It was as far as one could tell, an accurate, well-rounded portrait in depth of a complex personality. It was as far from square as *Time* is ever likely to get.

The only question that remains unanswered is: should it have been published?

I have discussed this with many friends in recent weeks, and the predominant feeling is that whether publication was justifiable or not, in the final analysis the effect of the story can only be damaging to jazz in general. It is debatable, at best, whether its value will be positive for the subject himself, though for a while it will no doubt be the indirect source of a few extra bookings and higher prices for Monk.

What one has to consider in assessing a piece of this type is not only its intrinsic worth as journalism but also its place in the context of U.S. society.

To get down to the nitty gritty, you have to imagine yourself a typical householder or housewife in South Bend or Tucson or Baltimore, an average square—Negro or white—who reads *Time* as if it were a complete reflection of the contemporary social scene.

To such a reader, who may have a son contemplating a career in music, the picture painted by this story can have only one effect on the image of jazz, which, God knows, has taken enough beatings over the last 50 years. For white readers with little knowledge of the racial components that shaped the background of the story, the damage can be twofold; here we are dealing with an image that has suffered not decades but centuries of damage.

There are the references to heroin and marijuana; there is the sentence: "Every day is a brand-new pharmaceutical event for Monk: alcohol, Dexedrine, sleeping potions, whatever is at hand, charge through his bloodstream in baffling combinations," a statement capable of so many interpretations that it is chilling to think how millions of *Time* curiosity-hunters will construe it.

A main motif of the piece, in fact, is the familiar refrain that "musicians are characters."

Looking at the cover portrait and studying the photos scattered through the five-page story, it would not be difficult to infer that, after all these years, we are turning back the clock and arriving at another funny-hat era. The days when the funny hat symbolized commercialization in music seemed at last to have left us; now Monk, with his variety of funny hats (not to mention the dance routine and other eccentricities elaborately detailed throughout the story), may be bringing them back.

"Aside from his hat," writes Farrell, "and the incessant shuffle of his feet, he looks like a perfectly normal neurotic." Not too long ago such verbs as shuffle and grin were part of the Southern white's primitive concept of the Negro. Are we to return to that also?

One wonders what were the forces motivating the battalions of *Time* editors at whose conferences presumably the decision was reached that here was the logical and desirable subject for a cover story about jazz. It should be borne in mind that *Time* never carried a cover story on Art Tatum, nor one on Erroll Garner, Count Basie, Dizzy Gillespie, Jack Teagarden, Oscar Peterson, or many others whose contribution at one time or another may have been, in the opinion of some students, quite considerable. But then, none of these performers has ever enjoyed what is presumably *Time*'s idea of a rich, full, adventurous, newsworthy life. Tatum and Teagarden never wore funny hats; Garner, Basie, and Peterson do not get up and dance in the middle of their performances; Gillespie does not arrive every day at a brand-new pharmaceutical discovery.

The argument in defense of the story, of course, is that Monk is a man of great talent and influence and that it is good to see him finally accorded the exposure he deserves.

I happen to agree with Farrell, who made a point in last issue's *Chords and Discords* that it was not fair to discount the story in advance;[1] yet in retrospect, examining it from every possible standpoint, but most of all pragmatically in terms of its meaning for the Negro and the jazz musician, I'm afraid Farrell's integrity and honest intentions will be broadly misconstrued. (Incidentally, even LeRoi Jones' piece in these pages, though essentially music-oriented, made numerous references to Monk's drinking, the shuffle dance, etc.)

It might have been better to let Monk continue to make his musical contribution without this blinding spotlight on him. In crucially sensitive times like these, there are extramusical factors to be taken into consideration—factors that could have been weighed more seriously before a jazzman was explained away to millions of Luce-minded readers as a lovable, dignified, jive-talking, honest, odd-hatted, unselfish weirdo.

27. *The Acceptance of Monk*

Leroi Jones's (Amiri Baraka) article in *Down Beat* appeared one day before the *Time* article. In the introduction to the article, Jones uses the occasion to vent some anger at the establishment; as with anything written by Jones, it is impassioned, opinionated, and informed. And it provoked a strong reaction from Farrell, who in a letter to the editor of *Down Beat* wrote:

> A poet-critic (or is it critic-poet?) who devotes six opening paragraphs to braying about an article he has not read is surely in need of a poet-editor, but when he speculates on the dark motives behind the imagined article, one wonders if he couldn't use an analyst as well. His presumption that any article about Monk in *Time* would be square, if not downright foul, shows all the intellectual content of a knee-jerk.[1]

The remainder of the article, however, is a commentary on Monk's extended stay at the new Five Spot (from June 1963 to February 1964) with candid observations about Monk's nightly stage routine. Jones is the author of what perhaps became the most-quoted and discussed book on black music, *Blues People* (1963). He is also a well-known poet and playwright, and has published numerous books of poetry and plays.

This article originally appeared as "The Acceptance of Monk," by Leroi Jones in *Down Beat*, February 27, 1964, pp. 20–22. It also appeared as "Recent Monk" in *Black Music* (New York: Morrow) in 1967, slightly revised, and as reprinted here. Reprinted with permission of *Down Beat*.

Time Magazine's cover of the 25th of November 1963 was scheduled to be a portrait of Thelonious Monk. But when President Kennedy was assassinated, another cover was substituted. The Monk cover was also to be accompanied by a rather long *Time* magazine specialty biography which was supposed to present Monk, at long last, to polite society, officially.

One thinks immediately of another jazz musician to be so presented, Dave Brubeck, and even though it seems to be impossible that Monk could ever even think to receive the kind of "acceptance," and with that, the kind of loot that Brubeck received because of his canonization, it did not seem too extreme an optimism to predict the swelling of Monk's bank account, etc., as a result of such exposure, though it was not certain the cover would ever appear. But the very fact that such a cover was scheduled does mean that Monk's fortunes are definitely still rising. The idea of seeing Thelonious

1. Barry Farrell, "Jones from Time's Viewpoint," in "Chords and Discords," *Down Beat*, April 9, 1964, p. 6. *Ed.*

Monk's face on a cover of *Time Magazine* would have seemed, only a few years ago, like a wild joke. As a matter of fact, seeing a dummy cover, as I did, my first reaction was that someone was trying to put you on. I'm still not absolutely sure they didn't.

But what remains puzzling, though not completely, is the reasons for such a step by the Luceforce. What can it possibly mean? (Aw, man, it means they figure they got to be *au courant*, like everybody else.) One understands *Time* promoting a man like Brubeck, who can claim jazz fugues and American college students to his credit, the wholesome cultural backdrop of which would certainly sit well with the *Time* editors who could project Brubeck into the homes of their readers as a genius of New Culture. But even taking into consideration Monk's widening acceptance by jazz taste-makers, and even the passing of his name around a growing audience merely by his Columbia recordings, it is still a wondrous idea that people at *Time*, hence, a pretty good swath of that part of the American population called "knowledgeable," now have some idea they can connect with Thelonious Monk.

And what, finally, does that mean? Has Monk finally been allowed onto the central dais of popular culture? If such is the case, one wonders why not put Miles Davis' picture on that magazine, since it is certain that after his last few Columbia efforts, Davis has definitely entered the larger marketplace. But Monk is Columbia property, too, and equally available through the record club, etc. That is, his music is now open to the most casual of tastes. But then, so is Mozart's.

I don't think the truism about success being more difficult to handle than failure is entirely useless. Certainly almost everyone must have some example, and within the precincts of American Jazz, of some artist or performer who, once he had made it safely to the "top," either stopped putting out or began to imitate himself so dreadfully that early records began to have more value than new records or in-person appearances. There are hosts of men like this, in all fields, around America. It is one of this country's specialties.

So Monk, someone might think taking a quick glance, has really been set up for something bad to happen to his playing. He came into the Five Spot for what turned out to be a six-month stay. That fact alone could have turned some musicians off just as easily, i.e., the boring grind such a long date might turn out to be, especially perhaps under the constant hammer of slightly interested audiences—the presence of which, in any club, is one symbol of that club's success.

But Monk is much harder than any of these possible detractions from his art. He is an old man, in the sense of having facts at his disposal any pianist, or man, for that matter, might learn something from. *Down Beat* says that Bill

Evans is the most influential pianist of the moment. I would suppose, by that, that they mean in their editorial offices. Monk's influence permeates the whole of jazz by now, and certainly almost none of the younger wizards just beginning to unfold, and even flower, have completely escaped Thelonious' facts. Young musicians like Cecil Taylor, Archie Shepp, Ornette Coleman, Don Cherry, Eric Dolphy and so many others acknowledge and constantly demonstrate their large debt to Monk. In fact, of all the bop greats, Monk's influence seems second now only to that of Charlie Parker among the younger musicians.

Even though Monk should be considered a jazz master, having piled up his credits since the early days of yesteryear, viz., at Minton's and contributing to the innovations that brought in the hard swing, it is only relatively recently that some kind of general recognition has come his way. Even though, for sure, there are still well-educated citizens who must think of Monk (*Time* or not) as incomprehensible. He's always had a strong reputation among musicians, but perhaps his wider acceptance began during his stay at the old Five Spot the late spring and summer of 1957, with that beautiful quartet consisting of John Coltrane, Wilbur Ware and Shadow Wilson. Anyone who witnessed the transformation that playing with Monk sent John Coltrane through (opening night he was struggling with *all* the tunes), must understand the deepness and musical completeness that can come to a performer under the Monk influence. It is not too far out to say that before the Monk job Trane was a very hip saxophonist, but after that experience, he had a chance to become a very great musician and an ubiquitous influence himself.

When Monk opened at the new Five Spot, the owners said that he would be there, "as long as he wanted." Monk also went out and bought a brand new piano, though after the long stay, there were hundreds of scratches, even gashes on the wood just above the keyboard, where Monk slashing at the keys, bangs the wood with his big ring, or tears it with his nails.

"No one," said Joe Termini, co-owner with his brother, Iggy, of the Five Spot, "draws crowds as consistently as Monk." And it seemed very true during the six months Monk spent at the new sleek version of the old Bowery jazz club. Most evenings there was a crowd of some proportions sitting around the club, and the weekends were always swinging and packed, the crowds stretching, sometimes, right out into the street. The crowds comprised of college students . . . by the droves, especially during the holidays . . . seasoned listeners, hippies, many musicians, tourists, explorers, and a not so tiny ungroupish group of people immediately familiar to each other, if perhaps obscure to others, Monkfans. For certain, a great many of the people who came and will come to see Monk come out of a healthy or unhealthy curiosity to see somebody "weird," as the mystique of this musician and his music, even as it has seeped down distorted, to a great extent, by the cultural lag into the more animated fringe of the mainstream culture, has led them to believe he is.

Of course many of Monk's actions can be said to be strange . . . they are, but they are all certainly his own. He is a very singular figure, wearing a stingy brim version of a Rex Harrison hat every night I saw him for the whole stretch of the date. All the old stories about Monk coming hours late for a job and never being able to hold a gig dissipated at the Five Spot to a certain extent. Certainly a six-month stand, if not the shorter stand at the old Five Spot, ought to prove he can hold a job. And after a while Monk kept adjusting his employers and his audience to his entrance times, and while someone might think, if it was his first time in the Spot, that the music should begin a little earlier, anyone who had been through those changes before, and gotten used to the schedule, knew that Thelonious never got there until around eleven. But he was very consistent about that.

Monk's most familiar routine at the Five Spot, was to zoom in just around eleven and head straight back for the kitchen, and into some back room where he got rid of his coat and then walked quickly back out into the club and straight to the bar. Armed with a double bourbon "or something," he would march very quickly up to the bandstand and play an unaccompanied solo. This would be something like "Crepuscule with Nellie" or "Ruby, My Dear" or a very slow and beautiful "Don't Blame Me," the last finished off most times with one of his best "James P. Johnson" tinkles.

After the solo, Monk would take the microphone and announce (which surprised even the Monkfans who by now have grown used to the pianist's very close-mouthed demeanor on the stand). But the announcements, for the most part, were very short: something like, "And now, Frankie Dunlop will play you some tubs." Then Monk would disappear out into the alcove, and a few fans who had waited for a long time, say a couple hours, to hear Thelonious, would groan very audibly, but would still have to wait for a while longer until the rest of the program was finished. After Dunlop's unaccompanied drum solo Monk would return to the stand, but only to say, "Butch Warren will play a bass solo," and gesturing toward Warren as he left the stand, returning to the alcove to walk back and forth or dance with the solo, he'd add, "You got it!" "Softly as in the Morning Sunrise" was what Warren usually played.

Finally, the entire group would come onto the stand together, Dunlop on drums, Warren the bassist and tenor saxophonist Charlie Rouse. Many many nights, the first tune the group did jointly was "Sweet and Lovely," which began as a slow Monkish ballad, only to take wings behind Charlie Rouse's breathy swing and easy lyricism. Before the night was over one was likely to hear that tune three or four times, but it never got wearing. An average set was likely to be comprised of about four tunes, maybe, "Rhythm-a-ning," "Criss Cross," "Blue Monk," ending each set with "Epistrophy." But almost everything heard throughout any given evening was a Monk piece, except for the few standards like "Tea For Two," "Sweet Georgia Brown," "Don't Blame Me," which upon hearing seem immediately and permanently transformed into Monk originals. But mostly he played tunes like "Misterioso," "Straight, No Chaser," "Off Minor," "Well You Needn't," "I Mean You," "Evidence," and other of his own now well-known compositions.

The group, by now, is very much a tightly connected musical unit. They have a unison sound that is unmistakable and usually the ensemble playing is close to impeccable. Monk and Rouse are the soloists, though each player did take a solo on almost each tune, and sometimes the other two players, Warren and Dunlop, did come up with a striking solo, but most times the solo force had to be carried by Monk and Rouse. (Dunlop is a light, occasionally dazzling, tapdancer of a drummer, who barely seems to touch the skins: Warren is a very young, very promising bass player who is still looking to find his way completely out of the Oscar Peterson bag.) Charlie's playing is almost artifact-like at times, sometimes detrimentally so, but when Monk was knifing through his polished dialogues with sharp, sometimes bizarre-sounding chords . . . always right though . . . then Rouse was stampeded into making something really exciting, for all his insouciant elegance. One night on "Criss Cross" this happened and Charlie went off into tenor saxophone heaven, he was tooting so hard.

But sometimes one wishes Monk's group wasn't so polished and impeccable, and that he had some musicians with him who would be willing to extend themselves a little further, dig a little deeper into the music and get out there somewhere near where Monk is, and where his compositions always point to.

Monk's playing is still remarkable. The things he can do and does do almost any night, even when he's loafing, are just out of sight. Even when he's just diddling around the keys looking for a chord to shake somebody . . . the rest of his group most times . . . up, he makes a very singularly exciting music. Critics who talk about this pianist's "limited technical abilities" (or are there any left?) should really be read out of the club. Monk can get around to any place on the piano he thinks he needs to be, and for sheer piano-lesson brilliance, he can rattle off arpeggios and brilliant sizzling runs that ought to make even those "hundred finger" pianists take a very long serious look.

While the other musicians solo, Monk usually gets up from the piano and does his "number," behind the piano, occasionally taking a drink. The quick dips, half-whirls, and deep pivoting jerks that Monk gets into behind that piano are part of the music, too. Many musicians have mentioned how they could get further into the music by watching Monk dance, following the jerks and starts, having dug that that was the emphasis Monk wanted on the tune. He would also skip out into the alcove behind the bandstand, and continue the dance, and from the bar it was pretty wiggy digging Monk stepping and spinning, moving back and forth just beyond the small entrance to the stand. You'd see only half a movement, or so, and then he'd be gone off to the other side, out of sight.

One evening after the last tune of the set, Monk leaped up from the bench, his hands held in the attitude he had assumed as he finished the number, and without changing that attitude (hands up and in front of him as he lifted them from the keys) he wheeled off the stand and did a long drawn out shuffle step from the stand completely around the back of the club. Everyone in the club stopped, sort of, and followed him with their eyes, till he had half circled the entire club. Monk brought the semicircle to a stop right at the center of the bar, and without dropping his attitude or altering his motion he called out to the bartender, very practically and logically, "Give me a drink." Somebody next to me said, to no one in particular, "Now, you get to that."

Monk goes on as he does, playing very beautifully, very often, and at least giving out piano lessons the rest of the time. (The last set of the evening, he would usually get into the remarkable part of his skills, and for some reason, when the club was down to its last serious drinkers and serious listeners, he, and the rest of the group because they sensed the leader's feelings, would get way up and scare most of us.)

Monk is a success now, and there's no getting around it, nor should there be, because he's one person and musician who deserves it very much. He's paid more dues real and mythological than most musicians are ever faced with paying. As a matter of fact, even at the height of his success at the Five Spot, Monk had to go downtown one day, and go through still more changes with the cabaret card people, and the word was that the whole routine wasn't really necessary and that those worthies just took Monk through the thing because they could. But Monk now is making his way into bigtime America, and he hasn't given his mind away on the way in. He's still "out there," and showing no signs of becoming anything other than what he's been for quite a long time now.

The last night at the Spot, I asked him when he was coming back. (Charlie Mingus replaced him.) He said, "You never can tell."

28. *Well, You Needn't*

This extraordinary essay about the *Time* feature article on Monk coherently ties together themes from the articles by Farrell, Feather, and Jones with penetrating and colorful commentary on the issues of cultural appropriation and in-group knowledge. Published seven years after the *Time* article appeared, Elder writes forcefully, in the vein of Leroi Jones, but more from the perspective of a radical minded middle-class intellectual, equally dismissive of *Time* magazine and all that it represents, but more willing to accept the notion that jazz does not belong to any one group. Elder's conclusion is that no matter how much we would like Monk to be the exclusive property of those in the know, there is no denying that his music's appeal cuts across many social barriers. Elder has had several volumes of poetry published, most recently *Hold Fire: Selected Poems 1970–1985*, has edited a work on Western fiction, and has contributed to several literary journals.

This article originally appeared as "Well, You Needn't," by Gary Elder in *The Journal of Popular Culture*, Vol. 4, No. 4, 1971, pp. 850–862. Used by permission of *The Journal of Popular Culture* and Gary Elder.

No one, creator, critic or connoisseur gets very close to the heart of the jazz scene without paying some very real dues—emotional, personal, racial, social, cultural, esthetical, and just plain financial. Whether one chooses or must, for whatever reasons, the paying of dues involves one in a special group dynamic: the jazz scene, *making it.*

The dues dynamic has been one important factor in the terrific hang-tough vitality of the jazz world-vision: no one who has truly hassled for that vision is likely to value it lightly; nor is he likely to put up understandingly with anyone who does, or might, given the chance. The very necessity of paying dues creates an impression of debt, of some value owing, to be filled; and a value to be fulfilled means, if not a sense of direction, at least an impulse to find one.

But the impression of debt is also liable to imply that everyone who has not paid, or not paid "as much," owes. So back off, Butterlip.

Whatever demerits this conjecture, it's a help toward getting focus on the general image of the jazz scene: the come-on that has put jazz music under a hermetic seal the dues-paid guardians of which tend to be, or seem, a) serious, honest, sincere; b) defensive, possessive, reactionary; c) put-down-prone; d) myopic, confined, sort of straightarrow-hip. These are descriptive not definitive qualities and you're welcome to miss or make it in the jazz world with any/all/none of them, but they clearly pervade the picture. And the picture, lest it seem misrepresented, is that seen by an informed observer, which I presume to be, not by a dues-paid club member, which I am not.

Jazz, or rather the fierce clan (leaders, followers, prophets and scribes) that has fought so hard for the valuable heart of it, has been so long on the defensive in the American Culture Game that it has become blindly self-oriented. And in this it has been so vigorously self-sustaining that the we-don't-need-it attitude has come naturally—and whatever it is, jazz probably doesn't *need* it. Only there is an unsubtle difference between the fact and the attitude.

Because it has been such a tight community, the jazz world is naively suspicious of all that is not endemic to itself, especially of the larger merely human community. Because he's hassled, the man whose life centers on or in jazz must take honor by putting Them down before they get the chance. Because of the dues dynamic and because jazz people accept it expecting no equal return, the jazzman who does make it with the mass culture is at very least suspect: "So now I'm supposed to say, 'He sold out, baby,' rather than say, 'Well, now isn't that great that he has a hit?'" as Maynard Ferguson put it in one of those interminable *Down Beat* group-interviews.

For a direct illumination of all this, consider the still-flapping noise in the jazz world over *Time*'s February 28, 1964, cover-story on T. S. Monk. I deliberately pick up this rather deflated bag with the hope that its very flatness might allow it to be examined without losing too many tempers. After all, not one of the dire forecasts Monk-in-*Time* has weathered true, but beyond that the whole thing offers a sharp etching of the jazz vision as applied to the square mass.

The most obvious aspect of the jazz view of Monk-in-*Time* is its focus on the fact, not the content, of the cover-story. There was nothing really bad about Barry Farrell's article; it was extensive, correct, made no slights and no blasphemy in vain of the high priest of jazz, and Farrell obviously loves Monk. The piece was blessedly lacking in keen *Time*isms and the effect was a bit mucky ("jazz—one of the loveliest and loneliest of sounds, the creation of sad and sensitive men") as are all *Time*'s efforts to make the scene, probably because the natural virility of the variform jazz argot beggars the strained-vocable style of *Time*. But overall the article was subtle as its subject ("The Loneliest Monk") and clearer, more felt, and more understanding than most of the huge litter of Monk tales.

There's only one real hangup: *Time* is a very national publication, baby.

And LeRoi Jones, who in 1964 was still trying desperately to burn out of his anger signals to mass white America, hung it right there when on February 27, beating *Time* itself by a day, he had the word on "The Acceptance of Monk" for the aficionados of *Down Beat:*[1]

> One thinks immediately of another jazz musician so presented, Dave Brubeck. . . . One understands such treatment for a man like Brubeck, who could claim jazz fugues and U.S. college students to his credit, the wholesome cultural backdrop of which would certainly sit well with the *Time* editors who could thus project Brubeck into the homes of their readers as a genius of New Culture.
>
> But even taking into consideration Monk's widening acceptance by jazz tastemakers, and even the passing of his name around a growing audience merely by his Columbia recordings, it is still a wondrous idea that people at *Time,* hence, a pretty good swath of that part of the population called "knowledgeable," will now have some idea they can connect with Thelonious.

Jones "understands such treatment for a man like Brubeck," but his understanding here amounts to nothing more than the natural impulsive reaction of his Ingroup attitude: Of *course* they'd cover Brubeck—Milhaud Student, Serious Musician, College Concerts, Clean-Living, Financially Respectable, Nice-Guy-Professor Image—he's One Of Them.

Monk on the other hand is the absolute epitome of a dues-paid jazzman. He belongs so deeply to the heart of jazz that he is one of its organic elements; so that the horrible sacrilege of a square national white-power-structured magazine presuming to claim Thelonious Sphere Monk public domain must be not only incomprehensible but invidious. And the insult of the injury is a kind of superstitious anguish among jazz people—who by rigid tradition consider Brubeck slight if not offensive—when confronted with Monk's permission to become as household a personality as Brubeck. Which would mean the desecration of one of the most dearly hermetic figures in the mythology of jazz. "What remains puzzling," as Jones so neatly obfuscated the matter, "are the reasons for such a step by the Luceforce. What can it possibly mean?"

Jones was in fact not at all worried about Monk copping out, or losing it, in the way of success-spoilt Rock Hunters. He closed his article with the assurance that Monk was finally as big-time as he's long had every right of dues

1. Jones's article has been reprinted on p. 163. *Ed.*

and stature to be, and that, "He hasn't given his mind away. . . . He's still 'out there,' and showing no signs of becoming anything other than what he's been for quite a long time now."

The "wondrous idea" that had everyone bugged was not so much Monk's "acceptance" as it was the thought of all them damned Luceland icecubes being dumped in the middle of Our Choicest.

Now all this might rate a quick, if considered, mental shrug if it were merely the stuff of that old Ingroup vacuum-bag: "Somebody's gonna get our goodie." It is that, but there is more where that came from.

It came to begin with if not from a closed mind at least from one so inwardly oriented that its peripheral vision is blurred. It is simply blind fallacy—albeit purposeful—to assume au Jones that nothing but *Time* magazine or some similar hobgob ever happens to create awareness out here on the American glacier. After all, leaving aside questions of dues and rites of passage, it's obvious that many of us who came out of the cultural sterility of the refrigerated white middleclass do deeply love jazz and are fascinated by the scene to the extent of possession, at times obsession, and even of total commitment. I am one possessed by the music, I claim it mine—to the extent that I may claim any music, since I was born with none—and I am from that swath of the population Jones considers *Time* country, out of the Pacific Northwest where the glacier spawned by the period of the gelid regina is still the whole fact of life.

We had heard of jazz up there, jazz, its argot and its names—Dizzy and Bird as well as Duke and Satch and all that big band thing. There was even a clue around that swing didn't and that black and white might mean some kind of musical tension. That was in the fifties, and high years of payola rock & roll, and I have no idea how we got onto such amazing underground secrets. The radio was rock and mush and country-western. No one I knew up there ate *Time* as a staff of life and we'd never heard of *Down Beat*. Possibly the leak was in the new men's magazines but then I didn't know anyone who *read* them, either. Jazz filmscores were beginning to happen—I first remember Gerry Mulligan from *I Want To Live*—but for the most part I suppose it was just a truelife instance of that weird thing that is always happening in war novels: Word Gets Out.

By the late fifties I was one of those "U.S. college students" you've read about, in a small liberal arts place up there, and we were *listening* to jazz records—not only Garner and Tjader and Brubeck (who then seemed hopelessly into his I'll-play-my-liltylicks-in-MY-group-if-I-WANT rut) but the sounds as well of a wild and wonderful man called Monk, whose name was not passed to us through Columbia Records Anonymous. We sometimes went 500 miles to Portland to get those Riversides and Blue Notes. Of course we could be easily put down for having no right even to like Monk's music, for being brittle young middleclass icicles we could not possibly have understood an nth of what Monk was saying. But in that bag Monk has no right saying it in public and we may as well all get off the earth (which of course is exactly what Jones has since recommended, in a colorful way).

We were anything but hip but we were aware and our awareness was hardly unusual. "I see," a friend of mine was informed by his next-apartment neighbor, a fubsy high school English teacher whose taste chewed Gregorian chants with Italian opera, "I mean I hear, humph, that you have quite a lot of that 'progressive jazz'—Thelonious Monk and the like." Monk, perhaps as the price of his marvelously befitting name, has long been a catchword in the general mind for post-swing jazz.

It may be that jazz music itself, even "mainstream" jazz, is still an undercurrent of the American glacier but it is an undercurrent that has channeled throughout that glacier, and *Time* magazine, which is merely an expression not a creator of "popular culture," has had nothing whatever to do with the forces that made those channels. Jazz people short-credit their own myths badly by promulgating the myth of Luce's dominion, by symbolizing under any other agency what is only their own efficacy.

Jazz and jazz figures have been names upon this land for quite a while now, and names no less widely dispersed than those of say, high society, or crime, or football.

Certainly the fact of general "public awareness" and the circumstantial phenomenon of "national recognition" are not identities. The manifest significance of *Time*'s Monk coverage was that responding to a bluntly-placed toe of public awareness when the editors of that "news" magazine finally got around to expressing that awareness. Shazam! There was national recognition of one of the fulcrum figures of modern jazz.

Still, wailed jazz folk, why Monk, why they gotta pick on our high priest, why not Miles Davis whose "last few Columbia efforts," according to Jones, in 1964, had "definitely entered the larger marketplace?" Assuredly Miles' "star quality" is one of the most brilliant in all jazz and it is mildly astonishing he's not more attended to particularly in the au courant ladies' mags; but Monk is, after all, the high priest, and the journalistic values of his most unconventional personality are obvious. It's pertinent also, as Jones well knew, that, "Monk is Columbia property, too, and equally available . . . to the most casual of tastes." Jones, with his most avant of critical ears, should know about the relativity of markets; but what is a "casual taste?"

Monk's music, the sound, the experience of Monk's music, is not that far out. If as Jones says, "for sure, there are still well-educated citizens who must think of Monk (*Time* or not) as incomprehensible," they are merely those citizens for whom jazz, or certain directions in jazz (or in any serious music for that matter) will remain incomprehensible anyway—*Time* or not indeed. But for anyone with any kind of open predilection or at least no overt hostility toward jazz, the pure delight and sometime joy in the immediate *sense* of Monk's music will be far more easily accessible than Miles' inimical esthetic distance or even, perhaps especially, the generally cerebral suit of Brubeck.

And here we are circling what should be a point of real concern for jazz people: that is, beyond the rather meretricious issues of public awareness and national recognition, there is the more essential matter of societal involvement, of Jazz and the Common Understanding. Surely the jazzman wishes his music to be heard. However his spokesmen and critics may articulate his stance, the jazz artist is engaged exactly as all artists in that finding and opening of strange doors we call the creative act; and the jazzman's opening, his invitation to us to come in and dig what he's found, must be just as indiscriminate as any other artist's. It happens in fact that because most jazzmen live virtually in and by their music, the jazz artist depends for his very survival upon a certain acceptance of his invitation, and for his well-being upon a wide, hopefully enthusiastic, acceptance.

But just at this point of invitation-and-acceptance the dues dynamic sets up a paradoxical mental blockade. That societal involvement for which jazz people continually plead—the lack of which, at any rate, jazz writers are always bemoaning—becomes in the instant of its occurrence social infringement of the jazz scene. Thus jazz people immediately heard the ominous overtones of Jones' title, "The Acceptance of Monk."

To understand this more exactly it helps to remember that the dues dynamic operates most importantly to balance the abiding precariousness of the jazz scene. The threat, the sense of dread under which jazz people have existed has not been illusory: given that the jazz scene has always embraced ideas, attitudes, elements inimical to certain areas of the establishment (rampant individualism, moral rebellion and ethical questing, freedom, sane sensuality as well as Dionysiac abandon, dope and its always-attendant crime); given that the jazz scene has always been a front line *and* avant garde of race relations—integration, interaction, conflict; and given the appalling financial precariousness of jazz music, or rather of those who live by it—despite the seeming vigor with which jazz has been capitalized by the recording industry, the returns of which somehow resolve to industrial capital much more than money for jazzmen.

Like people in most threatened groups—religious, political or cultural—jazz people tend to consider themselves embattled, often referring to their artist-heroes as warriors and describing their art in warlike terms or the sophisticated permutations thereof, pugilistics and all the brutal sports. The brotherhood of battle provides a comfortable if not very clear definition of identity, of Where We Are, and so it happens that most jazz people value the battle itself, the identifying separation, over any conceivable or real victory. And woebetide any artist-hero suspected of mucking about the enemy camp, or suddenly discovered to be a leader of both sides or of all sides. Any such shift, actual or potential, confuses and increases the precariousness of the embattled group; any such warrior has sold out his brothers, whether he has compromised his art or not. The economic facts of life being what they are for most jazzmen—narrowing circles of live performance gigs resolving to the recording of more and more lp's for sale to fewer and fewer people (the recording industry's gaderene overloading of the naturally limited jazz market in the past decade inspiring an overwhelmed public to greater apathy)—it's a rare warrior indeed who gets even the chance to sellout. So the dues dynamic provides the defense mechanism: you have just got to be scuffling to be where it's at, because that's Where We Are.

In a pleonasm, jazz people crave understanding but abhor being understood. Therein is the difficult problem of the jazz writer. It would seem at first glance that he is faced with the merely impossible task of explaining something which will not permit explanation and that insofar as his explanation is successful he must surely have consorted with the enemy. Undoubtedly all good jazz writers, assuming themselves dues-paid and loyal group members, must wrestle like saints with this problem which, however, has only to do with the honor of prophets in their own country. What is more important is that the jazz writer has an endemic function in the jazz community as spokesman, historian and sage. Whenever there is a crisis on the scene it is the duty of the spokesman to come forth in his robes pronouncing judgment, excommunication or forgiveness. It is his function to maintain the community's definition. That is what the young prophet LeRoi Jones was doing about "The Acceptance of Monk," restating the articles of dogma, reassuring the faithful that Monk-hero was unfazed by this insidious plot of the Enemy, and redefining the lines of battle. Equilibrium established, jazz folk could close ranks and battle onward.

But two months after the *Time* battle was joined there came flapping home from the front a most peculiar old bird of a Sage Feather, with his intelligence on the flourishing stalemate and warnings of portentious danger. Leonard Feather, who has been called everything from Dean of Jazz Writers to Arch-Establishmentarian-Whitey-Apologist-Mouldy-Fig, for the very good reason that he has been everything between, stands in a truly unusual relation to the family of jazz. An English expatriot who came over way-back-when because he just had to be in the country of Duke Ellington and Louis Armstrong, he's become through the sheer bulk and energetic projection of his verbosity the unquestioned champion popularizer of the music. As such he's been responsible for the good fortunes and perhaps even survival of many jazzmen, as well as for hexing a few. His dues paying has gone far beyond mere membership in the group, in a way he's one of the patriarchs; yet in another way the dues dynamic puts him at a remove from jazzfolk because of his popularizing success with the square mass. But an old sage hand like Feather understands the dues dynamic and what is more knows how to use it in his service as Guardian Colossus of the jazz scene. It is just in the gap of such a colossal stance, in the muddy currents between jazz and the mainland, that the ambiguity of the dues dynamic feeds into a stream of hypocrisy most definitely typified by Feather's estimation of Monk-in-*Time*. Granting, in his *Down Beat* "Feather's Nest" column of April 23, 1964, the good quality of Farrell's writing, still Feather insisted:[2]

> The only question that remains unanswered is: should it have been published?
>
> I have discussed this with many friends in recent weeks, and the predominant feeling is that whether publication was justifiable or not, in the final analysis the effect of the story can only be damaging to jazz in general. . . .

The objection of Feather and friends had to do with the very fact of Farrell's integrity, that he really severely tried to give the facts of Monk's being as completely and as straight-across as possible. Those facts happen to include dope, fuzz trouble, mental trouble, funnyhats, and all the uncomfortable realities of ghetto existence. "I'm afraid," said Feather, "Farrell's integrity and honest intentions will be broadly misconstrued." What he was afraid of was the United States of America, merely—the American people as he imagined them under the stress of the current moral revolution. "In crucially sensitive times like these, there are extramusical factors to be taken into consideration. . . ." And

2. Feather's article has been reprinted on p. 161. *Ed.*

most assuredly there were and always have been, but perhaps the most important factor of all remains that very "consideration" itself, its kind, quality, focus and direction.

Swallowing the Luceline-hook-and-sinker, Feather fantasied all the square land chugalugging all the bad goodies in Farrell's lines without even tasting the strong flavor of honestly sympathetic viewpoint. With particular piquancy he pictured his kind of archetypal "average square," this midwestern housewife-harpy, see? Shocked yet slavering over those tidbits of verboten information which she would accordingly use in her dark square ways against all that's right and true and hip.

The nip I take of that fantasy recalls my northwestern roots and damned if it tastes right. We knew, gee whiz, all about pot and horse and booze and sex and crime and the interrelated degradation of poverty. We knew that the jazz scene was supposedly permeated by such-like—*supposedly and such-like indeed*: It was precisely all those facts of matters we did *not* know, could not understand, that impelled our imaginations to fill the jazz world with impossible hippies (Old Slang) and svelte lascivious chicks souling through Jack Kerouac nightmares of gorgeously boring vice. Furthermore in terms of our own reality I do not believe our humane equipment was at all inferior to that of genteel cosmopolitans like M. Feather. I mean that given the apparatus of understanding we could muddle through in some kind of humanitarian manner. I mean that the American mass has had a regurgitative surfeit of popularizing, apologizing, glamorizing, dissimulating storytelling—ersatz of the scene Like It Is—and that Barry Farrell's "integrity" was a welcome and valuable, useable, antidote to the fantasy-ridden preachments dispensed to the masses by more "authentic" jazz writers—speaking extramusically, of course.

For what the Feather attitude requires is really nothing more or less than the benevolent blimp of censored propaganda; and Sage Feather, in the seemingly so sincere expression of his concerns, has come much closer than I'd care to consider funny to selling out jazz and Monk and the sum of the squares of black and white America. The "average square" has never been anywhere near so simple as the conveniently-bagged intellections of jazz argotry. The race maze in these "crucially sensitive times" is anywhere but underground and it has not for lo these ten years been a special hidden-corner province of jazz country. If the stratographic upheaval of this bewildered American continent is ever going to get us *anywhere* then the square mass will have to help heave and it will do no good to try to keep everything buried in the same old crap.

But in the five years since Monk was a *Time* cover-story the smell around us has much worsened, the burial matter has much deepened, and for all the apparent social chaos many of the eruptive strata have settled back down to grinding geologic conflict. Certainly the jazz scene has regrouped inwardly to the ambiguous extremities of its definition-by-separation—in connection with which it should be remembered that "the young prophet LeRoi Jones" was moving in social and cultural directions of his own that would shortly lead him out of the mass American mess, and the staggering perplexities thereof, into that definitive black nationality where the jazz scene is a clear racial context and wherein "the common understanding" of jazz is not even a possibility much less a problem—where indeed the very conception of jazz lies literally beyond the pale.

Now whether or not there is any point contending Jones' position or the definitions it poses (jazz is black music—well, okay. . . only black music is jazz—oh well . . .) there remains, still, one clear and abiding point the contest of which is proven in fact by Jones' stance itself: that common understanding, the comprehension of societal involvement, is a problem *especially* of a position which can be maintained only by constantly defining its separation. The fact makes its own comment that Jones publishes for popular culture books about jazz and the scene (*Blues People, Home, Black Music*—in the last of which, incidentally, he's included, under the title "Recent Monk," the *Down Beat* article we've discussed) and that those books sell pretty well.

Yet if the comment be made, still the point needs pursuit; yet again, it might better be removed from another argument with LeRoi Jones—simply and quite pertinently because everyone loves to argue with LeRoi Jones. Rather take it up in the estimable words of a jazzman contemporary of Jones, the brilliant (virtually, musically and verbally) tenorist Archie Shepp whose liner notes to his Impulse album *Mama Too Tight* commence with the following esthetic:[3]

> I play music out of an overwhelming need to play; to make the rains come; to abolish wars. The ultimate human sacrifice is to me, life, not death. Folk art reaffirms life. I consider myself a folk musician by dint of the fact that I play for masses of people, under the most formidable circumstances: when they are drinking, eating, swearing, fighting, etc. It is my responsibility to make order out of chaos without the specific aid of a gavel; that is, to capture a religious moment and convey it in the most intelligible language God inspires. . . . Undoubtedly some will take issue with me on the grounds that the music I play is not listened to by the "mainstream" of jazz listeners. Nothing, to my way of

3. *Mama Too Tight* (recorded in 1966) was issued as Impulse 9134. *Ed.*

> thinking, could be further from the truth. In fact it should be pointed out that in areas such as Harlem, even so-called "mainstream" jazz has been made virtually unavailable to the public. The point is that music which was endemic to—and once accessible to—people (I mean the poor) has now been taken away and systematically removed to the middle class, more commercially viable areas, with the result that many of today's youngsters in ghetto situations are totally unaware of their own contribution to world music culture. Indeed some look upon the work of Messrs. Coleman, Taylor, Shepp, Ayler as the alien artifact of an obtrusive "white" esthetic. Jazz needs as much to return to Bedford and Watts, as it does to "go to college." The defection of the artist from his community has obtained too long. . . .

No one can argue with Shepp's beautiful esthetic (indeed the esthetic of any artist is not an arguable matter) and without doubt his concern over the general, public, absence of jazz in ghetto communities is deeply important and valid (although it's interesting, and funny, that the U. C. Berkeley "Jazz '69" festival's artist-in-residence was none other than M. Shepp); but that, "The point is that music which was endemic to. . . people. . . has now been taken away and systematically removed to the middle class," strikes me as being very rhetorically questionable. The point, my point (rhetoric, dig), is that nothing worse than an anthropological culture exchange has occurred and nothing more than a *systemic* assimilation; that no music has been "taken away" in that ominously active sense but that it has been received else than whence it came; that the ingroup dues dynamic has been violated (check "the alien artifact of an obtrusive 'white' esthetic") and that will-or-nil the jazz scene has been engaged in the sprawling structure of America; that jazz has been democratized.

Jazz has been democratized: by which I neither mean nor believe that jazz or its scene or its people have been at all denatured, but, only, that jazz does not exist in its own vacuum, that jazz people can no longer claim their uniqueness in apartheid.

America has for so long now been hearing that its only true endemic art form is jazz music (and its rootforms and relatives, which jazz historians stretch to cover country-western—a compliment amiably returned by country folks) that the idea, at least, is generally if superficially accepted. It's time and past, then, that jazz people let us have what they expect us to claim and stop coming on like Nibelungs guarding the ring of doomsday. The jazz scene, unless it is to be passed through LeRoi Jones' metaphysical osmotics back to Africaland, must accept the fact of its own vitality in the American context and jazz people should realize that their identity needn't be threatened in the larger context as long as it is maintained and projected with that creative vigor which is the essence of jazz. If as jazz writers incessantly announce—and everyone but Leonard Bernstein agrees—jazz has come of age as Serious Art Music and jazz musicians expect to be taken seriously as artists, then jazz people must cut their share of responsibility with the other adults.

The naive hostility of the dues dynamic is no longer necessary. The dues dynamic itself will remain useful only so long as jazz people insist upon considering themselves and their thing beyond human ken. Whatever turns out, one of Monk's best titles bags the whole affair: "Well, You Needn't."

The Blindfold Test and a Last Interview

During the 1960s, Monk was a jazz star, a recognizable commodity touring the world and staying at the best hotels, always accompanied by his wife Nellie, and sometimes by his two children, Thelonious Jr. and Barbara. But even with the increased public expectations that accompany such world status, in most interviews Monk continued to be reluctant to speak seriously about anything. For example:

Interviewer: "Do you come from a musical family?"

Monk: "I come from a musical family, since my family is the world. And the world is musical, is it not? A musical world indeed . . ."[1]

It is clear that Monk genuinely disliked being interviewed and if it were not for Nellie, who was often present during the interviews, or in some cases Harry Colomby, we might have even fewer meaningful responses to not so meaningful and even meaningful questions. In some cases the responses may not have stemmed so much from Monk's impatience with the interview process or his general elusive and evasive behavior as from a misunderstanding about what others expected from him. In print, some of Monk's answers may seem decidedly off-putting, since the lost nuance in speech and facial and other bodily motions may give them another twist.

1. Francis Postif, "'Round 'Bout Sphere: Une Interview de Francis Postif," *Jazz Hot,* Vol. 186, pp. 22–25, 39, 41. Interestingly, during the rest of this particular interview, Monk's answers are verbose and informative (or at least it appears this way in the edited print).

As an example, in the film, *Thelonious Monk: American Composer,*[2] a French reporter asks Monk which of his compositions is his favorite, and he replies that they are all his favorites, and that he hadn't really thought about choosing a favorite composition. The expression on Monk's face during the questioning shows he is perplexed and somewhat amazed, thereby indicating that he really did not know how to answer the question, and this is precisely the kind of extra information lacking in these and other printed interviews.

29. *Blindfold Test*

Leonard Feather's blindfold test is considered by some to be an occupational hazard, because, if you are a jazz artist, you sooner or later are asked to take the test. You cannot fail the test, but you end up demonstrating your critical acumen and generosity, or, as it happens, your ignorance and parsimonious nature. Recordings are chosen to reflect a musician's interests or influences, and musicians generally comment on what they like and don't like about a record, whether they are able to recognize the performer or not. Feather minces no words in declaring Monk a difficult participant, and Monk certainly lives up to his expectations. But once they establish that he is not interested in rating the recordings, he begins to comment freely. In response to a record by Oscar Peterson, Monk demonstratively asks where the toilet is, clearly showing his disrespect. As with many other jazz players, Monk's conception of what jazz should be and how it should be played is radically different from Peterson's and has caused them both to denounce or complain about each other's music in public.

This article originally appeared as "Blindfold Test: Thelonious Monk," by Leonard Feather in *Down Beat,* April 21, 1966, p. 39. Reprinted with permission of *Down Beat.*

In the 19 1/2 years that the *Blindfold Test* has been published, Thelonious Monk had not been a subject. The reason primarily was that Monk is not the

2. *Thelonious Monk: American Composer.* 1991. Produced by Toby Byron and Richard Saylor, with Quincy Troupe. 60 min. BMG Video. Videocassette.

most voluble of personalities; therefore, it did not seem probable that an interview could be obtained.

During a recent trip to Los Angeles, the long silence was broken. Monk brought along Nellie Monk, his friend and neighbor since childhood and his wife since 1947. When moments of silence engulfed us, she succeeded in prodding him.

After the first minute of the first record, it became obvious that the only way to complete an interview and retain Monk's interest would be by concentrating mainly on other artists' versions of his own compositions. Accordingly, Records 2-6 were all Monk tunes. At this point, he seemed interested enough to listen to a couple of non-Monk works. He was given no information about any of the records played.[1]

1. Andrew Hill. "Flight 19." (from Point of Departure, *Blue Note).*

(After about two minutes, Monk rises from his seat, starts wandering around the room and looking out the window. When it becomes clear he is not listening, the record is taken off.)

TM: The view here is great, and you have a crazy stereo system.
LF: Is that all you have to say about that record?
TM: About *any* record.
LF: I'll find a few things you'll want to say something about.

2. Art Pepper. "Rhythm-a-ning" (from Gettin' Together, *Contemporary).*
Conte Candoli, trumpet; Pepper, alto saxophone; Wynton Kelly, piano; Paul Chambers, bass; Jimmie Cobb, drums.

TM: He added another note to the song. A note that's not supposed to be there. (*Sings.*) See what I mean?

1. Discographical information for the recordings discussed in this piece is as follows: Andrew Hill, "Flight 19," *Point of Departure,* Blue Note BLP 4167, Recorded March 21, 1964; Art Pepper, "Rhythm-a-ning," *Gettin' Together,* Contemporary M3573, Recorded February 29, 1960; Dizzy Gillespie, "I Can't Get Started," "'Round Midnight," *Something Old—Something New,* Philips PHM 200-091, Recorded April 24, 1963; Bob Florence, "Straight, No Chaser," *Here and Now,* Liberty LRP 3380, Recorded 1965; Phineas Newborn, "Well, You Needn't," *The Great Jazz Piano of Phineas Newborn,* Contemporary M3611, Recorded September 12, 1962; Bud Powell, "Ruby, My Dear," *Giants of Jazz,* Columbia CL1970, Recorded December 17, 1961 [Originally released as *A Portrait of Thelonious,* Columbia CL2292]; Oscar Peterson, "Easy Listenin' Blues," *With Respect to Nat,* Limelight LM82029, Recorded October 28, 1965; Denny Zeitlin, "Carole's Garden," *Carnival,* Columbia CL2340, Recorded October 28, 1965. *Ed.*

LF: Did I hear you say the tempo was wrong?
TM: No, all tempos is right.
LF: How about the solos? Which of them did you like?
TM: It sounded like some slow solos speeded up, to me.
LF: How about the rhythm section?
TM: Well, I mean, the piece swings by itself. To keep up with the song, you have to swing.
LF: How many stars would you rate it?
TM: (Indicating Mrs. Monk): Ask her.
LF: It's your opinion I'm asking.
TM: You asked me for my opinion, I gave you my opinion.
LF: Okay, let's forget ratings.

3. *Dizzy Gillespie. Medley: "I Can't Get Started," "'Round Midnight" (from* Something Old—Something New, *Philips). James Moody, alto saxophone.*

TM: Dizzy. He had a crazy sound, but he got into that upper register, and the upper register took the tone away from him. That was the Freddy Webster sound too, you know, that sound of Dizzy's. (*Later*) That's my song! Well, if that's not Diz, it's someone who plays just like him. Miles did at one time too.
LF: You like the way they put the two tunes together?
TM: I didn't notice that. Play it again. (*Later*) Yes, that's the Freddy Webster sound. Maybe you don't remember Freddy Webster; you weren't on the scene at the time.
LF: I remember Freddy Webster. And the records he made with Sarah.
TM: Remember "I Could Make You Love Me?" The introduction? Play that for me.
LF: I don't think I can find it. You think Freddy influenced Diz?
TM: Every sound influenced Diz. He had that kind of mind, you know? And he influenced everything too.
LF: You like the alto player on here too?
TM: Everybody sounded good on there; I mean, the harmony and everything was crazy . . . . play it again!

4. *Bob Florence. "Straight, No Chaser" (from* Here and Now, *Liberty). John Audino, lead trumpet; Herbie Harper, trombone; Florence, arranger.*

LF: You liked the arrangement?
TM: Did you make the arrangement? It was crazy.

LF: No.

TM: It was a bunch of musicians who were together, playing an arrangement. It sounded so good, it made me like the song better! Solos . . . the trombone player sounded good . . . that was a good lead trumpet player too . . . I've never heard that before. I don't know how to rate it, but I'd say it was top-notch.

5. *Phineas Newborn. "Well, You Needn't" (from* The Great Jazz Piano of Phineas Newborn, *Contemporary). Newborn, piano.*

TM: He hit the inside wrong—didn't have the right changes. It's supposed to be major ninths, and he's playing ninths (walks to piano, demonstrates). It starts with a D-Flat Major 9. . . . See what I mean? What throws me off, too, is the cat sounds like Bud Powell. Makes it hard for me to say anything about it. It's not Bud; it's somebody sounding like him.

LF: Outside of that, did you like the general feeling?

TM: I enjoy *all* piano players. All pianists have got five stars for me . . . but I was thinking about the wrong changes, so I didn't pay too much attention to the rest of it. Maybe you better play it again. (*Later*) It's crazy to sound like Bud Powell, but seems like the piano player should be able to think of something else too. Why get stuck with that Bud Powell sound?

6. *Bud Powell. "Ruby, My Dear" (from* Giants of Jazz, *Columbia).*

TM: That's Bud Powell! . . . All I can say is, he has a remarkable memory. I don't know what to say about him he is a remarkable person, musically.

LF: You think Bud is in his best form there?

TM: (*Laughs*) No comment about him, or the piano. . . . he's just tired. stopped playing, doesn't want to play no more. I don't know what's going through his mind. But you know how he's influenced all of the piano players.

LF: Of course. I was just questioning whether this is his best work.

Mrs. Monk: (*To Monk*) You don't think so.

TM: Of course not.

7. *Oscar Peterson. "Easy Listenin' Blues" (from* With Respect to Nat, *Limelight), Peterson, piano; Herb Ellis, guitar; Ray Brown, bass.*

TM: Which is the way to the toilet? (Waits to end of record, leaves room, returns . . . laughs.) Well, you see where I went. (*To Mrs. Monk*) Could you detect the piano player?

LF: How about the guitar player?

TM: Charlie Christian spoiled me for everybody else.

8. *Denny Zeitlin. "Carole's Garden" (from* Carnival, *Columbia). Zeitlin, piano, composer; Jerry Granelli, drums.*

LF: You liked that one?

TM: I like all music.

LF: Except the kind that makes you go to the toilet.

TM: No, but you need that kind too. . . .It reminded me of Bobby Timmons, and that's *got* to be good. Rhythm section has the right groove too. Drummer made me think of Art Blakey. Hey, play that again.

(*Later.*) Yeah! He sounds like a piano player! (*Hums theme.*) You can keep changing keys all the time doing that. Sounds like something that was studied and figured out. And he can play it; you know what's happening with this one. Yeah, he was on a Bobby Timmons kick. *He* knows what's happening.

30. *Monk Talk*

The interview with Pearl Gonzalez was done in Mexico City in April 1971, where Monk performed with his own quartet featuring his son and saxophonist Paul Jeffrey for the International Jazz Festival. Unlike with Feather or other well-known jazz critics, Monk is unusually candid and forthcoming, perhaps because Gonzalez appeared naive and nonthreatening—she was unaware of Minton's, for example, and her questions are of the sort that fan magazine interviewers ask celebrities. Nevertheless, the interview shows Monk at his best: witty and seemingly happy, with more serious comments interjected by his son, who was 21 at the time. Little is known about the interviewer or the circumstances other than what appears here.

This article originally appeared as "Monk Talk," by Pearl Gonzalez in *Down Beat*, October 28, 1971, pp. 12–13. Reprinted with permission of *Down Beat*.

Thelonious Monk came out from the wings alone and played a bawdy-house blues version of "I Love You" to an audience that didn't want to go home. Later, in the dressing room at Mexico City's Bellas Artes, he was signing autographs between wiping the perspiration from his face while being questioned like a fugitive from Interpol.

"Was that song your way of showing appreciation to the audience?"

"Yes, it was. Been playing it for 20 years and most people don't realize what I'm trying to say. Some of them don't even know the name of the song."

"What do you think the importance of jazz is?"

"It stimulates a lot of music you hear. All music. Everybody in all countries tries to play jazz. All musicians stimulate each other. The vibrations get scattered around."

"How do you select musicians?"

"Just hire them."

"You look tired. Can we continue this tomorrow at your hotel?"

Tomorrow at his hotel.

"Where were you born?"

He showed his passport. It said North Carolina, 1917.

"I started playing music," he said as his left foot seemed to be keeping rhythm with unheard music, "when I was 5. I always wanted to play the piano. A lady gave us a piano. The player-piano kind. I saw how the rolls made the keys move. Very interesting. Sounded pretty good to me. I felt I did not want to waste this person's gift, so I learned to use it. I learned how to read music all by myself. My sister used to take piano lessons, like all girls whose brothers take violin lessons. Only I stayed with the piano. I learned the chords and fingering on the piano. I figured it out. I jumped from that to reading. But I had to go further than that. I had a little teaching: you have to have some kind of teaching."

"Did any classical composer have any influence on you?"

"I don't know what you mean?"

"You know. Like Bach, Beethoven and so on."

"Oh, you mean Rachmaninoff, Stravinsky and guys like that," He laughed and added: "I only mentioned their names because you're wearing a red jacket."

"Well, did any of them impress you?" I asked after I stopped laughing at the humor of this really sweet, warm man.

"Well, not too much of the classical composers. But the jazz musicians impress me. Everyone is influenced by everybody but you bring it down home the way you feel it. I've never copied anyone, though; just play music."

"What do you think your sound is?"

"Music."

"Let's face it. You have your own style."

"Face? Is there a face in music? Isn't there a song like that? *Let's Face the Music?*"

Monk's saxophonist, Paul Jeffrey, was in the room and the two of us roared along with our cornball friend.

"Where were we?" I asked.

"We were facing the music. Well, you face the public all of the time. And it's something I always wanted to do. No one ever pushed me. If someone wants to play music you do not have to get a ruler or whips to make them practice."

"When was your first professional date?"

"It's so far back." He started laughing and scratching the back of his neck. "Time flies. Let's see. I was playing birthday parties. House-rent parties where they used to sell whisky during prohibition. They'd hire you to play in the house, same as a birthday party. They gave these house-rent parties to pay the rent. Then when Roosevelt came on the scene and brought whisky back I only played in the summer because I was going to school then. So I'd take a gig during the summer. Then I played in a three-piece band in a cabaret. No, I guess you'd call it a plain bar and grill."

"Was this in North Carolina?"

"No. I left North Carolina when I was 4 years old. My mother didn't want me to grow up in North Carolina so I grew up in New York City where I kept on playing music. Things kept right on happening. Gigs. Going on one-night gig jobs."

"Did you think about becoming a band leader?"

"All musicians are potential band leaders. Do you mean was I considered a professional? Union-wise, I guess."

"How do you feel about your influence on jazz?"

"I'm always surprised people dig it. I'm always surprised if someone requests some thing special."

"Where's the first big place you played?"

"You mean capacity, prestige? Every place can be big; a small place can become the biggest place. Did you ever hear of Minton's Playhouse? No?"

"When did you start to find an individual sound in the world of music?"

"I always believed in being myself. You have to notice and dig what other musicians do, though, even though you don't copy."

"What other interests do you have?"

"Life in general."

"What do you do about it?"

"Keep breathing."

"I hear you don't give out too many interviews, why is that?"

"I can't figure that one out myself. Sometimes I talk, and sometimes I don't feel like talking."

"Why?"

"I don't know. I'd like to know, too."

"Moods?"

"I don't know what makes people talk. Maybe it's whisky. A lot of people talk a lot full of whisky, in other words."

"Is whisky and drugs the atmosphere of musicians?"

"The majority of juice-heads and winos and junkies aren't musicians. Musicians are such a small minority. You have all types of people in all types of professions, like the motion picture actors. They drink. Why do they say this about musicians? These other people are very important in the entertainment world. So most people who do this are not musicians."

"How do you relax?"

"Playing ping pong. Sometimes I play back stage between performances."

"Have you had any problems because you are black?"

"The problems are there before you 're born. But you do not have to run into them. It never bothered me. I never thought much about race. I came up in the New York streets. There were all types of people. Every block in New York was a different city. Each block was a different town. Have this on that block and something else on the next block—that's the way it goes. People have gotten killed going to the next block to see their girl!"

"Worth it?"

"All of them are worth it."

"How did you meet Mrs. Monk?"

"You'd better ask her about that."

"How many children do you have?"

"My son, whom you met and who has been playing drums with me for a month. And my daughter's here too. She's 17 years old. She likes to dance. The family travels a lot with me when they can. My wife always does."

Thelonious Monk, Jr. came in and said "hi."

"Hi. Where did you go to school?"

"Stuyvesant High."

"Were you good in mathematics? It's so interwoven in music."

Monk, Sr.: "All musicians are subconsciously mathematicians."

Me to Sr.: "What do you feel like when you're writing music?"

Monk, Sr.: "Like I've accomplished something. Feel as if its a fulfillment. Something's been pulled through."

Me to Sr.: "Have you written words?"

Monk, Sr.: "Years ago. But they were never put out. Used that type, of words expressing—well . . . "

He looked a little shy so I noticed the ring on his finger.

Me to Sr.: "Where'd you get that fabulous ring?"

Monk, Sr.: "It's an opal I got in Hong Kong. We've been to Japan often. Hong Kong once."

Me to Sr.: "Is that where you got that wild yellow belted silk suit?"

Monk, Sr.: (Laughing). "The family had to force me to buy it. I like casual clothes much better. We've given a couple of concerts in Tokyo."

Me to Sr.: "What about that other ring?"

Monk, Sr.: "I had it made in New York years ago, in the '50s. I designed it." (It's a black onyx with the letters M O on top separated by two large diamonds followed by the letters N K underneath.)

Me to Sr.: "How do you feel about money?"

Monk, Sr.: "I don't worry about it. I just let the family spend a quarter of it."

Me to Sr.: "Are you interested in politics?"

Monk, Sr.: "That's all you hear about on the radio."

Me to Sr.: "What do you think about the Black Panthers?"

Monk, Sr.: "Why don't they call them the Black Leopards?"

Me to Sr.: "Ever think about writing a book?"

Monk, Sr.: "I thought about it because other people brought it to my attention. Coming to a decision is something else. I don't know."

Me to Sr.: "What do you want to do the rest of your life?"

Monk, Sr.: "I want to enjoy it."

Me to Sr.: "How?"

Monk, Sr.: "That's what I want to find out from reporters. If you know the best way to enjoy life, I'd like to know. I believe everybody would like to find out."

Me to Sr.: "How do you feel about God?"

Monk, Sr.: "Why bring religion into it?"

Me to Sr.: "It's part of you. How you feel about it. Are you a religious man?"

Monk, Sr.: "Cool it a while. Don't get me too fast. This is a very religious city, isn't it? Do Catholic priests still have to come in the streets dressed without their habits? I was brought up as a Protestant. I went to a lot of Baptist churches and a lot of Protestant churches, Sunday school and all that. I played piano in church in a choir. I once traveled with an Evangelist for a couple of years. It was in the Southwest, and I was a teenager."

Me to Sr.: "How long did you stay with him?"

Monk, Sr.: "It was a she. I stayed two years. When I came back to New York I started playing jazz. That's when it all started."

Me to Sr.: "Do you think much about religion now?"

Monk, Sr.: "At all times. You just know everybody goes for religion."

Me to Sr.: "How do you feel about *Jesus Christ Superstar?*"[1]

Monk, Sr.: "It's a gimmick."

Monk, Jr.: "It's gone too far for just a gimmick. I think it's healthy. The kids do not accept just anything. This is just another fight of the young."

Me to Sr.: "How do you feel about that?"

Monk, Sr.: "No comment."

Monk, Jr.: "The people who are running the church are saying one thing and doing another. Why, the Catholic Church can pay off the national debt."

Monk, Sr.: "How do you know? Have you seen their books?"

Monk, Jr.: "The Catholic Church owns everything inside the Catholic churches and all kinds of property."

Monk, Sr.: "This is a Catholic country, you know."

Monk, Jr.: "I can't help that. Look at Harlem. The church isn't helping the people. They throw people out. This is not an opinion, Dad, this a fact."

Monk, Sr.: "Well, I'm not a preacher."

Me to both: "Do you discuss these things at home?"

Monk, Sr.: "All kinds of things come up: Mostly they talk with their mother. You know. I did a gig in the Catholic Church way back, in the Village. Played the same kind of music last night."

Me to Monks and Jeffrey: "Do you think music reflects its time?"

Jeffrey: "Definitely."

Monk, Sr.: "It's not the same kind of music. You don't have as much fire and enthusiasm. It happens to everybody with age."

Me: "That wasn't exactly my question."

Monk, Jr.: "I think more than my Dad about what he said. There are changes a man goes through. You don't have to get old with years. You can get old because you get on something."

Jeffrey: "Music changes over the years."

Monk, Sr.: "You play the same records and it's not the same."

Jeffrey: "As long as you are living, time is going to have effect."

Monk, Jr.: "Music has to be different because everything is different. We're looking at different horizons."

Jeffrey: "Everything publicized is not necessarily good music. The public is fed so much malarky they don't know good music. Different people judge it different ways."

1. Gonzalez is referrring to the musical by Andrew Lloyd Webber, which was popular at the time. *Ed.*

Monk, Jr.: "The commercial aspects become dominant even in rock and roll."

Monk, Sr.: "Good music is something you enjoy. It's pleasing to you. It's good to your ear. Anything that sounds good to your ear, a nice type of sound, is music."

Monk, Jr.: "I agree. But I'll go one step further. Good music has a tendency to last."

Me to Jr.: "What are you studying for?"

Monk, Jr.: "I've graduated from a prep school in Darien, Connecticut, and I'm going to study music, and continue playing drums."

Charlie Bourgeois calls on the phone, and Monk, Sr. goes into the bedroom to answer. Bourgeois was managing the Monk group, which was taking part in the International Jazz Festival. Monk, Sr. came back into the room and said Charlie wanted to talk to me.

Charlie: "Let the guys out. You can finish the interview on the way to Bellas Artes."

I went back into the living room and announced:

"Charlie wants me to let you go to work."

Monk, Sr.: "There's still time. It's only across the street."

Me: "Well, I don't want to be responsible if you guys don't turn up for work, so just one more question," and I got up to put on the red jacket which Monk, Sr. helped me with. Then a chambermaid opened the door of the suite and the sound of mariachis was heard. Monk froze. He listened a while, then put his finger in the air and said:

"B flat."

After we recovered, Monk, Sr. said what was the question.

Me: "What do you think the purpose of life is?"

Monk, Sr.: "To die."

Me: "But between birth and death, there's a lot to do."

"You asked a question, that's the answer," he said with his back to me, staring out of the 12th floor that overlooked a valley once conquered by another kind of sound led by a chief with relatively few forces in his band.

Behind the Scenes

31. *Rehearsing with Monk*

The noted critic Martin Williams believed Thelonious Monk to be one of jazz's most important composers, along with Duke Ellington and Jelly Roll Morton. Williams was so enamored with Monk that he selected no fewer than five of his performances for the *Smithsonian Collection of Classic Jazz,* to the exclusion of other pianists such as Herbie Hancock, Oscar Peterson, and Keith Jarrett, to name but a few who have in one way or another—commercially or critically—played significant roles in the history of jazz. From liner notes and record reviews in the late 1950s to his last essay on Monk in the *Musical Quarterly* in 1992, Williams constantly promoted Monk's music.[1] The piece included here is one of two pieces by Williams that are ethnographic in nature, the other being an account of a 1963 appearance by Monk in the new Five Spot.[2] These pieces are quite different from Williams's usual fare in that he relies far less on opinions about the music and more on observation of surroundings and behavior. The rehearsal described here was for a concert held at Carnegie Hall on June 6, 1964. Afterwards, John S. Wilson reported in the *New York Times:*

1. Martin Williams, "What Kind of Composer Was Monk?," *Musical Quarterly,* Vol. 76, 1992, pp. 433–441.
2. The account was reprinted as "Monk at The Five Spot," in Williams's book *Where's the Melody? A Listener's Introduction to Jazz* (New York: Pantheon, 1969).

> In the final moments of the program, the large ensemble dug into Hall Overton's orchestration of one of Mr. Monk's tunes with a zestful exuberance that indicated the level on which the concert might have been played. But, although this group was onstage during the last half of the concert, its members spent most of their time sitting silently while one or another of the musicians played long solos accompanied by bass and drums.[3]

Dan Morgenstern's review in *Down Beat* was equally subdued, although it ended with "A special added attraction was Monk's splendid white, Texas-style hat, an exact copy of LBJ's."[4]

This article originally appeared as "Rehearsing with Monk," by Martin Williams in *Down Beat*, July 30, 1964, pp. 14–16. It was reprinted in *Jazz Masters in Transition 1957–1969* (London: Macmillan) in 1970. Reprinted with permission of *Down Beat*.

"What time does a ten o'clock rehearsal start?"

"Well, I think Jerome Richardson will be here soon. And Steve Lacy. They picked up their parts yesterday to take them home."

The speaker is Hall Overton. He is dressed in a rather baggy white shirt and dark trousers, standing next to a two-burner gas stove in the kitchen area of his midtown New York loft studio, three steep flights above its Sixth Avenue entrance, and as he finishes speaking he offers his visitor some coffee.

Out in the rather rugged two-room studio, two photographers are busy setting up their lights, attaching them to pipes and to the sides of the several bookcases that line one wall or placing them on the tops of the two upright pianos. Overton has a floor-through, which means the front windows would overlook Sixth Avenue if they were not largely covered by blinds against the morning sun. The two rooms are one in effect, since they are separated only by a wide arch. In the center of the rear room there are set up two rows of four chairs, plus as many music racks and stands as are available.

At 10:15 a.m. the first two players arrive. Thad Jones and Phil Woods are neatly dressed, and both look bright and wide awake. After greetings, Jones and Woods take chairs, get out their horns, look over their music, meanwhile exchanging stories about somebody's embouchure and somebody else's pet dog and cat.

3. John S. Wilson, "Monk's Jazz Group Heard at Carnegie," *New York Times*, June 8, 1964, p. 33.
4. Dan Morgenstern, "Caught in the Act," *Down Beat*, July 30, 1964, p. 17.

Overton continues to prepare and offer coffee in the kitchen alcove. He explains, "We are going to do 'Thelonious' and 'Monk's Mood,' which are not too hard. We will be doing 'Four in One' at the concert, but we can't rehearse it today because I don't have the score yet. And we have another tough one, 'Little Rootie Tootie,' though it's not quite as hard as 'Four in One.'"

"Didn't you do that at a Town Hall concert a few years ago?" Jones asks.

"Yeah. Monk misplaced the score, and I had to do it all over again. Of course, our instrumentation this time is different."

As Overton speaks, trombonist Eddie Bert arrives, quietly, as is usual with him.

The reason for the Thursday morning rehearsal is revealed in a poster on the side wall of the studio: "THELONIOUS MONK Orchestra at Carnegie Hall. Saturday, June 6 at 8:30 P.M." It is to be Monk's second concert of the season, a kind of follow-up to his much-praised evening at Lincoln Center last December.

Again, Overton has done the scores for the orchestra, working not only with Monk's themes but also with written variations based on Monk's recorded piano solos on a couple of the pieces—these are what make up the difficult portions of "Four in One" and "Little Rootie Tootie."

It is the third such collaboration of Overton and Monk, the first being the 1959 Town Hall concert that Jones remembered.

As planned, the Carnegie concert is to open with a Monk solo. Then Monk's quartet is to play several pieces—the quartet currently consisting of Monk, tenor saxophonist Charlie Rouse, bassist Spanky DeBrest, and drummer Ben Riley. The orchestra is to appear in the second half, and the evening will end with a second Monk piano solo.

It's now about 10:25, and Steve Lacy has arrived.

"Of course, a ten o'clock rehearsal starts at eleven," somebody says. Woods is playing the piano. Overton is explaining how jealously Monk guards his own scores: he usually asks for them immediately after a concert performance and puts them away at home but often can't find them again when he needs them.

At 10:30 Richardson enters, offering hearty and boisterous greetings to the others.

Overton is now going over a part with Bert. Nick Travis arrives, looking mildly genial as usual, and is soon in joking conversation with Jones. From time to time the phone rings, and Overton speaks quietly into the receiver, "Well, right now we're about to . . ."

Rouse has still not arrived, but at about 10:35 the six horn men assemble in their chairs by unspoken agreement to begin the rehearsal. It turns out that the saxophones need a little more light on their parts, and some lamps get moved around.

"Hall, have you got a piece of sandpaper? This reed is a little. . . ." It is Richardson. Lacy has a piece and passes it over.

Overton faces the group and indicates that they may as well start with the hard one, "Little Rootie Tootie."

"Let's try it at this tempo right here," he says crouching slightly and patting his right foot. "I'll give you a measure and a half."

They begin the train whistle effect that opens the piece.

"Hold it! Steve, come down. Phil, I'd like you to accent the G-flat and the A."

They start again. Halfway through the chorus Overton stops them again, saying:

"Phil, right there—you got the right sound. But hold it a bit and give it a little vibrato."

"Put a little crescendo on it?"

"Yeah, maybe like a dotted quarter."

The phone rings. "Hello . . . He's not here . . . I'm not sure—he should be here any minute."

They begin again: "One, two, three, four. Cut off at three. But get the swell."

"At the fifth measure of B," Overton says indicating a section of the score, "baritone, two trumpets, and trombone. Got it? Okay."

The four horns execute a fat chord.

"Now, all of it again. We are missing the tenor, an important sound here, of course."

They are also still missing a rhythm section, but an ensemble swing is definitely developing.

"That was right, but let's try it at B once more—in the sixth measure. That G should be louder. Now once more at B."

They have the opening chorus down now, and it is time to move to the hard part, the closing ensemble choruses based on Monk's solo. Overton indicates the section, saying, "Okay, let's get started at E."

Spontaneously, Jones and Travis begin the chorus with no cue from Overton, using the previous tempo. The others join. The phrases link together. There is laughter at one passage, caused by its difficult—and its unexpected musical logic. Hall shouts "diminuendo" over the ending.

The group has awakened to a musical challenge. "Can we go back to I or J?" Richardson asks.

"Right now let's get this part here—you have to accent every one of those triplets," Overton says to the group generally.

A few minutes later Thad Jones is asking, "Let's start back at E again."

Overton agrees now. But before the group begins, Jones and Travis are running off one of the most difficult passages together.

"That was crazy!"

"It is kind of ignorant, ain't it?" says Jones, laughing broadly.

As they go through it again, Overton goes to the piano and stands at the keyboard, reaching down to add the continuing train whistle responses to the ensemble.

"Hey," Richardson says at the end, "it's moving! It'll walk by itself now!"

Rouse enters, to general greetings and a "Hey, Roustabout!" from Jones.

He takes his place between Richardson and Woods, and Overton asks if Woods can lend his instrument case for a substitute music stand.

Once more Jones and Travis begin the closing variations, and the group joins them. They have set the tempo faster this time. A mistake breaks up a couple of the players, but the music continues.

"Is that where you're going to put it?" asks Richardson about the new tempo.

"No," Jones replies. "Just to try it."

"Nothing wrong with it," Richardson responds. "Feels good up there too."

"Hey, let's tune up," says Overton going to one of the pianos to sound an A. After the general din, he takes his place in front of the group again, saying, "From the top, now that we've got everyone here."

Afterwards: "Once more, from the top. But didn't we get a train whistle sound on this introduction before?" He is addressing Woods who had played "Little Rootie Tootie" at the Town Hall Concert. His answer comes from all sides, as various of the players try wailing and bending their opening notes. Then there is one more run-through, and it comes off well.

"How about this way, Hall?" Jones asks, and then runs off a slightly revised and reaccented version of one of the trumpet phrases. He had made the passage less pianistic, pronouncing it the way a brass man would.

"Fine—now at the end of your part," Overton continues to the group methodically, "I have written out four chords. We can use these for backgrounds. You play each three times, like the opening. Let's try the first one." He gives a downbeat. "Now the second." Another downbeat followed by another triple wail.

"Man!" somebody interjects, "that's a weird sound."

At the end of the fourth, the sudden clanging and wailing sound of a fire engine swells up from the street below.

"That's the whistling sound we want!" says Richardson over general laughter.

They are about to set aside "Rootie Tootie" for the time being.

"Hall, can we have some coffee or something?"

"Sure." There is a break while coffee is prepared.

"Got anything to eat? I didn't get any breakfast."

"I think there's some cookies."

"That'll do fine."

"This music is hard to phrase right," Overton muses in the kitchen alcove.

"Yeah. So many of Monk's things are traditional, but he uses them in such an original way. If you play them the old way, they don't sound right at all."

At about 11:30 drummer Riley arrives with his set, apologizing for his lateness. He moves a little stiffly and explains that he caught a cold early in the week and then aggravated it by going out in the rain to pick up his daughter after school.

A couple of minutes later, Jules Colomby, who is to produce the concert, enters. With him are Spanky DeBrest and Thelonious Monk. Monk walks in, staring rather vaguely in front of him and not looking at anyone in particular. He returns Thad Jones's greeting and twirls around in a kind of dance movement. Lacy approaches him, and they exchange greetings. Then for a moment he looks out of the back windows of the studio. Soon he speaks to Overton: "How's it going?"

"So far pretty good. There are some problems with the horns . . ."

Monk is still in his hat and raincoat, which is buttoned all the way up tightly around his neck, the collar turned up.

DeBrest warms up by reading his part. Riley sets up his drums.

"Thelonious," Overton is saying, "I scored out some chords at the end of 'Rootie Tootie.' When you hear them you might want to pick a couple for backgrounds for the solos."

Monk nods.

The coffee break is about over, and the group is reassembling in the chairs as Overton tries to set future rehearsals: "Let's have another tomorrow morning."

"I can't come," someone says. "I have to teach, and I have a job tonight that will keep me out late besides,"

"Neither can I—I have a show to do," Bert says almost shyly.

"Maybe we could get substitutes for you two—wait a minute!" Overton remembers. "I can't either. I forgot I have something I can't break. Well, it'll just have to be Saturday morning before the concert. Here. Ten o'clock?"

There is general nodding.

"Then we'll have to get to the hall early to set a balance. We can get Carnegie during the afternoon for rehearsing, too, if we want."

"No, let's not rehearse in the afternoon. Our chops will be worn out before the concert."

"We ought to do 'Thelonious' and 'Monk's Mood' today," Overton says. "Shall we do them and then go back to 'Little Rootie Tootie'?"

Monk is walking, pacing the room, skirting the musicians, dancing a little, waiting to hear. He still has his coat on, and his collar is still up.

They run down "Thelonious," Monk's intriguing theme built around one note. At the end, Overton turns to Monk and says, "That goes faster than that, doesn't it?"

Monk moves to the piano, apparently to give the question a complete answer, and begins to play the piece himself, a bit faster, very forcefully, and with fascinating harmonies and successions of sounds pivoting off that one note.

At the end, Overton asks, "Are you going to take all the blowing on this?"

"Anybody can blow it if they know the chords."

"Well, did it sound okay?"

"Was everybody in tune?" Monk asks. "Yeah, it sounds okay." Overton turns to the group again and says, "Let's decide about the solos later. Now we'll try 'Monk's Mood.'"

As the players get out their parts, Overton confers with Monk. "We'll do it this way," he says finally. "We'll begin with a solo chorus by Monk. Then the band. Then Charlie Rouse. Then Monk. Then the band again, and out."

As they go through "Monk's Mood" again, the composer moves to the rear of the group to listen and probably to have more room for his rhythmic pacing as well.

"Try for a feeling of triplets right here," Overton instructs. "Okay, from the top again."

Some of the players move their feet in a kind of suggested 6/8 time to get the proper feeling during the triplet passage.

"Is something wrong with your part there in the first eight?" Overton asks. "Let's see your copy, Charlie."

One more run-through, with Bert's trombone again opening up the theme and the group picking it up. They now have rehearsed their ballad for the evening, "Monk's Mood."

"Okay, let's go on to 'Rootie Tootie' again," Overton says. "Monk, I'd like you to hear those chords now. Maybe you could think about how you would like to use them for background?"

Monk nods. And paces. And turns. His tread is becoming heavier and more varied.

"Okay, here we go, chord number one."

A piercing collection of sounds.

"Now number two. Three times again. Number three. Number four." Overton looks up at Monk, who continues stepping and turning. "I think number one and number four work out," Overton says finally. "Maybe we can use them in the background. Okay, now from the top of 'Rootie Tootie.'"

They run through it once, and it goes well. As they are about to begin again, Overton says, "Hey, Thelonious . . . ," gesturing toward the piano.

Monk seems uninterested. He still has on his coat and hat and is perspiring, especially around the collar. Jones and Richardson start off again, with no signal from Overton, who crosses to the piano to play the continuing train whistle responses to the orchestra's figures. He is backed by accents from Riley.

At the end, Monk says, "Everybody ought to hold that last note."

"But fade it out gradually, right?" Overton asks.

"Yeah."

"Now for backgrounds to the solos. The last time we did it this way. For the first eight, we play A once. For the second eight nothing. Then play the bridge. Then lay out for the last eight. Then do it the other way."

"In other words," Woods says, "alternate eights."

"Yes, but first one way, then the other. See what I mean? Let's try it. Thad, you blow two choruses."

Jones starts to blow with the group for eight bars, then off on his own for eight, back with the group for eight more, and so forth. Jones is just riding along for rehearsal's sake, of course, but he sounds good.

"Don't use the last eight," comments Travis at the end, "because it's up an octave. Use the first there."

Monk's movements, feet complemented by flying elbows, are developing into a kind of tap dance. At the same time, he still seems to be executing counterrhythms and special accents to the piece as they play it. Overton crosses over to him for a quiet discussion—a discussion on cigarettes, one might think from the concentration with which both of them are smoking.

Moving back to the front of the group again, the orchestrator says, "We've got exactly a half hour left. We don't have the parts on 'Four in One.' How would you like to spend it?"

"Let's work on 'Tootie,'" Jones says. "At E."

There is general agreement. But the musicians spend a short moment to chat and joke a bit beforehand; it is as if the group were gathering strength for a difficult task.

Then after a couple of minutes, Overton says, "Okay, here we go at E. One . . . two . . . one, two, three, four."

The choruses go well, but there are still rough spots.

"I want to take it at H."

To the rear, Monk is decidedly tap dancing now, in an unorthodox but effective way. The collar of his raincoat is quite wet. His face is still expressionless—or perhaps a bit solemn. And he seldom looks directly at anyone unless he is speaking to them—as if he were too shy to but not quite admitting it. He is listening, and his movements still seem to be a way of participating in the rehearsal—encouraging, feeling if it's right. From time to time, one or two of the players will turn to watch him briefly after a particularly heavy stomp or tap or a triplet.

"Could I have J, slower?" Overton asks, moving beside Riley, humming the band part and gesturing with his right hand to indicate snare accents.

"That's not the problem, playing that part there," suggests Richardson. "It's getting that accent right at a faster tempo."

"Once more this way, and then we'll do it fast."

As they go through it again, Overton lays his conductor's score aside and crosses to the piano. He sits down this time to play, and as he bends over the keys in playing Monk's part he almost takes Monk's piano position.

At the end, he turns to Woods and asks, "What do you think, Phil?"

"It's coming. Can we do the whole thing?"

"Good. Let's do it all, and, Thad, do two choruses solo, with the background. Then into E. Okay, right from the top. And Phil, you cut it off at the end, because you'll have to at the concert. They can all see you."

They play "Rootie Tootie" from the top, and suddenly the piece seems whole—from the opening ensembles, through the backgrounds through Jones' chorus, blowing into the variations at the end. The only thing missing is Monk.

"Hey, Phil," someone chides. 'That wasn't a very classy cut-off."

"Don't listen to him—that was fine, Phil"

"Thanks a *lot*!"

"Okay," says Overton, smiling lightly at the banter. See you on Saturday at ten o'clock, here."

To the rear, Monk's percussive steps and patterns continue.

Critical Summaries

32. *Monk in Perspective*

Although the titles of Thelonious Monk's compositions often made reference to the people he knew and the world he lived in, the music also very distinctly represented specific solutions to musical problems, and in this sense his musical thought was as abstract as it could be. His solutions always proved to be cleverly inventive, unconventional, and economical, whether dealing with rhythm, sound, or harmony. Ian Carr's summary of Monk's work, written when Monk had more or less stopped composing, provides a clear and succinct overview of his compositions. Although not classifying or categorizing all of his works, he gives us a plausible framework to which most of what Monk wrote can be placed—blues, abstract themes, and modal pieces. It gives us a musician's insight into how Monk may have viewed the process of writing music. Carr is a well-known British jazz trumpeter who has authored a critically acclaimed biography of Miles Davis and the biographical dictionary *Jazz: The Essential Companion.*

This article originally appeared as "Monk in Perspective," by Ian Carr in *Jazz Journal International*, Vol. 20, No. 1, in 1967, pp. 4–6.[1] Used by permission of Ian Carr.

1. The biographical material at the beginning of the article has been omitted, since this is covered elsewhere. *Ed.*

Monk the Pianist

Monk grew up with the swing era, and according to the evidence of the recordings at Minton's in 1941 in the company of Charlie Christian, the trumpeter Joe Guy, and drummer Kenny Clarke, he seems to have been a good run-of-the-mill swing pianist without much individuality. On the tune "Stompin' at the Savoy," for example, his left hand strides rather in the Teddy Wilson manner, while his right delivers persistent flowing figures. There is none of that use of space which was to become so characteristic a few years later. When his style matured in the middle and later 1940s, Monk retained all the rhythmic power of swing music without any of its monotony. No other pianist has a stronger beat than Monk and very few have exploited the rhythmic pulse as subtly or as freely as he. Sheer swing seems to be the most important single ingredient of his music, and he is quoted as urging his band, "When you're swinging—swing some more!"

But perhaps the most important influence on Monk was Duke Ellington. There are many traces of the Duke in Monk's piano: the bravura runs down the keyboard with their odd intervals, the rangy stride left hand which both of them use occasionally for dramatic effect, and the peculiarly loose conjunction of right and left hands. Indeed, in 1940 the Duke played more "Monk" than Thelonious himself. In the fifth chorus of "Jimmy Blanton's Blues" which he recorded that year, Ellington goes through a whole cycle of chords which are voiced and played in a way typical of the mature Monk.

Also like Ellington, Monk improvises more on the melody than on the harmonic sequence of a tune. This approach has always separated Monk from the out-and-out be-boppers who, after playing the theme simply created a whole series of improvised melodies on the chord sequence. Ironically, although he was dubbed "The high-priest of Bop" during the late 'forties, he was in many ways more rooted in tradition than his contemporaries. This predilection for improvising on the melody is fundamental to his whole conception of jazz. Once, while rehearsing one of his bands, his trumpeter (I believe it may have been Donald Byrd) persisted in playing only on the chord changes of one of Monk's tunes. Monk stopped him and said, 'You can make a better solo if you know the tune.'

In a Monk piano solo the "feel" of the original melody is nearly always present: wisps of it will appear in the solo, or the whole tune will be restated with embellishments, or the solo will be built on the rhythmic pattern of the theme. His most successful band recordings have been made with horn players who can adapt themselves to this approach—for example, the two or three tracks made with John Coltrane on tenor sax in 1957, of which "Trinkle, Tinkle" is perhaps one of the most perfect performances by a Monk quartet.

The *Monk Meets Mulligan* LP (1957) is a glorious failure, simply because Gerry Mulligan does not—or cannot—play the Monk way.[2] Mulligan plays very well, and the whole record is full of excellent Monk piano, but the two men are traveling (albeit superbly) in different directions. "I Mean You" has a brilliant solo by Monk. The Ellington touches are there: the bravura runs, the loose, rangy conjunction of right and left hands, the magnificent embellishments on the melody. This whole solo swings relentlessly, ending with a triumphant Dukish run down the keyboard.

When Monk plays without a rhythm section he often uses a stride left hand, producing a sort of benign parody of Swing-era piano, though he does slip in his characteristic harmonies, dissonances and idiosyncratic runs. A perfect example of this is his solo, "When It's Darkness on the Delta" on the 1963 *Big Band and Quartet in Concert* LP.[3] When he is playing with bass and drums, however, he often treats the keyboard like an abstract expressionist painter treats his canvas, splashing on colors and shapes with great drama. We become much more aware of space as he gradually heightens the tension by the length of his pauses, the varying lengths of his phrases, or by alternating very sparse passages with huge "sheets of sound". . . a phrase which, though coined to describe Coltrane in the late 1950s, aptly describes some of the things Monk has been doing since the late 1940s.

Monk's solo on "Swing Spring," recorded in December 1954 with Miles Davis, Milt Jackson, Percy Heath and Kenny Clark, is an excellent example of his more abstract approach.[4] He begins tentatively by repeating a dissonant phrase which occurred towards the end of Davis' second solo, he pushes it around a bit, leaves it, fills up the middle eight bars with massively stated chord changes, then rises to a powerful climax with intensely rhythmic sheets of sound. He has been called "the master of tension" and this solo is one of his masterpieces.

Monk the Composer

Monk was fully formed as a pianist and composer by about 1947. Since then there have been the occasional big band interpretations, and some almost

2. Originally released as Riverside RLP 12-247. *Ed.*
3. Originally released as Columbia CL 2164. *Ed.*
4. Originally released on Prestige LP 7150. *Ed.*

perfect performances of his tunes by his various small groups, but there's been no organic development, because there's been no need for any. In 1947 Monk was more complete, bigger in conception than any other small group mind. The bulk of his compositions (and there are about sixty of them) were done in the late 1940s or early 1950s and they bridge the gap between Traditional Jazz and today's avant-garde.[5] Monk seems to accept the values of earlier eras, while his method points to the future. John Coltrane has said that he came to realize Monk was a "musical architect of the highest order." Rollins called him "the old master painter." There isn't a superfluous note or line or color in a Monk composition. Furthermore, his work has powerfully constructed innards. It is not just that the melody is good, that the bass-line and rhythms are strong; it is that a Monk composition (or performance) has an important harmonic core. This is so vital to his conception that he often has a horn duplicating a counter-line which he's playing with his left hand beneath the actual melody of the piece. One of the first instances of this occurred in "Monk's Mood," recorded in 1947, where the trumpet and piano play a descending line in unison behind the alto which is carrying the melody.

Perhaps the most striking single characteristic of Monk's compositions (and of his performances—because improvisation is a form of composition) is their *honesty*. This quality seems to be an integral part of Monk's personality, so much so, that it is something beyond his control. He doesn't choose to be honest: he simply is honest. The ability to act a part is totally lacking in him. He hasn't got a series of masks which he wears in different situations—as for instance Gillespie has. Dizzy Gillespie can adopt many poses and this makes his approach to life more flexible, if less direct. He can be a buffoon, a wit, a serious talker, a man of the world, almost at will. Monk has only his hats to change and they sit above exactly the same face.

Similarly, the kind of sophisticated detachment which lay behind the conception of the George Russell Sextet when it recorded Russell's ironically titled tune "Honesty," is beyond Monk. This does not mean that Russell and Gillespie are wrong, whereas Monk is right. It means only that they are different: if you are naive, the difficulty is in surviving; if you are sophisticated the problem is not survival so much as keeping your creative potency. Monk has survived; Gillespie seems to have kept his potency. We should be equally glad about both these things. Monk's music is a perfect expression of his personality. As Quincy Jones has pointed out, "Monk is not familiar with many classical works or with much life outside himself, and because of this he doesn't

5. See footnote 2 on p. 26. *Ed.*

create on a contrived or inhibited basis." There are no displays of virtuosity for its own sake, "no ambiguous folksy ties, no sycophantic debt to European Culture," to quote Stanley Dance.

From the very beginning, Monk's compositions have divided into three main types:

1. Re-workings of the traditional twelve bar blues, e.g. "Straight, No Chaser," "Misterioso," "Blue Monk," "Ba-lue Bolivar Ba-lues-Are."

2. Abstract Themes. These are compositions which have their genesis in a basically musical idea. They may have an original chord sequence as in "Trinkle Tinkle" or "Brilliant Corners;" or they may be based on the harmonies of a standard tune—"In Walked Bud" is based on the old song "Blue Skies," and "Evidence" is based on the harmonies of "Just You, Just Me." Other examples of his abstract compositions are: "Epistrophy," "Rhythm-a-ning," "Humph," "Four in One," "Who Knows," "Hornin' In," "Skippy," "Gallop's Gallop."

3. Mood pieces, or descriptive pieces. These always have an original harmonic structure. Perhaps the finest examples are: "'Round Midnight," "Crepuscule with Nellie," "Ruby, My Dear," "Monk's Mood."

1. The Twelve-Bar Blues

Monk really felt the blues and was fully aware of their tradition. Although he could write the more abstract kind of blues such as "Straight, No Chaser," which is a fairly neutral springboard for improvisation, he also wrote some themes which generate a powerful blues atmosphere. "Ba-lue Bolivar Ba-lues-Are" is savage and sexy, and this feeling has to be enhanced by the solos. "Blue Monk" is like an extension of the very old tune "Apex Blues" but it has more elegiac splendor than the older theme. "Misterioso" was written in 1948—or even earlier—and is unlike any blues written by the Bop musicians. It harks right back to the technique of early blues pianists, using as it does, the three traditional chords of the blues, and the old trick of "walking" up and down the keyboard in octaves—except that "Misterioso" "walks" in sixths and this forms the tune, not the bass line. Again, this tune demands improvisation within the limits of its gentle though slightly sinister mood. In the 1948 recording, after the theme is played, Milt Jackson goes straight into a solo which could have been played on any blues at that tempo and it is very noticeable that Monk keeps slipping in chords and phrases which lift the vibraphonist's solo out of its ordinary rut.

2. Abstract Themes

These show the huge variety of Monk's approach. "Evidence," for example, is a theme of almost unbearable tension because of the very sparseness of the melody which consists of an intermittent phrase slowly rising and becoming more insistent, but never resolving into a complete melodic statement.

On the other hand, "Four in One," which is perhaps the most complex theme Monk has ever written, consists of huge "sheets of sound" alternating with pauses, longer notes, or lean phrases. The middle eight offers some relief from the tension because we are given more simple, more repetitive phrases, but the last eight of the tune again bombards us with sound. It is an absolutely brilliant composition, and anyone wishing to know how far Monk has traveled could do no better than to compare the 1951 small group version of this tune with the 1963 big band version. It is immediately clear that Monk has become more and more himself. He has not really changed—or rather the French paradox applies: *Plus ça change, Plus c'est la même chose*. The more it changes, the more it's the same thing. In the later version we are given something that is pure Monk from beginning to end—theme, interludes, solos, everything. The middle eight of the theme has the whole band playing in unison with the soprano sax on top, and it sounds very like an Arab ensemble. The tune has always seemed to suggest this, but it was not achieved in the earlier recording. Also in the later version, the backing to Thad Jones's trumpet solo is a marvelous adaptation (by Hall Overton) of Monk's piano approach. Charlie Rouse plays one of his very best solos, brilliantly paraphrasing the tune in the best Monk tradition. Monk himself rephrases the melody in his solo (no mean feat) and treats us to some of his Swing piano style before the final ensemble . . . and the final ensemble is one of the most exhilarating things I've ever heard. Overton has scored out a Monk piano solo for the whole band. It is full of odd bar lengths, sheets of sound. changing rhythms, and pushes the instrumentalists to their limits.

Other early recordings of Monk's abstract compositions, particularly the lesser known ones, show an amazingly rich imagination. In particular "Humph" (1947), "Hornin' In" (1952) and "Skippy" (1952), seem to anticipate in essence and organization, the sextet recordings made by George Russell ten years later.

3. Mood Pieces, or Descriptive Pieces

"'Round Midnight," first recorded by Monk in 1947, has been called "the most outstanding depiction of scene and mood by any musician since Ellington." There have been many beautiful versions of this tune by many musicians, but I think the best version of all is by the George Russell sextet featuring Eric Dolphy.[6] This is a great tribute to Monk. It is very rare for the most outstanding performance of a jazz theme to be done by anybody other than the composer himself. Russell and Dolphy seem to explore the whole essence of the composition. Their version, recorded in the early 1960s begins with the chaos of night sounds, from which slowly emerges Dolphy's alto playing the introduction to the tune. From then on it is all Dolphy until, at the end, the whole thing disintegrates once more into the chaos of night. "Crepuscule with Nellie" is remarkable for its slow organic development which perfectly evokes a twilight. Monk takes great pains with the middle of his tunes (he calls it the "inside") and it took him a whole month to perfect the middle of this one.

Monk's Influence

Monk influenced and inspired Bud Powell, and therefore has had a direct or an indirect influence on every modern pianist who matured after about 1945. He inspired both Parker and Gillespie and he taught harmony to the young Miles Davis who later stated: "Monk has been a big influence in giving musicians more freedom. . . . Monk has been using space for a long time." Sonny Rollins served a valuable apprenticeship with Monk, and Coltrane found himself completely while he was with Monk in 1957. A touring American tenor saxophonist once said to me, "If I'd been with Monk then, I'd be where Coltrane is now!"

The "sheets of sound" which became a characteristic of Coltrane's style in the later 'fifties, had in fact been used by Monk in his compositions at least ten years earlier, and had also been an integral part of Monk's piano style. Monk vastly widened the technical horizons of jazz because he insisted that phrases which were natural to his piano style could be played by front-line instruments.

Many of Monk's tunes have become jazz standards—blues such as "Blue Monk," "Straight, No Chaser," and "Misterioso"; mood pieces such as "'Round

6. Recorded on May 8, 1961. Originally released on Riverside RLP 375. *Ed.*

Midnight"—which must surely be in every jazz musician's repertoire; abstract themes such as "Well, You Needn't," "I Mean You," "Evidence," "Rhythm-a-ning," "In Walked Bud." The only reason why others have not gained general currency is because they are too difficult. Monk has all the jazz virtues. He has relentless depth; he swings powerfully. He may perform indifferently but he is never facile. We get the impression that there is a tremendous mind at work, but there is also the feeling of *sensuous* enjoyment. . . . he feels jazz with his big body. He will test the success of a performance by his little solo dance—indeed, it's said that at recording sessions he chooses "takes" by dancing to them and seeing which ones are best to move to. Finally, Monk is *pure* because he contains nothing but himself.

33. *Modern Jazz in Search of Maturity*

First published in the widely read *The Jazz Tradition,* and drawing on previously published reviews, this article represents Williams at his best—as a critic who provides intellectual substance to otherwise vague feelings about significant musical events and processes. Of the many vivid arguments, the comments about Monk's virtuosity—rhythmic and pianistic—his recomposition of jazz standards, and his innate understanding of musical form are thoughtful analyses of essential features of Monk's music. Form in particular occupies a central position in Williams's discussion. But his true colors come through in his emphasis on Monk's role as a jazz composer, alongside Duke Ellington and Jelly Roll Morton, an angle used by several commentators as a means to accept and sanction Monk's music. Williams won the ASCAP-Deems Taylor Award for *The Jazz Tradition* in 1973; since then it has been published many times and revised for a second edition in 1983.

Originally appeared as "Thelonious Monk: Modern Jazz in Search of Maturity," in *The Jazz Tradition*, by Martin Williams (New York: Oxford, 1970 [second edition, 1983]). Reprinted by permission of Oxford University Press.

The rediscovery of Thelonious Monk in the late 'fifties is surely a curious event in the admittedly short history of jazz. The fan and trade press, which once dismissed his recordings with a puzzled or scornful two or three "stars," began to wax enthusiastic at the slightest provocation and listed his name in popularity polls where it had seldom appeared before. Musicians who once dismissed him as having long since made his small contribution to jazz listened attentively for ways out of the post-bop dilemmas. They found that his music had continued to develop through the years of his neglect, that it provided a highly personal summary and synthesis of fifteen years of modern jazz, and that it suggested sound future paths as well. And a public which had once barely heard of this man with the intriguing name soon began to buy his records and attend his public appearances.

It is fitting that so unusual a thing in jazz as belated discovery should have come to so unusual a man as Monk. Monk's is one of the most original, self-made talents. Unlike almost every other jazzman, Monk was not only a productive musician after more than fifteen years of musical activity, but seemed still to be a growing artist exploring his talent and extending his range. Such a thing just does not happen in this music, one is apt to say; if a jazzman can simply maintain the level of his first maturity, he is exceptional.

Monk's first recordings were not released until 1947 and are ours by accident. Jerry Newman was "on location" in the back room at Minton's Playhouse in 1941 to record guitarist Charlie Christian, and, above the din and through the low fidelity, he happened to take down some accompaniments and solos by Thelonious Monk. As it turned out, the two solos he subsequently issued indicate the basis for much of what was to come. On "Topsy" (called "Swing to Bop" on the LP recording) Monk plays a solo based on the melody itself; on "Stompin' at the Savoy" he improvises on the chords of the tune but with an original, harmonic, and rhythmic looseness. The pianist's "comping" accompaniments and those of drummer Kenny Clarke sometimes involve unusual displacements of the regular four-beat pulse of the performance and of the period.[1]

The style of the "Savoy" solo is curious: it stems more or less from Teddy Wilson's fluent, many-noted approach. That solo, the ones he recorded with Coleman Hawkins in 1944, and such later variations as those on "Straight, No Chaser" and "Who Knows," should answer the question of Monk's "technique." Obviously Monk sacrificed techniques of manual dexterity for techniques of expressiveness—for the techniques of music, specifically of his own music.

Not that Monk's whole-tone runs are easy to play, with the unorthodox fingering that gives him the sound he wants. Not that his fast successions of

1. These were originally released on the Vox label. See the article by George Hoefer reprinted on p. 14. *Ed.*

ringing note clusters built on fourths are easy either. But Monk's virtuosity, and he has real virtuosity, has developed in the specific techniques of jazz. As when Monk offers a simultaneous, "inside" trill with the first fingers of his right hand, while playing melody notes with his outer fingers. Or when Monk actually *bends* a piano note: offers, by a special manipulation of fingers, piano keys, and foot pedal, a true blue note, a curving piano sound, not two tied-notes or a momentary resort to minor. Or most important, in the virtuosity of Monk's jazz rhythm.

When the records with Hawkins were released in 1944, Monk's introduction and solos on "Flying Hawk" and "On the Bean" (based on "Whispering") showed that an original talent was emerging. But the records were obscure, had limited distribution, and were pressed on fragile wartime material with extremely poor surfaces.

Thus Monk was known about long before he had really been heard by anyone but a handful of musicians and insiders. He was always named as one of those who had contributed to the evolution of the bebop style of the mid-'forties during those jam sessions at Minton's, but it was fate that he happened to be there—Monk had been hired as the "house pianist."

Monk did not record again until 1947 when the series for Blue Note records began. Meanwhile, whatever the truth of the matter, it seemed that bebop was a kind of virtuoso style full of fast tempos, cascading and jerky melodies, rapid runs of short notes, and was based on a certain few linear and chordal devices. In this setting, Monk's records were received with puzzlement and confusion; he did not seem to compose or play the way it had been decided he should. There is hardly a bop cliché in the whole early Monk series, and the ones that do appear are either deliberate parodies (like "Humph") or they are in two pieces Monk himself did not write. Whatever his contributions to bop had been, Monk was not a bopper. He had been working on something else all along. And those Monk recordings from 1947–52 seem among the most significant and original in modern jazz.

In the first place, they establish for jazz a major composer—the first that jazz had had since Ellington—and one whose best work extends the concept of composition in the idiom. In speaking of his writing, the usual procedure is to point out that "'Round Midnight" is a beautiful piece and has long been a jazz standard, and to say that "Straight, No Chaser," "I Mean You," "Ruby, My Dear," "Off Minor," "Well, You Needn't," "Epistrophy," etc. have been used by other jazzmen and groups. Popularity often determines value for the bookkeepers of jazz. But not all of these seem the most significant works in the series. It is in pieces like "Four in One," "Eronel," "Evidence," "Misterioso," and "Criss Cross" that the real import of Monk's composing emerges.

The ragtime pieces of Scott Joplin and James Scott are instrumentally conceived in comparatively simple ways. So are the best jazz works of Morton and Ellington instrumental *compositions*, not "tunes" and certainly not "songs." In modern jazz, most of Charlie Parker's best pieces are instrumental lines whose purpose is to set up a chord structure for improvising (most frequently a borrowed chord structure).

Joplin leaned heavily on the tradition of European and American dance melodies, polkas and marches; Morton leaned on the same tradition. Ellington often works within the idiom of American (or more properly, Viennese-derived) show tunes. Even when Monk writes within the framework of a thirty-two-bar, AABA song form, his conception is not only instrumental but compositional; he writes for instruments in the jazz idiom. Even when Monk borrows a popular song's chord structure, he transmutes it compositionally. Perhaps the best approach to this aspect of his music are his blues pieces. While they are as fundamental as Jimmy Yancey's, they have absorbed and transmuted the vocal background of the blues, and have gone beyond the facile excitement of the riff-style blues, restoring and extending the instrumental conception of such pieces as Morton's "Dead Man Blues" and Ellington's "Ko-Ko."

Try to hum "Misterioso." The instrumental quality of Monk's writing is easy to grasp, the best rule of thumb being that we come away, not wanting to hum such pieces so much as wanting to hear them played again.

The compositional aspect is most succinctly revealed in the fact that the melody and the harmony of a good Monk piece do not, almost cannot, exist separately. In order to play Monk's pieces well, one must know the melody and Monk's harmony, know how they fit together and understand why. Most of Monk's melodies are so strong and important and his bass lines (even those bass lines that are fairly simple, straightforward or traditional) so integrated with their structures that it is almost impossible for a soloist to improvise effectively on their chord sequences alone: he will do better also to understand their themes well and, one way or another, make use of them. When Monk uses AABA song form in things like "In Walked Bud" or "I Mean You," he is often careful to integrate the B, release, or "bridge" melody by basing it on an elaboration or development of bits of the final phrases of the A part.

It is even more striking that a close look at Monk's pieces shows that they are often unexpected elaborations, extensions, recastings of simple musical phrases, traditional jazz phrases, sometimes even clichés. This is obviously true of pieces like "Epistrophy," "Shuffle Boil," "Straight, No Chaser," but it is also less obviously true of pieces like "Misterioso" and "Criss Cross."

Monk's sense of form is innate and natural, and therefore extends beyond composition to performance. Monk had perhaps no less a sense of group form than had Jelly Roll Morton or Duke Ellington, but in his smaller groups the form is looser and more spontaneous—the "orchestration," one might say, is extemporaneous. Two of Monk's best compositions are, in their early recorded versions, two of the best overall performances of Monk's music. They are "Misterioso" and "Evidence," both, one should note, done in 1948.[2]

"Misterioso" opens with Monk's blues theme, a succession of "walking" sixths, and a striking reassessment of a traditional blues bass figure. It is offered by Milt Jackson and Monk, the bass and drums phrasing with them. As the theme ends, Jackson begins to improvise on the blues, as the bass and drums begin to walk behind him, more or less conventionally now. But Monk is determined that this is not merely the blues, however beautifully Jackson can play the blues, but Monk's blues "Misterioso." Monk accompanies the vibraphone, not with the comping, but in a stark, orderly pattern built on the next implied note, if you will, the "missing" note of his theme—the seventh. The sense of continuity continues in Monk's own improvisation, which is built around a commanding ascending figure, echoing the upward movement of the main theme. When that theme returns at the end of the performance, Jackson carries it, with the rhythm once more phrasing with him, as Monk spreads out the sevenths of his previous accompaniment across the theme, in melodic and rhythmic counterpoint.[3] Monk thus ties together all elements of the performance in a strikingly original, compositional, yet improvisational conclusion.

With "Evidence," a little hindsight is an advantage; that is, the recording is even better if we know Monk's melody, at least in its later manifestations. Here it appears in Monk's introduction, darts in and out of Monk's fascinating accompaniment to Jackson's solo, is held in abeyance during Monk's relatively conventional solo. Then at the end of the performance, in the interplay between Monk and Jackson, this apparently jagged, disparate, intriguing tissue of related sounds has at last emerged, but not quite—a theme of great strength and almost classic beauty for all its asymmetry and surprise.

2. These were originally released on 78 rpm disks as Blue Note 560 and 549. *Ed.*

3. This fine ending to one of the two takes of "Misterioso" may have been based on a sublimely handled mistake.

On "Criss Cross," done in 1951, Monk allows the firmness of his harmonies and the percussive accents of Art Blakey to carry the performance once the opening theme is stated and the solos take over. But as the last soloist, Monk himself (entering at a quite unexpected point, by the way) realized it was time to reassert the claims of continuity and form, time to begin rebuilding his theme. He suggests it and then improvises on it more directly, preparing for its restatement. "Criss Cross" is perhaps Monk's classic piece, the one which above all others extends the idea of jazz as an instrumental music.[4]

The early records also place Monk's piano style historically and establish his heritage in jazz. His earlier Wilsonesque solos don't fit that picture too well. Even if it were not for the stride bass line sections in "April in Paris" and the near-parody "Thelonious," it should be clear that Monk's style (like Ellington's, an influence whose later development has been strikingly parallel to Monk's) is a development of the style of Harlem stride men like James P. Johnson, Willie "the Lion" Smith, Fats Waller, and the rest.

The link between pianists like James P. and Monk is Count Basie. Basie's earliest work is either Earl Hines piano or Fats Waller stride piano, but in the 'thirties he modified or dropped the stated beat of his bass line and developed a rhythmic variety which modified the regular (not to say monotonous) accents of the Harlem school.

We are always brought up a bit short when a phrase or a quality in Monk's playing reminds us of these earlier stride players, because their work depends so much on the regular fulfillment of the expected. Monk's (somewhat like Lester Young's) depends on the surprise twist, the sardonically witty phrase, and the unexpected rhythmic movement seem fitting and inevitable once one has heard them. Monk was authentically a blues man, as none of the older stride men were.

Monk, like the other great jazz composers, is a unique and largely unorthodox accompanist. He forms a frequently "simple," polyrhythmic and nearly polyphonic, horn-like line *between* the percussion (bass and drums) and the soloist or front line horns. Even when Monk does "comp" chordally, he is a subliminal melodist. The best introduction to his very personal approach is probably his accompaniments to Milt Jackson, with whom he works excellently. And as we have seen, such accompaniments involve something that was noticed in his work only later: Monk can hold both performances and inspiration together by the continuity he gives to his accompaniments. He is a kind of improvising orchestrator.

4. Originally released on a 78 rpm disk as Blue Note 1590. *Ed.*

The only American critic who understood Monk in the 'forties was Paul Bacon, who wrote:

> His kind of playing isn't something that occurred to him whole . . . beyond its undoubted originality, it has the most expressive and personal feeling I can find in any musician playing now. It has cost Monk something to play as he does—not recognition so much . . . I believe his style has cost him 50 per cent of his technique. He relies so much on absolute musical reflex that Horowitz's style might be unequal to the job. . . . What he has done, in part, is quite simple. He hasn't invented a new scheme of things, but he has, for years too, looked with an unjaundiced eye at music and seen a little something else. . . . At any rate, Monk is making use of all the unused space around jazz and he makes you feel there are plenty of unopened doors.[5]

As a matter of fact, to make his playing as personally expressive as he wished, Monk had even altered his way of striking the keys, his finger positions, and had largely converted his piano into a kind of horn which was also capable of stating harmonic understructures. And he did not fake, doodle, decorate, or play notes only to fill out bars or fill time.

The core of Monk's style is a rhythmic virtuosity. He is a master of displaced accents, shifting meters, shaded delays, and anticipations. Therefore he is a master of effective pause and of meaningfully employed space, rest, and silence. Fundamentally his practices in harmony and line are organized around his insights into rhythm. And as rhythm is fundamental to jazz, so one who develops its rhythms also develops jazz along just the lines that its own nature implies it should go. The work of Lennie Tristano and his pupils and of the "cool" post-Lester Young tenormen shows, I think, that if attempts to impose innovations in harmony and melodic line are not intrinsically bound to innovations in rhythm they risk distorting some secret but innate balance in the nature of jazz.

Actually, I am not sure that the term "harmony" is accurate when applied to Monk; he seems much more interested in sound and in original and arresting combinations of sounds percussively delivered, than in harmony per se. And this aspect has also saved him from the neo-Debussyan sentimentalities of many of his fellow modern jazz pianists. When he undertakes an unlikely popular ditty like "You Took the Words Right Out of My Heart," he keeps the

5. Paul Bacon, review of "'Round About Midnight" and "Well, You Needn't," *Record Changer*, Vol. 7, No. 5 (May 1948), p. 18. *Ed.*

performance fairly straightforward melodically, except for Monkish nuances of accent and dynamics, but he pivots almost every sound around a single tonic note. Monkian alchemy somehow distills granite from sugar water.

In the early 'fifties, Monk's music and his recordings were even more misunderstood and ignored than before—after all, hadn't the question been settled that Monk had little to offer? But the records show that Monk was still productive and still growing.

He had not before recorded so obviously earthy a blues as "Blue Monk." "Think of One" is, like the earlier Thelonious, ingeniously built on the metrical-accentual variations and harmonizations of one note. Pieces like "Nutty," "Reflections," "We See," and "Gallop's Gallop" have melodies that maintain the good standards of "Introspection," "Ask Me Now," etc. "Trinkle Tinkle," like "Four in One," is built on the ingenious twisting of a fast run of short notes. "Let's Call This," one of his most satisfying lyric melodies (on the chords of "Sweet Sue," by the way), is continuous throughout, technically unresolved until its thirty-second bar.

Perhaps the greatest achievement of the time is Monk's exceptional 1954 recomposition of Jerome Kern's song "Smoke Gets in Your Eyes" into a piece for instruments.[6] One might call the performance a miniature concerto, with Monk's improvising piano leading the horns in their written parts, but with both sharing in the total effect. The notes Monk adds do not have the effect of embellishments but integral parts of a recomposition, a new piece based on "Smoke Gets in Your Eyes." Monk's splitting of the theme, his altered chords, his deeply forceful playing, his implicit humor, his commitment only to the best aspects of the original, rid it of its prettiness and its sentimentality and leave it with only its implicit beauty.

When Monk's solo on take 1 of "Bags' Groove" (1954) and his recital *The Unique Monk* appeared (1956), the reevaluation of his work had begun. These recordings made more obvious what had been true all along: in Monk's work the changes in the melody, harmony, and rhythm of modern jazz were being ordered and organized. Monk was apparently the first modernist in whose work elements of the style were assimilated enough so that they could begin to be used in a compositional continuity, beyond the requisite continuity and order of a good soloist. Far from being "difficult" and "obscure" or "eccentric," Monk's performances were logical and structured. And so was the music of his groups.

His work had obviously long had a sense of *emotional* completeness. Perhaps the highest tribute I have ever heard paid to Monk's music was offered

6. This was originally released on Prestige PRLP 180. *Ed.*

by a novice who said, after first hearing recordings by Bud Powell, Parker, and Monk: "Monk seems to finish things, to get them all said. I feel satisfied and sort of full when one of his things is over."

Monk's long improvisation "Bags' Groove" is based on the sustained exploration of a single musical idea and on an ingenious use of rhythm and silence.[7] It is a strikingly spare, suspended, hardly self-accompanied line, full of musical space and air, but it soon appears that Monk has brilliantly elaborated his opening phrase into a continuum of variations, turning it this way, that way, rephrasing it to fewer notes, elaborating it with more notes, hinting at contrasting phrases, but returning to the original, and all the while suggesting rhythmic patterns perhaps yet unheard.

A similar but less subtle *tour de force* is Monk's first version of "Functional," a sustained nine minutes of original variations on a traditional six-note blues phrase.

The improvisations on the LP *The Unique Monk* are rhythmic and thematic variations in interrelated, developing sets, based directly on the melodies of standard popular tunes.[8] "Just You, Just Me" is exemplary for its continuity. The version of "Tea for Two" also brings Monk's otherwise subtly penetrating but pervasive humor to the fore. Monk approaches the piece in parody, beginning as if he were doing a wildly witty version of an old-style jazz pianist. But soon one realizes that the joke is not so much on jazz as it is on the kind of listener who thinks that the jazz pianist is someone who plays a ditty like "Tea for Two" in a corny, ricky-tick style. However, everything Monk is playing is entirely and unfrivolously musical. And by the end, Monk has converted the respectful joke into a performance of Pirandello-like dramatic seriousness and penetrating melancholy, in a brilliant stroke.

Monk's penchant for making his variations directly on a theme itself in a sense echoes earlier practice: the embellishment styles of the 'twenties, as continued by Art Tatum, and the probing melodic paraphrases of Louis Armstrong. But Monk has his own perceptive ability in getting inside a melody to seek out its implications; he can elaborate, expand, reduce, or abstract a theme to an intriguing sketch and tissue of notes. At the same time he approaches a standard piece, as we have seen, not as a melody plus harmony, but as a point of departure for a two-handed, semi-improvised composition for piano, a logical, self-contained succession of unique, pianistic, musical sounds.

7. See Ran Blake's article reprinted on p. 248 for a transcription and analysis of the solo. *Ed.*
8. This was recorded in 1956 and released as Riverside RLP 12-209. *Ed.*

We have spoken of Monk's sense of form as a composer, as leader of a group performing a semi-improvised music, and as an extended soloist. But orderliness is innate with him, and we ought to make at least a brief mention of Monk's more inventive, nonthematic variations. There is a two-chorus solo by Monk on "I Mean You," as a "guest" with the Art Blakey Jazz Messengers, that has a striking inner logic.[9] Monk bases his first chorus on a descending motive which he handles variously. The second chorus he bases on a brief, contrasting riff figure, which is turned several ways, is subjected to a counter-riff or two, and finally is complemented by a descending fragment which alludes to the first chorus and ties the two together. Once again Monk's music benefits from Blakey's presence and rapport, as it had on "Four in One," "Criss Cross," "Eronel," "Blue Monk," "Just You, Just Me," "Tea for Two," and the rest.

In the immediate foreground of Monk's rediscovery and subsequent popularity was an engagement with a quartet—Monk; John Coltrane, tenor saxophone; Wilbur Ware, bass; and Shadow Wilson, drums—at a New York club called the Five Spot during the summer of 1957. It was surely one of the most important and exhilarating events in jazz history. The group did record three selections, strong experiences and exceptional jazz, even if they are not as good as the performances one heard those summer nights at the Five Spot, when each man played with great enthusiasm, at the peak of his abilities, and through Monk's music each discovered and expanded his potential.[10]

The leader and his saxophonist had exceptional emotional rapport. Technically they were something of a contrast. John Coltrane's techniques are obvious; Monk's piano techniques more subtle. And at the same time that Coltrane, with showers of notes and scalar "sheets of sound," seemed to want to break up jazz rhythms into an evenly spaced and fairly constant succession of short notes, Monk seemed to want more complexity, subtlety, and freedom. Monk is a melodist; his harmonies are intrinsic but his playing is ultimately linear and horizontal in its effect. Coltrane played vertically; he found harmonic stimulation in Monk's music, and he seemed to know where Monk was headed, as well as where he *was*, as very few players did then. But he also knew, as the recording of "Ruby, My Dear" shows, that Monk's melodies are strong and that it isn't enough merely to run their chords. Monk's pieces often disciplined Coltrane and ordered his explorations as weaker material did not. "Ruby" is a knowingly embellished performance, and Coltrane's opening solo

9. Recorded in 1957 and released as Atlantic SD 1278. *Ed.*

10. These were originally released as Jazzland JLP 46. For more information on these takes, see p. 91ff. *Ed.*

finishes with a beautiful, Monkish effect of suspension. Monk's decision to begin his own solo with a lightly implied double-time was a beautiful stroke of musical contrast: Coltrane's many notes at a slow tempo, then Monk's fewer notes at a faster tempo.

Wilbur Ware was, like Monk, a melodist also able to find surprise twists in a use of traditional materials. Wilson, whose work once had the even smoothness of a Jo Jones, responded to Monk's music with some appropriate polyrhythmic comments.

Monk got a variety of textures from his four pieces, by playing with the saxophonist, by playing contrapuntally against him, by "laying out" and leaving him to the bassist and drummer: sometimes to one of them predominantly, other times equally to both.

On their version of "Nutty," Coltrane having strayed further and more elaborately into the harmonic implications of the piece, the composer typically enters for his own solo with an eloquent reestablishment of the theme in paraphrase.

He does the same on "Trinkle Tinkle," with an even more intriguing recasting of that intricate melody. "Trinkle" is the best of the recorded performances by the group. Its melody, unlike most of Monk's melodies, is conceived perhaps a bit too pianistically to be fully effective on saxophone. But at the same time, its somewhat scalar quality suits Coltrane's style. The spontaneous interplay between Monk and Coltrane in the performance is exceptional, but Monk's intuitive logic in knowing just when to stop it and let the saxophonist stroll alone against bass and drums is intuitive perfection.

From this point on, Monk was heard and reheard carefully and widely. What could be so "difficult" about a man who often based his variations on melodies themselves? And what is so difficult about an improvisation based not on melody but on a chord sequence, if it worked out the single phrase or idea that it announced when it opened? In the face of this kind of basic continuity, what trouble could his unusual revoicings of chords and his rhythmic displacements cause? A listener who can follow a melody, and who is not put off by Monk's uncompromising emotion, need not know immediately how intrinsic are Monk's dissonances, harmonies, and rhythms. Form will guide him eventually to sense those things.

"Brilliant Corners" showed the innovative Monk still at work. Its basis is the alteration of the tempos; "Brilliant Corners" theme is effective played slowly and then exactly twice as fast, and the abrupt shift in pace does not interrupt the flow of the performance. It succeeds, partly because its melody notes dart about at unaccustomed intervals so that the changes of tempo are almost anticipated by the nature of the melodic line. In turn each player—Sonny Rollins, Monk, Ernie Henry, and Max Roach—is required to improvise at the alternate speed but has to keep the performance continuous.

Monk's first version of "I Should Care" is his piano solo masterpiece and a uniquely pianistic performance.[11] Again Monk transmutes a popular song into a composition for piano. And he conceives this composition as a striking, resourceful tissue of unique piano sounds, in a kind of free tempo in which each phrase seems to have its own momentum. Among its several virtues "I Should Care" is evidence that Monk has carried the jazzman's concept of individuality of sound further than any other player on his instrument; indeed, he has carried it almost as far as the hornmen.

Thelonious Monk learned to explore and develop an original and unorthodox musical talent. And he endured years when his music suffered neglect and even disparagement. Neither of those things is easy, and especially not for an American. Then Monk was signed by a major record company, and his appearances began to draw crowds, and he was faced with perhaps the severest test of all—success, personal popularity, the problems of facing an audience night after night, the problems of sidemen and of keeping the right group together. Many a popular artist (and many a fine one), faced with the recognition he has awaited, is tempted to relax, admire his laurels, and pause now and then to count the house. And during the years of success there were indications that Monk was all too willing to coast a bit too.

His second version of "Bolivar Blues" does not have the anguish of the original, but Monk's solo is something of a minor wonder, moving from tripling dissonances (quasi-amateurish and quite humorous), through sustained splashes of sound which spread out in rings from a center (and echo his earlier accompaniment to tenor saxophonist Charlie Rouse on the piece), ending in quick spurts of sound that abruptly disappear beneath the surface, leaving no trace.[12]

A new version of "Just a Gigolo"[13] condenses a range of sound into a quite brief solo performance by Monk, and again reveals, through Monk's left hand, that he belongs with the earlier Harlem stride players.[14] Then, when

11. Monk's first recorded version was actually with his quartet in 1948, for Blue Note Records. Williams is referring to the version recorded in 1957 and released as Riverside RLP 12-235. *Ed.*
12. Recorded in 1962 and originally released as Columbia CL 1965. *Ed.*
13. A scholarly (and thoroughly unimportant) essay might be written on Monk's affinity for Bing Crosby's repertory. Or Sonny Rollins's for Al Jolson's.
14. Recorded in 1962 and originally released as Columbia CL 1965. *Ed.*

his bass figures get a bit melodramatic, Monk kids them beautifully with a rattling tremolo in his right hand. "Sweet and Lovely," another of the out-of-the-way standards in Monk's repertory, is perhaps better than his first version. He develops it to the point where his left hand boldly sings out an abstract of the melody line, while his right hand offers glittering pianistic embellishments above. On a solo version of "Body and Soul" Monk has the daring to simplify a stride bass to the point of apparent amateurishness, yet its effect is of a powerful, incantive, yet humorous series of sound clusters, as accompaniment to a shimmeringly original paraphrase of the theme.

Then there is a new version of "Five Spot Blues," on which an archaic triplet figure is elaborated within the traditional blues framework.[15] It is perhaps a measure of Monk's talent that he is willing to undertake something so totally unpretentious. And yet in his solos, he stretches out that little triplet motif, then abruptly condenses it into half the space it is supposed to occupy, embellishes it until it is almost lost, then rediscovers it and restores its unapologetic simplicity. I think that anyone with an ear for melody and rhythm could follow him exactly yet in its small way "Five Spot Blues" is perhaps a measure of his sense of order, of his rhythmic virtuosity, his originality, and his greatness.

On a 1964 "in concert" recording, containing the best realization of Monk's music for a large ensemble, there is a grand moment that shows the pianist's commitment to improvisation in his sudden, wildly witty interjections on Hall Overton's scoring of his theme, "Epistrophy," a piece which Monk has obviously played many hundreds of times.[16] And in the same recital, there is once again his innate sense of form, in his punctuations, his solo, and his accompaniment (particularly with Phil Woods) on "Evidence."

It would not take too much psychological subtlety to see what Monk's achievement means. It means that some of the sensibilities that Parker, Gillespie, Powell, and Monk himself came upon and expressed with such masterful intuition could be made more ordered and rational, and could be handled with greater choice. Obviously a sense of form does not mean conventionality or depreciation of the idiom. Imagination, improvisation, spontaneity, and feeling—the fact that form for the smaller groups of modern jazz is more improvisational—these things alone might counter stylistic rigidity. At the same time, Monk's unresting harmonic, rhythmic, and melodic explorations have already led to further reorganizations of jazz. And within his own idiom

15. Ibid. *Ed.*
16. Originally released as Columbia CL-2164. *Ed.*

Monk long continued to maintain the precarious, spiritually dangerous status of an innovator.

But, most important, and the thing that shows that it is all not a matter of mere "techniques," Monk at his best is a deeply, uncompromisingly expressive player. He is not an "entertainer"; he does not "show" us anything. Everything he says, he says musically, directly, unadorned; he is all music and his technique is jazz technique. His greatest importance lies in the fact that Monk is an artist with an artist's deeply felt sense of life and an artist's drive to communicate the surprising and enlightening truth of it in his own way. And he has the artist's special capacity for involving us with him so that we seem to be working it all out together.

Jazz has had precious few of his kind.

After Monk (1982–Present)

When Monk died in a New Jersey hospital on February 17, 1982, of a brain hemorrhage, his picture appeared in the bottom right corner of the front page of the *New York Times* the next day, with a reference to a tribute by John Wilson called "Thelonious Monk, Created Wry Jazz Melodies and New Harmonies." The funeral was held at Saint Peter's Church in New York City, with performances by several of Monk's former sidemen in various combinations, some of the most respected interpreters of his music (Barry Harris, Randy Weston, and Tommy Flanagan), and the Rutgers Jazz Ensemble. The service was conducted by the Reverend John Gensel, whose church has been a gathering point for the jazz community since the early 1960s. Ira Gitler's eulogy, read at the funeral, was later reprinted in *Jazz Times,* recounting many anecdotes and reminiscences.[1] The program notes for the funeral recounted the facts of his life and cited his honors—various awards; his appearances on television; the *Time* cover; citations in *Who's Who in America* and other reference works—all evidence of Monk's acceptance into mainstream society. It also stated that "contrary to popular rumor that he was a 'self-taught' musician, Thelonious studied theory, harmony, and arranging at the Juilliard School of Music while he was in his late teens."[2] For someone who had stood outside of this mainstream for

1. *Jazz Times,* April 1982, pp. 9–11.
2. There is no evidence that Monk studied at Juilliard, but it seems plausible that the organizers of the funeral service used this story to enhance a formal occasion.

so long, following his own path and eventually withdrawing from the world altogether, it was an ironic ending.

On the day of Monk's death, Columbia University's FM Station, WKCR, began a 33-hour marathon tribute to Monk, with music, interviews, and commentary. *Jazz Magazine,* the leading journal from France, included a 20-page feature on Monk in its April issue, with reprints of interviews with Monk, Charlie Rouse, and Pat Patrick.[3] *Keyboard* magazine dedicated an issue to Monk in July 1982, including pieces by Orrin Keepnews, Bob Doerschuk, and Ran Blake, as well as praise and anecdotes from Max Roach, Gerry Mulligan, McCoy Tyner, Sonny Rollins, Horace Silver, Chick Corea, and Phil Woods.[4]

The number of tributes to Monk and his music, in the form of articles, poems, fiction, and especially albums dedicated to his music, has steadily increased over the last decade, bearing out Monk's quote that the public would catch up with him—eventually.[5] Early believers like Steve Lacy, who recorded an album entirely dedicated to Monk's works in 1958, and Bud Powell, who did the same in 1961, were harbingers of what was to become, by the 1990s, a merit badge for the more adventurous practitioners in the jazz record industry. Currently there are dozens of albums devoted solely to Monk's music available, ranging from solo interpretations on piano to big band arrangements to cross-genre experimentations.[6] And, as an indication of the kind of nonmusical inspiration drawn from Monk, the literary journal *Brilliant Corners,* launched in 1996, uses Monk as its patron saint. Moreover, Monk has been a consistent subject of poetry, beginning with Art Lange's 1977 volume *The Monk Poems.*[7]

3. See "Thelonious Sphere Monk: 1920–1982," *Jazz Magazine,* April 1982, Vol. 306, pp. 3–20.
4. The Swiss magazine *Du: Die Zeitschrift Der Kultur* produced for their March 1994 issue what is perhaps the most attractive and varied collection of material ever gathered on the subject of Thelonious Monk. The issue includes (mostly in German) interviews, analyses, photos, poems, and essays about Monk, including much original research.
5. See the article by Grover Sales, reprinted on p. 100.
6. Artists who have dedicated albums to Monk's music include Arthur Blythe, Anthony Braxton, Chick Corea, Évidence, Tommy Flanagan, Jerry Gonzalez, Barry Harris, ICP Orchestra, Kronos Quartet, Carmen McRae, Paul Motian, Randy Weston, and Hal Willner (producer).
7. *The Monk Poems* was published in New York by Frontward Books. For a summary of poems that use Monk as subject or inspiration, see Sascha Feinstein's article "Epistrophies: Poems Celebrating Thelonious Monk and his Music," *African American Review,* Spring 1997, Vol. 31, No. 1, pp. 55–59.

Why did it take almost 50 years for musicians and the public alike to fully accept Monk's music? Perhaps because he was the embodiment, as André Hodeir has said, of the "first jazzman who has had a feeling for specifically modern aesthetic values."[8] But it is also because his music exhibits an underlying complexity, or strangeness, that does not match up easily with conventional musical thinking, regardless of whose values are represented. In other words: The chords, rhythmic patterns, harmonic progressions, and melodic gestures are all familiar but have been assembled and presented in an original but unfamiliar manner. Playing Monk's music, as well as listening to it, is consistently challenging to the ear.

8. See the article by Hodeir reprinted here on p. 118.

In Memoriam

34. The Talk of the Town

Of the numerous eulogies that appeared after Monk's death, Whitney Balliett's piece, in his regular column for the *New Yorker,* stands out for its apt and skillful encapsulations of the essence of Monk's music, and is a moving tribute to the man and his music. There are some particularly insightful statements describing Monk's use of melody. The phrase "His improvisations were molten Monk compositions, and his compositions were frozen Monk improvisations" shows up repeatedly in articles about Monk and seems to sum up in a very succinct yet poetic manner one of the essential features of Monk's music.[1] The last part of the article contains a brief account by the Baroness Nica de Koenigswarter of Monk's remaining years in Weehawken, New Jersey. Balliett's extensive journals of the concert and club scene in New York, profiles, and interviews with jazz musicians have been published in more than a dozen books, beginning in the early 1950s.

1. Balliett has truly coined some imaginative phrases in describing Monk's music, another jewel being "His songs ripple with dissonance and rhythms that often give one the sensation of missing the bottom step in the dark." See his chapter on Monk in *The Sound of Surprise* (New York: Penguin, 1959).

This article originally appeared as "The Talk of the Town," by Whitney Balliett in *The New Yorker* on March 1, 1982, pp. 37–38. From *Goodbyes and Other Messages: A Journal of Jazz* (New York: Oxford), copyright © 1982 by *The New Yorker Magazine, Inc.*

The pianist and composer Thelonious Monk, who died last week, at the age of sixty-four, was an utterly original man who liked to pretend he was an eccentric. Indeed, he used eccentricity as a shield to fend off a world that he frequently found alien, and even hostile. A tall, dark, funny, bearish, inward-shining man, he wore odd hats and dark glasses with bamboo frames when he played. His body moved continuously. At the keyboard, he swayed convulsively back and forth and from side to side, his feet flapping like flounders on the floor. While his sidemen soloed, he would stand by the piano and dance, turning in slow, genial circles, his elbows out like wings, his knees slightly bent, his fingers snapping on the after-beat. His motions celebrated what he and his musicians played: Watch, these are the shapes of my music. His compositions and his playing were of a piece. His improvisations were molten Monk compositions, and his compositions were frozen Monk improvisations. His medium- and up-tempo tunes are stop-and-go rhythmic structures. Their melodic lines, which often hinge on flatted notes, tend to be spare and direct, but they are written with strangely placed rests and unexpected accents. They move irregularly through sudden intervals and retards and broken rhythms. His balladlike tunes are altogether different. They are intense and graceful art songs, which move slowly and three-dimensionally. They are carved sound. (Monk's song titles—"Crepuscule with Nellie," "Epistrophy," "Ruby, My Dear," "Well, You Needn't," "Rhythm-a-ning," "Hackensack"—are as striking as the songs themselves. But none match his extraordinary name, Thelonious Sphere Monk, which surpasses such euphonies as Stringfellow Barr and Twyla Tharp.) His improvisations were ingenious attempts to disguise his love of melody. He clothed whatever he played with spindly runs, flatted notes, flatted chords, repeated single notes, yawning silences, and zigzag rhythms. Sometimes he pounded the keyboard with his right elbow. His brilliant style protected him not only from his love of melody but from his love of the older pianists he grew out of—Duke Ellington and the stride pianists and the likes of Art Tatum. All peered out from inside his solos, but he let them escape only in the form of parody.

Monk hid himself so well behind his music that we know little of him. He was brought from North Carolina when he was little, he eventually settled in the West Sixties, and he lived there until his building was torn down. He married the Nellie of his song title, and he had two children, one of whom became a drummer. He began appearing in New York night clubs around 1940, but he achieved little recognition until the late fifties. (He was often lumped with Charlie Parker and Dizzy Gillespie; however, he did not have much in common with them outside of certain harmonic inventions.) Part of the reason for Monk's slow blooming was his iconoclastic music, and part was the fact that he was unable to perform in New York night clubs from 1951 to 1957—the time when Charles Mingus and the Modern Jazz Quartet and Gerry Mulligan were coming to the fore. (The police had lifted his cabaret card, because he had been found sitting in a car in which narcotics were concealed.) But he exploded when he returned to the scene, and he suddenly seemed to be everywhere—on record after exceptional record, at concerts and festivals, at the old Five Spot and the Vanguard and the Jazz Gallery. He filled us with his noble, funny, generous music. His attendance record in night clubs was spotty (he was often late, and sometimes he didn't show up at all), but the cumulative excellence of his playing made him a standard against which to measure all jazz.

Then, in 1973, he vanished again. There were rumors that he was ill and had been taken in by his old friend and mentor the Baroness Nica de Koenigswarter, who lives in a big house in Weehawken, New Jersey. The rumors turned out to be true, and this is what the Baroness had to say about Monk one day last fall: "No doctor has put his finger on what is wrong with him, and he has had every medical test under the sun. He's not unhappy, and his mind works very well. He knows what is going on in the world, and I don't know how, because he doesn't read the newspapers and he only watches a little telly. He's withdrawn, that's all. It's as though he had gone into retreat. He takes walks several times a week, and his wife, Nellie, comes over from New York almost every day to cook for him. He began to withdraw in 1973, and he hasn't touched the piano since 1976. He has one twenty or thirty feet from his bed, so to speak, but he never goes near it. When Barry Harris visits, he practices on it, and he'll ask Monk what the correct changes to 'Ruby, My Dear' are, and Monk will tell him. Charlie Rouse, his old tenor saxophonist, came to see him on his birthday the other day, but Monk isn't really interested in seeing anyone. The strange thing is he looks beautiful. He has never *said* that he won't play the piano again. He suddenly went into this, so maybe he'll suddenly come out."

But Monk must have known he wouldn't. His last public appearance, at the Newport Jazz Festival of 1976, was painful. His playing was mechanical and uncertain, and, astonishingly, his great Gothic style had fallen away. His very soul had gone, and he never found it again.

35. *Thelonious Monk: A Remembrance*

Orrin Keepnews's piece for the July 1982 *Keyboard* issue devoted to Monk recounts his years as a record producer for Monk. The excerpts reprinted here focus on how Keepnews—like many musicians—viewed Monk as a teacher, a guru, and they describe some of his personal feelings for Monk. In fact, Monk's role, beginning with his stay at Minton's, has often been cast as that of a teacher or mentor, with musicians dropping by his apartment at all hours of the day during the 1940s and 1950s, asking him to write down some of his musical ideas for them. It was not only musically that Monk exerted tremendous influence over people, but on an interpersonal level as well. Keepnews, perhaps more than anyone else in the record business, knew Monk well and managed to maintain a good working relationship with him, ensuring that Monk's work in the late 1950s was recorded and promoted. In the 1980s and 1990s, he was involved with several major reissues of Monk's music, including *The Complete Riverside Recordings,* which was awarded Grammy Awards for Best Historical Album and Best Album Notes.

This article originally appeared as "Thelonious Monk: A Remembrance" in *Keyboard,* July 1982, pp. 17–23. It has been excerpted and edited for this reprint. Used by permission of Orrin Keepnews.

[Monk's] last recording project with me was more than two decades ago, in 1960; thereafter I had little direct contact with him. In the '70s, like most people, I hardly saw or heard Monk. However, in the years since we stopped working together I have remained constantly aware of the man and of his stature and value and influence. It is an awareness that has consistently been shared and talked about and utilized by a great many of the musicians I've been associated with during that time. Several of these men—most notably saxophonist Sonny Rollins—have shared my belief that Thelonious was in reality one of the great teachers, even though he undoubtedly never gave a formal lesson in his life. And it remains a source of pride to me to feel that I can count myself as one of his pupils. . . .

I have only recently become aware of a Sonny Rollins interview in which he recalled his late '60s retirement of sorts, involving some time in India.

"When I . . . found out what a real guru was—how they were treated and what they represented—I realized that Monk was my guru and it was . . . time to get back to work on what I do best." Even though Sonny may not have realized it until then, he really had been acting on that belief for many years—just as in my case, although I hadn't made the comparison before reading his remarks, it was equally true that in the late 1950s Monk had been *my* guru. In recent years Rollins and I have talked more than once about Thelonious' importance as a teacher, and it is clear that in very different ways he contributed greatly to the early shaping of both Sonny's career and mine.

For me it was initially a matter of a very tough period of on-the-job training, of apprenticing myself to a hard master. In the liner notes to only my third album with Monk, I described him as "a perfectionist . . . who drives the others as hard as he drives himself—which is possibly a little unfair of him." In writing that, I was unquestionably referring to myself as much as the players. The music was tough; the artist knew exactly what results he wanted (regardless of whether his associates considered those results to be possible); and he was as uncompromising as he was unconventional. The other musicians were driven by their own pride as well as their feelings of respect, awe, and/or love (although not always of understanding) for this man. Such a combination inevitably led to a good deal of tension in the studio. I soon learned that it was my responsibility to relieve that condition as swiftly as possible. Looking back at that period, I realize that things were made somewhat more difficult by some of the ground rules and economic necessities of the era. For one major example, neither the time nor the money for adequate rehearsal was likely to be available; for another, it was nevertheless assumed that a jazz album could be recorded in a single day, almost everything done in one take. I eventually worked my way through to a formula that combined those incompatible elements. For the most part, I accepted the requirement of working too quickly and without rehearsal, but insisted on at least two days in the studio and as many takes as the leader and I considered necessary. It was my work with Thelonious more than anything else that helped shape this approach. It was also from sessions with him that I got my priorities straight about a number of other things.

It is possible that, as with the 1948 interview, I was able to survive and succeed because I was too ignorant to be properly afraid. Perhaps, too, the fact that I really valued his music got through to Monk and helped—and over the years it has become an iron-bound law for me (one that I rarely break, and invariably regret it when I do) not to attempt to deal with a musician whose work I don't feel strongly about. I do know that I would have been in serious trouble if I had attempted an authoritarian pose in the studio, but I saw my primary role as that of a catalytic agent, providing optimum conditions for the expression of his creativity, and that attitude has worked out pretty well for me ever since. This involves a basic premise I suspect some producers have never come to understand, that in jazz (maybe not everywhere, but certainly in jazz) the artist is what it's all about. His music and personality are what you are trying to express, not your own, that each one you work with may call for a different approach, a separate working relationship. Flexibility is far more valuable to a producer than a specific personal style.

Being aware of the circumstances of Monk's early career made it easy enough for me to understand that he might well be carrying a very large chip on his shoulder and easily get rather testy and belligerent during a session. Among the lessons this should teach a young producer is: If the artist in the studio is feeling a draft, for whatever reason, that's your problem rather than his; you're supposed to remember that your primary goal is to produce the best possible record.

There is of course a corollary to that lesson, also Monk-taught: don't roll over and play dead either. The scheduled initial session for our fourth album, a solo date, never took place because he arrived at the studio nearly an hour and a half late (following a series of "he's on his way" phone calls). More in anger than in sorrow, I delivered a fairly pompous lecture about my need to respect myself and informing him that, while I'd accept a half-hour lateness as close enough for jazz (a timeframe I've held to ever since), he needn't bother to come any later than that because I would have left. We set a new date; I arrived about fifteen minutes early; and there in the control room sat Thelonious, waiting for me. He gave me that huge slow smile of his and asked, very quietly: "What kept you?" It was an extremely successful session.

Life with Monk was not often very relaxed but once I had—with his help—gotten through my apprenticeship and become a well-schooled professional, it was a lot less tense. Having survived his basic training, having become aware that severe crises, last-minute major adjustments, and personality clashes are the routine facts of recording life, I could never be frightened by any musician or shaken up by any in-studio problem. I like to think that my overall attitude and philosophy is fundamentally a product of my own instincts, intellect, and taste. But that is certainly part of what Sonny Rollins meant by choosing the term "guru" rather than simply "teacher"—much of Monk's special magic lay in the fact that you gain from him whatever you most needed to enhance what was already at least potentially there. Sonny, for example, clearly found reinforcement in his own belief in the importance of humor in his music. And in the course of developing from a young player often accused of harsh and unemotional tone into a mature master of the art of balladry, he surely had absorbed a basic Monk message on how to add beauty and lyricism without losing toughness.

In a 1960 *Down Beat* article in which Coltrane refers to the time he spent with Thelonious, there is an extremely appropriate reference to Monk's uniquely oblique way of knowledge without actually appearing to instruct. "I felt I learned from him—through the senses, theoretically, technically. I would talk to Monk about musical problems, and he would sit at the piano and show me the answers just by playing them. I could watch him play and find out the things I wanted to know. Also, I could see a lot of things that I didn't know about at all." . . .[1]

My last words with Monk came about two years before his death. While on a trip to New York, I had a sudden impulse to telephone him; the conversation ran approximately like this:

"Thelonious, are you touching the piano at all these days?"

"No, I'm not."

"Do you want to get back to playing?"

"No, I don't."

"I'm only in town for a few days; would you like me to come and visit, talk about the old days?"

"No, I wouldn't."

When I repeated this to Barry Harris, the pianist who was much closer to him than anyone else in the last years, he said: "You're lucky. You got complete sentences. With most people he just says, 'No.'"

If I were to make a guess, I'd conclude that he may just have worn down and stopped caring, that the roller-coaster aspects of being a performing artist in our times had finally taken its toll. From an early '60s peak that even saw his picture on the cover of *Time* magazine, this once-obscure pianist had slid back towards obscurity. To someone who had never really cared all that much about communicating with the public, it couldn't have seemed worth the effort to start climbing again. Towards the end he reportedly had ignored or rejected some very fancy offers from would-be promoters of comeback concerts. I hope those reports are accurate; I would like to think that he simply felt he had said all he cared to say to any of us.

The legacy he left remains very much in evidence: his recordings and compositions, the work of those he influenced in various ways. He taught quite a

1. "Coltrane on Coltrane," *Down Beat*, September 29, 1960, pp. 26–27. *Ed.*

few people, directly or indirectly, some very important lessons: to play the way you feel you have to, to be intolerant of musical (and other) conventions and dogma, not to compromise—admonitions that are, for most of us, impossible to follow completely. But even to add a little of his approach to your music or life can be very valuable. Thelonious Monk was a very unusual human being and extremely good at what he did. I'm glad that I was able to know him and work with him.

Reflections on Monk

36. *Thelonious Monk: Gothic Provincial*

Perhaps more than any other jazz musician or composer, Thelonious Monk has been the inspiration for cerebral expositions drawing on ideas and material far removed from traditional discourse about music. The essay by Gerald Early from which this excerpt was taken is about two distinct themes: being a black male in America and losing the creative edge in old age, specifically as exemplified by the lives and music of Charles Mingus, Sonny Stitt, and Thelonious Monk.[1] He critically examines the commonly stated notion that Monk displayed childlike behavior that commentators have used to explain his eccentricities. Although not wishing to reduce Monk's personality to social or racial factors, Early notes that there are parallels between

1. In the introduction to the original essay, he states: "It was nearly unbearable to hear about the decline of Mingus and Monk and the faltering of Stitt in their later years. And their deaths were untimely and tragic not only because they meant the closing of the book on a period of great music and the passing from earth of a type of masculine vitality not bound to resurge any time soon, but also, and most important, because these men died without having the luxury of ceasing to work. They saw their genius stretched to the point of softness and serene decay; they were not able to die secure in what they had accomplished or in the recognition of that accomplishment. They will always be the old men who lost it" (p. 24).

the manner in which Monk is portrayed and the manner in which the black male has been described in America. Concerning Monk's creativity, he sees a steady decline since the first Blue Note recordings in the late 1940s and early 1950s. Finally, Early characterizes Monk's personality as "gothic provincialism," or a dark, limited view of the world, a defense mechanism used to survive in mainstream America. Gerald Early has written extensively on African-American culture, including books on Motown, Muhammad Ali, and American culture in general. He teaches English and African-American Studies at Washington University in St. Louis, Missouri.

Excerpt from "The Passing of Jazz's Old Guard: Remembering Charles Mingus, Thelonious Monk, and Sonny Stitt," by Gerald Early, originally published in *The Kenyon Review*, Vol. 7, No. 2, Spring 1985, pp. 21–36. Used by permission of Gerald Early.

When I heard on February 17, 1982, that Thelonious Monk, the great bebop pianist, had died of a stroke, I felt not only saddened but, oddly enough, relieved. It had seemed, for such a long time before his death (excluding the few years of artistic silence that preceded it), that Monk had become tiresome. How many times could one stand to hear him play "Straight, No Chaser," "Ruby, My Dear," or "'Round Midnight?" For so many years, actually since the late forties when Monk recorded his first two albums for Blue Note, nothing really new emerged from the Monkian imagination. The fifties saw Monk refine and distill his art, perfecting his expression in an extraordinary canon of albums for Prestige and Riverside ranging from solo piano versions of Tin Pan Alley stuff to big band arrangements of his own compositions. The arrival of the sixties was the arrival of Monk: a cover story in the February 28, 1964, issue of *Time* magazine and a lucrative contract with Columbia records. Then Monk proceeded to commit the terrifying mistake that has beset so many great artists, from Hemingway to George Cukor: he repeated himself; he tried to recapture the moment of his greatest triumphs and he failed. Some of the Columbia records were quite good; most were merely competent; and many were, finally, boring, heartbreakingly so. The slow decline, the quaint staleness began to pervade his music, and his most aware fans realized that the "put-on" had finally and most devastatingly fooled the confidence man himself. Monk's music had been reduced from the controversy of uncompromised artistic engagement to the slouch of bedeviled laziness.

I suspect that Amiri Baraka (LeRoi Jones) knew that Monk would cease to be vital once he gained wide acceptance, and so Baraka wrote the essay called

"Recent Monk" which appeared in *Down Beat* in 1963, an essay which said in one breath that success wouldn't spoil T. S. Monk, while saying in another breath, "say that it ain't so, Thelonious, that you sold out to the moguls on the hill."[2]

But success did spoil Monk in a way that it spoils, destroys really, a fair number of black men in this country. The very persona that Monk encased himself in as the opaque, weird, high priest of the zombies in the forties, a persona so unacceptable to mainstream America then, became quite acceptable in the sixties. What initially made Monk just another outcast black jazzman eventually rendered him attractive and interesting, cute even, to, as Baraka put it, "a pretty good swath of that part of the American population called 'knowledgeable.'" Once Monk was accepted, he was trapped in the image of what made him an "interesting" black man to the white majority. This sort of thing happens very often to many performing black men: Richard Pryor and Muhammed Ali are two recent examples. When Monk was trapped in the image, he was no longer able to grow as an artist. Indeed, Monk, to the popular, simplifying mind, had even ceased to be a man; he had become an innocent primitive. Nat Hentoff, a usually very perceptive jazz critic, in an essay in his book, *The Jazz Life*, referred to Monk as a "child," and the *Time* article made it clear that Monk, after the death of his doting and overprotective mother, had simply transferred his allegiance and his need to be mothered to his doting and overprotective wife.[3] Underneath all of this was the fairly hoary thesis that Monk was the product of black matriarchs and maybe even a white one, if one is to consider Monk's friendship with the Baroness Nica de Koenigswarter (for whom Monk wrote a lovely tune called "Pannonica").

If Monk had become, by the sixties, the noble innocent, then he was simply reenacting a sort of Nigger Jim-Queequeg role for the larger white public. It is quite in keeping that this black man-child, neurotic and mother-dominated, should have an exterior which white people found frightening. Perhaps it is because the appearance is so frightening that the figure has to be reduced: the Southern racist calls him a "boy," the Northern liberal, a "child." Nat Hentoff describes the incident which led to Monk's temporary stay in an insane asylum:

> . . . in spring of 1959, he was booked for a week at Boston's Storyville. He had been up for some three days and nights without sleep. When he arrived, he

2. Jones's essay was actually titled "The Acceptance of Monk." It has been reprinted on p. 163. *Ed.*
3. Nat Hentoff, *The Jazz Life* (New York: Dial Press, 1961).

> came to the desk of the Copley Square Hotel, where Storyville was then located, with a glass of liquor in his hand after having flitted around the lobby rather disconcertedly, examining the walls. He was refused a room, and at first also declined to accompany his sidemen to the Hotel Bostonian where they were staying. At about ten o'clock, he finally went on stand. The room was nearly full of expectant but patient admirers. He played two numbers . . . and then sat motionless at the piano for what seemed like half an hour. His bewildered sidemen had left the stand after about eight minutes.
>
> Monk began wandering around the club, obviously disturbed at not having a hotel room. He finally registered at the Bostonian, didn't like the room, and left. He tried the Statler, was refused there, and took a cab to the airport with the idea of going home, collecting his wife, Nellie, and taking a room with her for the rest of the week. By that time of night planes were no longer running, and he was picked up by a state trooper to whom he would not or could not communicate. Monk later did reveal who he was, but it was too late, and he was transported to Grafton State Hospital near Worcester for observation.[4]

The passage seems to abstract the entire Monkian personality: the brooding, sullen demeanor, the dependency on his mothering wife, the inability to communicate through language. I feel deeply ambivalent about the entire episode. There is little reason to doubt the accuracy of Hentoff's account; he was a very close friend of Monk and probably got this account from both Monk and his wife. To be sure, there is no denying the fact that Monk was emotionally disturbed, at least temporarily so.

I do not wish to sound like the overly sensitive minority person, but I believe that one cannot overemphasize the fact that Monk was committed to a mental institution mostly because he was a black man who refused to cooperate with authorities. Monk was surely not arrested because he acted like a child. To speak of the black male personality as being childlike—any black male's personality—is merely to describe euphemistically what white society perceives as the black male's psychopathology. Hentoff quotes jazz critic Paul Bacon as saying in reference to Monk that "to become an adult it's necessary to make a lot of concessions." There is a certain amount of truth in this assertion, but it fails to examine the complex depth of cultural resonance in precisely what it means to call a black man a child or the meaning of any black male's refusal to make "concessions." Surely, any half-thinking black male realizes it is only as an adult that the act of refusing to make concessions has

4. Ibid., pp. 190–191.

any meaning beyond merely asserting the ego, in that such an act acquires a political aspect. Anyone who knows the history of the black male in America—the constant attempt by white society to reduce and restrict his impulses and personality, to make him submissive and tractable—anyone who knows how much black males hated this insultingly familiar diminution would realize that Monk, whatever his emotional disorders, was no child.

I would not even try to explain the whole of Monk's personality in racial terms for he is much too complex a human being for that. But part of the manifestation of his psyche was largely an attempt to personify and symbolize, albeit subconsciously, the very unknowable-ness of the black male personality. Monk's actions as a public performer were a precise equivalent, a precise cognate for the function of slang or of the X in a Black Muslim's name. For so long had the black male been unrecognized—and I believe bebop symbolized this—that he chose, in response to years of invisibility, to be unrecognizable. In short, Monk is locked up not because he is a child but because he is a threatening, inscrutable black adult. The real ambiguity in role-playing here is the inability of many observers to understand that Monk's willful and somewhat deranged dependency is not synonymous with childishness. It is more closely akin to a distraughtly played game of deception.

It is in the great racial overtones of this story that one finds the true source, the touchstone, of Monk's personality: his gothic provincialism. One is reminded, when thinking of Monk, of those Poe heroes, so tortured yet so frightfully self-absorbed. That gothic provincialism had allowed Monk to survive and to operate in a white-dominated society.

Monk was born in the South but was raised in New York City and, indeed, lived there all his life. He spent his entire life in practically the same neighborhood, almost on the same block. (That sort of insulation is common with poor urban blacks. I remember working with some tough black kids for a social service agency and discovering that few of them knew how to get downtown. They had never been there!) He seemed to have little inclination to do anything but play the piano and compose, and he wrote many of his best pieces while he was still a very young man. His style of playing may have developed as an act of self-defense as much as for any other reason. He was very familiar with Art Tatum, whom he called "the greatest piano player I ever heard," and the recently deceased Earl Hines, and once hearing these men he realized that there was no need or even possibility of going the virtuoso route. One jazz critic called Monk's playing "fey" but, at times, it almost seems (to me) cowering in its effort to avoid being in any way "artistic."

When his music went unheard and unaccepted, Monk simply clammed up and waited. This was, in a sense, a very brave thing to do. It was, moreover, not only a sign of the depth of his determination but also of the intensity of his provincialism. While waiting, he showed little interest in doing anything else or in approaching anything differently. The cloistered environment of the black in the inner city made that kind of attitude possible. It is difficult to know whether this is lassitude or inner strength. The bourgeoisie have decided that if a poor boy succeeds, then it is inner strength; if he does not, then it is lassitude.

In Monk's case, we have a combination of both. Monk was surely a very great piano player in his way and a profoundly brilliant composer, but the music which was lauded by musicians and fans as being so rife with possibilities finally became quite narrow and restricting, just as Monk's gothic provincialism proved to be a source of tenacious inspiration and, eventually, the pathway to a kind of amazingly busy sloth. The problem lies in the fact that Monk never found a proper avenue for his musical expression. Many thought that Monk was a bluesman, pure and simple, and, to be sure, he was. Yet the essence of his music, where it was really tending, was toward the show tunes and songs of a W. C. Handy, a Will Marion Cook, and a Fats Waller. Most of Monk's music cries out for lyrics, and in another age his music would have been songs with lyrics sung from a stage. By the mid-sixties, Monk's days as a composer of new material and as a stylistic innovator on the piano were over. At this point, Cecil Taylor of the new school and Duke Ellington of the old school were much more bracing to listen to, both as pianists and composers. But the body of material that Monk wrote could have been mined in other ways. What if Monk had hired a lyricist to pen words to his songs? What if someone could have constructed a book around Monk's tunes and created a musical? It is an idea that might yet be realized but without Monk guiding and supervising such a project, it will be fairly much an empty exercise in commercializing the art of a heavyweight. But when I speak of making real songs from Monk's material, I do not mean to commercialize it but rather to extend further the aesthetic content, to *lyricize* formally a music already rich in lyricism.

It is often said that Monk was ahead of his time but he really was not. His music was a distillation and recapitulation of all the Afro-American *songwriters* before him. Only a man of considerable genius could have realized how much his cultural past was filled with the sounds of singing and could have exploited this realization with such unassuming deftness and quiet profundity.

37. *Master of Space*

Usually music is accompanied by words or other programmatic devices to convey extramusical associations or meaning, but with Monk this does not seem to be necessary. Consider the following titles of recent articles that take Monk as their point of departure: "The Beauty of Building, Dwelling and Monk: Aesthetics, Religion and the Architectural Qualities of Jazz" or "Improvisation, Individuation and Immanence: Thelonious Monk."[1] These are intriguing topics, regardless of whether or not they deliver what they suggest. It is along these lines that Gene Santoro draws an unusual set of far-flung yet related connections between Monk's music, postwar suburbia, John Cage, physics, and Sun Ra. The question of musical and physical space is central to the discussion, as is the question of humor, irony, and satire. Santoro, a music critic for *The Nation* and regular contributor to numerous other magazines and journals, has had his essays published in several books, the most recent being *Stir it Up: Musical Mixes from Roots to Jazz,* a remarkable collection covering important musical figures drawn from a wide range of musical styles.

This article originally appeared as "Master of Space," by Gene Santoro in *The Nation,* Vol. 258, No. 14, pp. 498–500. It also appeared in *Stir It Up: Musical Mixes from Roots to Jazz* (New York: Oxford) in 1997. Reprinted with permission from *The Nation* © 1994 and Gene Santoro.

Like a motif, the scene recurs during the course of *Straight No Chaser*—one of the most compelling, poignant, and informative films ever made about a jazz musician. Thelonious Sphere Monk, wearing some kind of outré hat as always, gets up off his piano stool and begins to spin around, like a kid playing the old schoolyard game "I'm Busy Getting Dizzy." He does this for indeterminate, variable lengths of time. Meanwhile, his quartet carries on, pianoless but led by his twirling figure. The rhythms of his spins have no necessary or

1. Steven Richter, "The Beauty of Building, Dwelling and Monk: Aesthetics, Religion and the Architectural Qualities of Jazz," *African American Review,* Vol. 29, No. 2 (Summer 1995), pp. 259–69, and H. J. Roberts, "Improvisation, Individuation, and Immanence: Thelonious Monk," *Black Sacred Music,* Vol. 3, No. 2 (1989), pp. 50–56.

apparent correlation with the rhythms of the music being played. And yet it's clear that to Monk, at least, some deep syntax of the beat is what's driving him round and round.

Meet Thelonious Monk, Master of Space.

Over the last few years, Monk has come increasingly into his own again, as reissues of his music have come tumbling out. His reputation as a composer has grown, and more and more jazzers have scrambled to record versions of his classic tunes. So it's worth remembering that Monk, whether as a composer or as a player had no easy time of it for much of his performing life, especially in his earlier days. What he wrote, like his highly eccentric piano attack, was considered by kindlier critics to be at best refreshingly primitive, and by nastier types to be an oddball if not unfathomable byway along jazz's main superhighway of historical development. (Much later, after he'd been accepted into the jazz pantheon, folks complained that he and his touring quartet just played the same pieces over and over again. Sometimes you just can't win.)

His contemporaries in the 1940s and 1950s were right to be confused by Monk—although they weren't right, by and large, about why. (The exceptions—which, according to Monk's longtime producer Orrin Keepnews, included Coleman Hawkins, Duke Ellington, Nat King Cole—were musically big enough themselves to have room for the not immediately explicable.) Monk's tunes and improvising attack both differ drastically from those of his bebopper peers like Charlie Parker and Bud Powell.

It's a difference that doesn't require a degree in musicology to hear. As the late jazz historian Martin Williams put it, in his influential essay on Monk included in *The Jazz Tradition*: "Perhaps the highest tribute I have ever heard paid to Monk's music was offered by a novice who said, after first hearing recordings by Bud Powell, Parker, and Monk, 'Monk seems to finish things, to get them all said. I feel satisfied and sort of full when one of his things is over.'"[2]

The key reason for this is Monk's veering and gyring and utterly unique sense of rhythm. As Williams also pointed out, "In all the stylistic developments of jazz a capacity for rhythmic growth has been fundamental."

Let's over-schematize history's inevitable slips and slides, glitches and sidesteps and tentative probes to make the point clearer. Early New Orleans jazz was largely organized around its inheritance from marching bands, the two-beat bar. (So were Harlem's stride piano stylings, which derived from ragtime's similar beat.) With its increased emphasis on a different format for dancing—the ragtime period's cakewalk doesn't have much in common with

2. Williams' chapter is reprinted on p. 210. *Ed.*

the foxtrot, rumba, or lindy—the Swing Era smoothed those somewhat herky-jerky two-beat measures out to a more easily flowing four-beat bar. Bebop, rhythmically as well as harmonically, upped the ante: eighth notes became the common currency of rifts and solos, with triplets and dotted eighths appearing as frequent spikes to break up the rhythmic flow, prevent it from becoming too mechanical—although in the hands of the many Little Birds, it often did.

Monk's sense of rhythm was like no one else's, in his writing or his execution. Partly that's due to his roots, which ran deep in Harlem stride piano, filtered through later influences like the spare, crisp keyboard work of Count Basie. It was from these influences that Monk began to develop what would become one key aspect of his sonic signature: the jagged, floating spaces that erupt and spread between his angular phrases and crushed chords. It was almost as if his notion of harmonic space (especially his favorite intervals, the flatted seconds and ninths) was collapsing into ever tinier increments, while the space between runs and even individual note choices was becoming ever more unpredictable. In that sense, listening to Monk's music is like having the burgeoning notion of entropy in the universe enacted in sound.

So you could say that space defined Monk, especially vis-a-vis his bebop contemporaries. Like Miles Davis, Monk was grouped with the beboppers but was not really of them. They frantically sought to overpower space with sound, to filigree it with a latticework of harmonically structured ideas—an attempt to control the inevitable. Monk and Miles, on the other hand, both sought to incorporate space into the essence of what they did. Space created relief, texture, definition—even humor. This discovery parallels the moment when physicists and chemists realized that space was one of life's essences, that each molecular building-block (and whatever results from their bonding) is made up far more of space than it is of the mass and particles that space defines.

As John Litweiler puts in his invaluable book *The Freedom Principle*, "This tension of space and sound is an ancient mystery of the spirit in solitude, a mystery that was always immediate to Monk."[3] Now Monk, introspective as he and his music no doubt were and are, may have often been oblivious to the outside world's most mundane demands. One of the touching scenes in *Straight No Chaser* comes when his wife Nellie is trying to get him dressed, and one of the funniest is when an officious bellboy tries to take his order for dinner, with Monk steadfastly refusing to yield what he wants to the limits of the hotel's menu. But even if he didn't always seem aware of the reality of

3. John Litweiler, *The Freedom Principle* (New York: Quill, 1984), p. 19. *Ed.*

his immediate surroundings, Monk's musical vision saw through the accidents of day-to-day life and projected a penetrating topography of the postwar world.

"Space is the place," as Sun Ra, a contemporary of Monk's (one of the few far-out enough in his own terms to seriously grasp what Monk was up to), and his Arkestra used to chant on their way to and from the stage. And indeed, in the twentieth century, the concept of space in music, especially in American music, became an idea and technique whose importance would be hard to overestimate. In that sense, Monk was tapping into a mental shift that was occurring across especially the post-World War II American musical landscape regardless of stylistic faultlines.

Space in America was changing dramatically. Once the soldiers came home in 1945, suburban sprawl began in earnest. Cities, for millennia the hubs of civilization, gradually began to erode, not just in physical terms but in more intangible ones. Power flowed out from urban to suburban areas, following the flow of money. People no longer lived where they worked, where they shopped, where they sent their kids to school. The pace of life itself, which had been picking up relentlessly since the Roaring 20s, accelerated yet again. Ironically, that undercut one of the main points of suburbia, which was to regularize life, to use the larger sense of individual space that suburbs could offer and cities couldn't in order to make life safe and predictable.

It was an idea that, not surprisingly, many of America's best artists reacted against at the time, implicitly or explicitly. Monk was among them. All it takes is one hearing for any listener to realize that Monk's music rides the irony and accumulated knowledge that has traditionally been the mark of the urban sophisticate.

Like all his most important contemporaries, Monk had clearly listened to all kinds of music, including classical music from both the U.S. and Europe. Jazzers from at least Gershwin and Ellington onward had been lured and fascinated by the shimmering, suggestive harmonies of Impressionists like Debussy. But there are few overt signs of a direct classical influence on Monk's work. What there is, however, is the sense of a confluence, a feeling that often happens during the evolution of a culture at key points: that more than one person or group is confronting a particular problem from different angles, and that their ideas, however couched in their individual idioms, have an overlapping set of concerns.

Thus it is with Monk and his American cousins in the barbaric yawp, composers like Harry Partch and Henry Cowell and, of course, John Cage. Among Cage's most famous works is *4′ 33″*, which amounts to a challenge to the audience as well as to notions of composition itself. Basically, for slightly over four minutes of silence, listeners are forced to contemplate the meaning of the space that surrounds sound. In the process, they come to understand that sound is like the old pictorial conundrums cited by art historians like E. H. Gombrich that outline either a duck or a bunny depending on which way you look at them. In short, silence and sound are two sides of the same coin, mutually defining terms.

Now, dynamics are no news in music, and dynamics are, from one angle, simply relative indexes of sound and silence. But the absolute nature of Cage's I Ching-inspired experiment revealed some other aspects to the relationship. What if, for instance, you became fascinated with the rhythm of your own pulse during the piece? Or were gradually alerted to the random pockets of noise that burst into our lives in more or less erratic ways during a typical day simply because there was no other dominant noise (or music) to mask it? In that way, listening to Cage becomes a reflection on the random nature of the universe and its building blocks, the intrusive and affective nature of creation and observation itself—a kind of representation of Heisenberg's uncertainty principle at work.

Like Cage's, the jagged humor of Monk's musical concept reflects a playful but informed sense of just how chance becomes irony—the irony of, say, the unexpected, the uncertain, the unpredictable. (The unpredictable is, of course, one of the key ingredients of jazz at its best anyway.) In his music Monk, like Cage, was building implicit social satires that undercut the post-war American Dream via his prickly eccentricities—especially his playful, satiric concept of space.

The Music

Jazz analysis, at least the musicological species, remains a multifaceted and loosely structured area of study, with much borrowing of ill-fitting analytical and theoretical tools and concepts. Monk's music has consequently not fared well in analysis, or for that matter, simple transcription, since his compositions never did fit the conventional melody-and-chord-changes method of notation used by the majority of jazz fake books. The voicings and accompanying figures were simply too integral to each piece to be omitted in transcription, and the means by which Monk employed these musical ideas was far beyond orthodox thinking.

Ran Blake's 1982 article in *Keyboard,* later reworked and published in *The Wire,* was the first purely descriptive analysis of the salient features of Monk's music. It was followed by Lawrence Koch's 1983 review of Monk's compositional techniques, a good summary of musical techniques laid out in unadorned and essentially non-evaluative terms.[1] Peter Niklas Wilson's article for *Jazzforschung* in 1987 attempted to define the "Monkish influence," including notions about musical cells, reduction, and sound

1. Lawrence Koch, "Thelonious Monk: Compositional Techniques," *Annual Review of Jazz Studies,* Vol. 2, pp.67–80. Koch's analysis provides a good starting point for an inventory of ideas and techniques used by Monk in his compositions. Similarly, "Monk Composition" by Phillippe Baudoin in *Le Jazzophone,* Vol. 13 (1982), catalogues Monk's themes.

production.[2] The 1990s saw more ambitious efforts, with discussions of motivic cells, form, and theoretical notions of rhythm, but at the turn of the twenty-first century, there were still no book-length studies of Monk's music, other than a few largely inaccessible dissertations.[3]

Does Monk's music elude meaningful musical analysis? Certainly there is enough to talk about, but it appears difficult to apply analytical terms to his music. Verbal descriptions relying on metaphor and imagery have often been more successful in conveying Monk's musical ideas. Subtleties in rhythm and sound production are never quite captured through analytical tools, especially with Monk's piano playing. In fact, musicological discussions of timbre, or the production of sound, suffer from a decided lack of coordination between theoretical notions and psychoacoustical phenomena. A telling anecdote about Monk's sound is recalled by Bill Crow, who describes meeting Monk at a rehearsal:

> I told Monk that some of his intervals surprised me. They would sound unusual, but when I checked them out, they were ordinary fifths, sixths, sevenths. It was his touch that made them sound different. He nodded and said, "It can't be any new note. When you look at the keyboard, all the notes are there already. But if you mean a note enough, it will sound different. You got to pick the notes you really mean!"[4]

Add to this that Monk was a music theory autodidact and the problem of analysis compounds itself. To recall his telling remark as quoted by Grover Sales: "Music theory? Well, when I was a kid, I only knew I wanted to make it better."[5]

2. "Versuch über das 'Monkische': Zur musikalischen Ästhetik Thelonious Sphere Monks und ihrem posthumen Weiterwirken," *Jazzforschung/Jazz Research,* Vol. 19 (1987), pp. 41–59.
3. See, for example, James Kurzdorfer, "Outrageous Clusters: Dissonant Semitonal Cells in the Music of Thelonious Monk," *Annual Review of Jazz Studies,* Vol. 8 (1996), pp. 181–201; and Mark Haywood, "Rhythmic Readings of Thelonious Monk," *Annual Review of Jazz Studies,* Vol. 7 (1994–1995), pp. 25–45. As evidence of the peculiarities of the bibliographic universe, a little-known and largely inaccessible (in the sense of getting it in hand) master's thesis proves to be one of the clearest analyses of Monk's music: Laila Rose Kteily-O'Sullivan's "Klangfarben, Rhythmic Displacement, and Economy of Means: A Theoretical Study of the Works of Thelonious Monk," Master's thesis, University of North Texas, 1990.
4. Bill Crow, *From Birdland to Broadway* (New York: Oxford, 1992), p. 148.
5. See the article by Grover Sales reprinted here on p. 100.

38. *The Monk Piano Style*

Ran Blake is one of those rare individuals who has been able to successfully combine performance, scholarship, and administration into one career. He has performed and recorded extensively as a jazz pianist, and his interpretations of Monk's compositions rank among the best; he wrote the entry on Monk for the *New Grove Dictionary of Jazz,* the first authoritative reference source on jazz to venture into musical-analytical territory; and he is chair of Contemporary Improvisation at the New England Conservatory of Music. This article was originally published for a 1982 memorial issue on Monk for *Keyboard Magazine,* and later revised for *The Wire;* it has been slightly edited for this reprint. Blake presents a brief but lucid analytical tour of the features of Monk's composing and piano playing, with discussions of his accompaniment, recomposition, use of rhythm and harmony, and his more or less improvised "liquid compositions." Noteworthy is an analytical description and transcription of the much-discussed "Bags' Groove" solo, alluded to in several other articles in this reader.[1]

This article first appeared as "The Monk Piano Style," by Ran Blake in *Keyboard Magazine,* July 1982, pp. 26–32. It has been slightly edited for this reprint. The musical transcriptions were done by Jim Aikin. It also appeared in a reworked form in *The Wire Magazine,* December 1984. Reprinted with permission of Ran Blake and *Keyboard Magazine,* July 1982, All Rights Reserved.

Giants abound in the history of American improvised piano, which is studded with the talents of innovators and consolidators. In addition to such acknowledged masters as Jelly Roll Morton, Fats Waller, Earl Hines, and, of course, Art Tatum, I would include Count Basie for his rhythmic drive and sparseness, Bill Evans for his highly innovative linear improvisations, and dozens of other vitally important figures.

But I know of no pianist as personal as Thelonious Monk. As with Ben Webster's sax playing and Billie Holiday's singing, there is never any doubt who is at the keyboard. It may be a delayed attack on a chord, a cluster that

1. Hodeir's discussion of the "Bags' Groove" solo in "Monk or The Misunderstanding," reprinted on p. 118, is the most prominent example.

pounces like a tornado, or a jagged snippet that asserts itself under a number of guises. Monk's methods of reworking the raw material of a tune are unlike anybody else's.

Pianists and other musicians can gain a great deal by studying and considering Monk's sense of melodic connections between chords when comping behind a soloist, his use of the melody of a composition as the *cantus firmus* to be referred to constantly during a solo in place of the more common practice of creating new melodies that outline chord changes, and above all, his magnificent use of space. These are a few of the important elements of Thelonious Monk's piano style. His approach to the keyboard was a radical departure from what had gone before, and he unquestionably qualifies as one of the great jazz innovators, though fewer people were prepared to adopt the Monk vocabulary than learned and repeated Charlie Parker's virtuoso licks. In addition, Monk's respect for tradition, especially the strangely refracted blues feeling that pervades much of his work, qualifies him as consolidator of what had gone before. Some musicians have discarded the old to arrive at the new, while others have made their main contribution by distilling and perfecting the contributions of others. Monk did both.

Monk's solos are superb examples of what I call "liquid composition." He always seemed to be aware, when playing a solo, of where he had been and where he was going, and he almost never resorted to spinning out lead lines merely to be filling space. When he felt that he had nothing to say,Monk was quite willing to let the space remain empty. . . .

Jazz writer Whitney Balliett offers another perspective: "His [Monk's] improvisations were molten Monk compositions, and his compositions were frozen Monk improvisations."[2] This is an important perception, emphasizing the essential unity of everything Monk did. But it is also true that his compositions were concise, tightly structured gems, in which to alter one note would be to change the shape of the whole. His solos were more laconic and often more deeply emotional, though there are certainly tunes like "'Round Midnight" and "Crepuscule with Nellie" that showed Monk's lyrical side, while solos like the superb blues "Bags' Groove," which will be discussed in more detail below, are as tightly constructed and brilliantly developed as any composition.

Since Monk had a habit of re-recording compositions he had written and recorded years before, it is sometimes possible to see the principles of economy in his composition at work. In the 1951 Blue Note version of "Criss

2. Balliett's article has been reprinted on p. 227. *Ed.*

Cross," for example, Monk presents the theme completely, with a repeating eight-bar A section, an eight-bar B section, and a reprise of the A section. But in the early 1960s Columbia version of the same tune, he omits the last two bars of the bridge, transforming the structure drastically. Since the B section contains a three-bar phrase that is repeated, followed by a two-bar tag phrase, omitting the tag phrase emphasizes the asymmetry of the three-bar phrases and gives the return of the A section an unexpected jump.

There are many aspects of Monk's music that merit discussion. I'd like to talk about his compositions, his rhythmic and harmonic ingenuity, and his improvisations, and also give examples of his pianistic technique and his roots in the Harlem stride piano tradition in which he grew up.

Let's start with technique. How often have you heard musicians say, "Monk writes good tunes, but he can't play the piano"? This is a common misconception, but his recordings frequently contain short keyboard passages that are actually a great deal harder to play than they sound. Consider his solo piano recording of "Eronel" (ex. 38-1).[3] At the beginning of the first solo chorus, and again at the beginning of the second, he plays a trill with the thumb and index finger of his right hand while his fourth and fifth fingers articulate the accented melody notes. The left hand is also playing some low chords, so there is no question that the right hand is doing both parts. This feat of pianism certainly merits the term 'virtuosity,' and a little listening is enough to detect other instances of similar technical precision.

To those who aren't familiar with jazz keyboard work in general, Monk often sounds clumsy or deficient in technique because of his predilection for split notes (minor or major seconds played simultaneously as though they were a single note). This is a standard jazz technique, used to provide variety of articulation in a line, but it's true that Monk used more split notes than almost any other jazz pianist. When we look at *how* he uses them, however, we find that they were clearly intentional, and not the result of sloppy fingering. The seventh chorus of "Bag's Groove," for example, is built entirely on the idea of hitting a minor second and then letting one of the two keys up. Elsewhere, as in "Hornin' In," Monk composes a unison line for the horns and then doubles it on the keyboard in major seconds, playing both the horn notes and the notes above them.

Several piano players, notably Earl Hines and Bud Powell, borrowed the kind of lines played by horn players (Louis Armstrong and other trumpeters in the case of Hines, and Charlie Parker in the case of Powell) and adapted

3. Recorded on June 7, 1954 and originally released on Vogue 500104. *Ed.*

38-1 Two excerpts from "Eronel." Copyright © 1962 (renewed 1990) Thelonious Music Corp.

them to the keyboard. But Monk's idiom was both intensely personal and intensely *pianistic*. It's hard to imagine much of his music being conceived for or executed on any other instrument than the piano. You can sometimes hear the horn players he worked with struggling to play his music, because it's *not* horn music. And in learning Monk tunes for a memorial concert we did recently, I was amazed to find how well they fit under my fingers.

We can also discover, once in a great while, Monk acknowledging his debt to stride piano. In his solo in "Thelonious," (ex. 38-2),[4] for example, after a first chorus that consists mostly of a high B-flat octave played over and over, Monk abruptly launches into a stride statement of the changes, with a typically laconic Monk phrase in the right hand. With the possible exception of the left-hand chord on the fourth beat of bar 8 of the example, which doesn't

4. Recorded on October 15, 1947 and first released on Blue Note BN 542. *Ed.*

38-2 A portion of Monk's solo on "Thelonious." Copyright © 1965 (renewed 1993) Thelonious Music Corp.

seem to fit with the C-flat 7 harmony of the third beat, there is certainly nothing in this passage that could be called sloppy or technically deficient.

Turning to Monk the composer, we find different tunes revealing different facets of his thinking. His well-known predilection for whole-tone scales, and their associated flat-5th and sharp-5th chords, was a way of organizing pitch material that, carried to its logical conclusion, allowed him to develop a high degree of harmonic ambiguity while retaining the familiar jazz cycle-of-fifths feel. In other words, since there are only two whole-tone scales, it's possible to write music that sounds as though it is following a cycling chord progression by merely shifting back and forth from one scale to the other, without clarifying where the roots of the chords are.

A clear example of this is seen in "Hornin In" (ex. 38-3),[5] a rarely played Monk composition and one I believe he only recorded once. The transcription shows the entire orchestration (except for drums) of the first run-through of the 'A' section. What is remarkable about this tune is that until the cadence arrives in bar 7 there is nothing to tell the listener what key the tune is in. The familiar II-V progressions are absent (though when bar 7 arrives, we can look back and see that the tenor was playing the 3rd of II in bar 5 and the 7th of a V in bar 6). Instead, Monk uses the E-flat whole-tone scale for the first two bars, then dodges away to the other (outlined by the E and B-flat in

5. Recorded on May 30, 1952 and first released on Blue Note BN 1603. *Ed.*

38-3 Ensemble orchestration of the 'A' section of "Hornin' In." Copyright © 1978 Thelonious Music Corp.

bar 3). Bars 3 and 4 especially are in a twilight zone at the border of tonality; the tenor implying some sort of harmonic movement, but we are unable to say what the chords would be.

For the ears of musicians who were steeped in the swift melodies of Bird and the blues of Mahalia Jackson in the early '50s, this was entirely new, even shocking. While composers working in the European concert music tradition had been experimenting with diffuse tonality or even atonality for several decades, jazz had remained a firmly tonal music. Along with a few other pioneers like Duke Ellington and Billy Strayhorn, Lennie Tristano, Richard Twardzik, and George Russell, Monk was responsible for loosening the grip of tonality and thus paving the way for the later free jazz experiments of Ornette Coleman and others.

In the mid-'50s, having severed his connections with Blue Note Records and later Prestige Records, Monk began recording with the sympathetic support of Orrin Keepnews of Riverside Records. In this fertile period he composed three of his finest compositions, "Brilliant Corners," "Pannonica," and "Crepuscule with Nellie," as well as such catchy tunes as "Jackie-ing" and "Worry Now Later." "Pannonica" is dedicated to the legendary Baroness Pannonica de Koenigswarter, who inspired a number of other compositions by Monk and a great many other musicians (a partial list would include "Nica's Dream" by Horace Silver, "Nica's Tempo" by saxophonist Gigi Gryce, "Blues for Nica" by Kenny Drew, "Tonica" by trumpeter Kenny Dorham, "Nica" by

Sonny Clark, and "Nica Steps Out" by Freddie Redd). "Pannonica," which incidentally marked Monk's debut on celeste, is a composition that haunts; its granite beauty has a devastating impact on listeners, even those not fully convinced by Monk. The melody of "Brilliant Corners" stalks around a circular path. Shifts in tempo and Sonny Rollins' fine sax solo add to Monk's uncompromising mood.

In addition to the Baroness, Nellie Monk was a great source of strength to her husband. "Crepuscule with Nellie" (ex. 38-4),[6] written while she was recuperating from an illness, may be Monk's most harmonically rich composition; the parallel sixths in bar 1, which set the mood, are certainly not a typical Monk device. Here again, however, he creates harmonic ambiguity by starting on a II major chord, not even introducing the flat 7th for a couple of beats. The dissonant interjection at the end of bar 2 is probably something that only Monk could have thought of. At first glance it seems foreign to the rest of the tune, but in fact it provides the vital spur that keeps listeners on the edges of their seats.

Monk composed a large library of music, making it difficult to single out any one composition over the others, but many fans agree that "Criss Cross" is among his best (ex. 38-5). I particularly like the second note in the figure, which gives a Lydian quality to the melody. But the harmonic structure is less important here; what is striking is the rhythm of the melody. In his four-bar intro, Monk sets up a three-beat pattern that crosses the bar lines, with stressed long notes that form a rising chromatic scale. Beginning at the repeat sign (the actual beginning of the 32-bar structure of the tune), the piano and alto seem to be merely repeating what Monk has already played—but with an exquisite sense of timing, Monk dodges away in bar 7, first leaving an unexpected hole with the eighth-rest and then jumping up past the high point of the previous line (the A-flat in bar 4) to an A-natural. A new figure is introduced in bar 12, its descending chromatic scale perfectly mirroring the rising chromatic scale in the first four bars.

The stark economy and clarity of organization of Monk's improvised soloing are plainly audible in just about everything he recorded, but "Bags' Groove" (ex. 38-6)[7] may be an especially good example of the Monk genius at work. This is a standard 12-bar blues, and instead of referring directly to the melody of the head, Monk creates his own "molten composition." In the first chorus, he introduces a simple two-note idea and plays with it for a

6. This is Monk's only through-composed piece, so no specific recording is referenced here. *Ed.*

7. Recorded on December 24, 1954, and originally released on Prestige PRLP 7109. *Ed.*

38-4 "Crepuscule with Nellie."

38-5 The lead line of "Criss Cross."

while, finally expanding the interval of a fourth to an augmented fifth to create a momentary dissonance with the F-sharp before resolving back to the two notes with which he started. In the second chorus a more "melodic" figure appears, but after only a few bars he abandons it in favor of a series of sixths and sevenths in laconic syncopations. At the end of the chorus, however, these larger intervals collapse back to a fourth, making it clear that Monk was only continuing the development of his first idea.

The fourth is also the basis of the next chorus, but here it is played in sixteenth-notes as a sort of tremolo, as the music becomes more agitated. The upper notes in this section, the D, E, F, and E-flat, outline a melodic idea, and Monk quickly abandons the sixteenth-notes in favor of this more powerful element, combining it with the upward interval leaps from the previous chorus in a series of more dissonant and more rhythmically staggered fragments. At the end of this chorus he returns to earth momentarily with a tag phrase that is almost corny. What redeems it is that it serves as the springboard for the block chord chorus, which is the most abstruse material in the whole solo. Notice how the block chords elaborate the rhythmic idea of the preceding tag phrase, twisting it around and taking it in unexpected directions.

Having emerged triumphant from this jungle of dissonant voicings, Monk returns to the triplet figure he abandoned in the second chorus. At first this

38-6 *"Bags' Groove" by Milt Jackson.* Piano Solo by Thelonious Monk.

38-6 Continued

38-6 Continued

seems to be a whimsical little idea, but the downward leaps at the ends of the phrases become more and more bizarre, while the rigid use of rests between phrases creates mounting suspense. In these two choruses also we can see how Monk deliberately omits selected notes in the triplet figures. The ear of the listener tends to supply the missing notes, however, so that in some sense not striking a note at all is simply another variety of keyboard articulation, as effective and as characteristic of Monk as the three-note cluster near the end of this passage.

In the last chorus transcribed (actually, the solo goes on for two more choruses after this one) Monk tries out a new idea as spare as the one he started with, striking two notes at a time and then releasing one of them to create a pitch-bending effect. At this point he is using only his right hand, letting the bass sketch in the blues structure without adding any left-hand chords. And given the superb balance of the lead line, any left hand at all would have been superfluous.

Monk's repertoire also embraced a number of standard tunes, such as "Carolina Moon," "Smoke Gets in your Eyes," and "April in Paris." We don't have space to transcribe them here, but they are worth listening to and studying in detail because of the way Monk altered and developed the material; in effect, he "recomposed" practically every standard he played. In recomposition, a high degree of the personality of the artist permeates the subject matter, without destroying or obliterating the original. The "recomposer" explores new horizons, not merely embellishing but using the structure of the tune to create something new. In film, Luis Buñuel, Carlos Suara, and Alfred Hitchcock are considered *auteurs*. They are more than innovators—their films possess a special recognizable style. Monk too possesses this quality of uniqueness. Although we recognize the old tunes when he plays them, they become in a musical sense his property.

There is much that can be learned from Monk, and much to emulate, even for musicians operating outside the straight-ahead jazz style. Among the greatest lessons he has to teach us are the ways in which he uses space—both intervallic space and temporal space. In two minutes or less, he can paraphrase a melody, lovingly or sarcastically altering the landscape by adding or subtracting a note or two, emphasizing an accent, allowing the silences a chance to breathe. Such minute but crucial transformations are close to the essence of Monk's music. On a broader scale, we can study how Monk developed the ingredients that were fresh and vital to him, how he assimilated and molded them into a new perspective, pruning away whatever was irrelevant, both in his improvisations and in his compositions. He created his own universe; and if we can't enter it completely, still, we can share it with him for a while by listening to his recordings. There is only one Monk.

39. *"Nice Work if You Can Get It": Thelonious Monk and Popular Song*

That Monk was a highly original composer and pianist, seemingly without any obvious direct musical influences, has always been accepted as a given, although commentators often mention remnants of the New York stride tradition in his piano playing. His compositions reflect the deliberate use of typical modernist devices such as whole-tone scales, rhythmic displacement, and the exposed tritone, but the manner in which he has used these devices has been idiosyncratic. When questioned about his influences, Monk always gave the impression that he developed his style independently of others, but as musicologist Scott DeVeaux demonstrates in his examination of Monk's treatment of standard repertory songs, there may be direct borrowings from the popular song tradition that helped shape Monk's compositional and pianistic style. Monk was known to labor long and intensively in developing interpretations of certain jazz standards, trying out runs, fills, harmonizations, and accompanying figures endlessly until he would be satisfied with the right sound. The result was always an individualistic and unique interpretation, or, as many have commented, a recomposition. Scott DeVeaux teaches at the University of Virginia and has written several articles and books on jazz and American music, the most recent being *The Birth of Bebop: A Social and Musical History.*

This article was submitted simultaneously to the Spring 2000 issue of *Black Music Research Journal* and for inclusion in the present reader. Used by permission of Scott DeVeaux and *Black Music Research Journal.*

Thelonious Monk is primarily celebrated as a composer: the creator of a unique body of music that counts as one of the cornerstones of modern jazz. When we think of him as an improviser, it is primarily in the context of his own compositions. As Whitney Balliett once put it: "His improvisations were molten Monk compositions, and his compositions were frozen Monk improvisations."[1]

Yet over the years, Monk made numerous recordings of Tin Pan Alley popular songs. It may seem odd to single out these performances for special attention, since playing popular songs or "standards" was the basic procedure for a jazz musician of Monk's generation. But these are genuinely odd performances in any case. They are typically played as solo piano pieces in the stride piano tradition, but without the extroversion or virtuosic bravado of that idiom. Some are curiously out of tempo, as if Monk were fumbling at the

1. Whitney Balliett, *Goodbyes and Other Messages: A Journal of Jazz* (New York: Oxford, 1991). (The quote can be found in Balliett's article on p. 227. *Ed.*)

keyboard or giving to the unfolding of each chord an uncommon weight. Others seem stiffly and mechanically in tempo. Passages that are unnervingly banal are juxtaposed with the most unsettling and inexplicable dissonance. Even stranger, they often sound less like improvisations than faithful, if idiosyncratic, renderings of the songs.

The pop songs that Monk chose to record throughout his career were not contemporary, but tunes of a certain vintage. As shown in Table 1, none was older than 1945. The majority were originally published in the late 1920s and early 1930s, making them already "standards" by the time that Monk (who was born in 1917) would have first heard them. To be sure, some of the choices are hardly surprising. Tunes like Fats Waller's "Honeysuckle Rose"or George Gershwin's "Liza" (both from 1929) had long ago been absorbed into the repertory of virtually every gigging jazz musician. More often than not, Monk performed this kind of song with his quartet, trading off solos with his saxophonist. But other selections—the ones for solo piano—often seem pointedly archaic. By the late 1950s, and well into the 1960s, solo versions of such chestnuts as "Just a Gigolo," "Memories of You," and "(I Love You) Sweetheart of All My Dreams" had become a regular adjunct of his usual stock of original compositions as performed by his quartet. When performed (as they often were) as the opening number of a nightclub set, they were triply set apart: as solo piano pieces, as popular songs, and as a repertory that referred several decades into the past.

The application of Monkian dissonance to tunes like "Lulu's Back in Town" is usually construed as a kind of irreverent nostalgia or cheerful parody, the eccentric humor of an artist who, like the cubist collagists, enjoyed deploying discarded scraps of popular culture in the service of a modernist aesthetic. "There's Danger in Your Eyes, Cherie" was apparently just such a "found object." According to Orrin Keepnews, Monk had stumbled across the tune in an old songbook shortly before his "outrageous interpretation" of it on a 1959 recording session.[2] Even songs that were presumably well known to him are treated with a broad, campy humor that is immediately enjoyable. His 1956 version of "Tea for Two" for Riverside is a good example: the familiar melody, verging on triteness, is retrofitted with a bizarre harmonic scheme in which the circle-of-fifths movement of the original seems to have come unhinged.

2. Orrin Keepnews, *The View from Within: Jazz Writing 1948–1987* (New York: Oxford, 1988), p. 141.

Table 1: Popular songs recorded by Monk

This table lists recordings, commercially released under Monk's name, of popular songs registered under another composer's copyright. It therefore does *not* include compositions by Monk based on harmonic progressions that are derived in whole or part from preexisting popular songs, such as "Evidence" ("Just You, Just Me"), "In Walked Bud" ("Blue Skies"), or "Bright Mississippi" ("Sweet Georgia Brown"). The table also omits the anomalous 1955 Riverside album devoted exclusively to Ellington compositions.

Dates in bold, to the left of titles, show years in which the songs were published. Dates following titles give the years of Monk's recordings (multiple recordings in a year not listed), with those in italics indicating solo piano performances. Dates in brackets [1941] indicate live recordings from Minton's Playhouse mentioned in the text.

Source: Leen Bijl and Fred Cante, *Monk on Records*, second edition (Amsterdam: Golden Age Records, 1985).

1909	"Meet Me Tonight in Dreamland" *1971*
1912	"My Melancholy Baby" [1941], *1971*
1924	"Tea for Two" 1956, 1963
	"All Alone" *1957*
	"The Man I Love" *1971*
1925	"Dinah" *1964*
	"Remember" *1959*
	"Sweet Georgia Brown" [1941]
1928	"Carolina Moon" 1952
	"(I Love You) Sweetheart of All My Dreams" *1964*, *1966*
	"Sweet Lorraine" [1941]
1929	"Just a Gigolo" *1954*, *1958*, *1961*, *1962*, *1963*, *1966*
	"Liza" 1956, 1964
	"Just You, Just Me" 1948, 1956, 1964
	"Honeysuckle Rose" 1956, 1964, 1965
	"There's Danger in Your Eyes, Cherie" *1959*
	"Star Dust" [1941]

1930 "Memories of You" *1956, 1964*

"Body and Soul" [1941], *1961, 1962*

"I'm Confessin'" *1964*

1931 "Sweet and Lovely" 1952, 1962, 1963, *1964*, 1966

"I Surrender, Dear" *1956, 1964*

"Between the Devil and the Deep Blue Sea" *1967*

"I'll Follow You" 1952

1932 "April in Paris" 1947, *1957, 1961*, 1964, 1965

"Willow Weep for Me" 1951

"You Are Too Beautiful" 1956

"(I Don't Stand) A Ghost of a Chance" *1957*

"I'm Getting Sentimental Over You" *1957*, 1960, 1961, 1963, 1964, 1966

"(When It's) Darkness on the Delta" *1963*

1933 "Smoke Gets in Your eyes" *1954*

"Don't Blame Me" *1963, 1964, 1970*

1935 "These Foolish Things" 1952, *1964*

"You Took the Words Right Out of My Heart" *1959*

"Lulu's Back in Town" 1964, 1966

1937 "Nice Work if You Can Get It" [1941], 1947, *1964, 1971*

1938 "I Hadn't Anyone Till You" *1964*

1939 "All the Things You Are" 1948, 1964

"Darn That Dream" 1956, *1965, 1971*

1941 "Everything Happens to Me" *1959, 1964, 1965*

1942 "Easy Street" 1968

"Lover Man" *1971*

1944 "I Didn't Know About You" 1966

1945 "I Should Care" 1948, *1957, 1964*

But as so often with Monk, parody and eccentricity act as a mask concealing deeper levels of meaning. Among other things, one can view these performances as an avenue into Monk's musical autobiography. The repertory, after all, points to a crucial and otherwise largely hidden phase of Monk's creative life: the decade before 1947, when recordings for the Blue Note label first introduced his music to the general public. We know that from1940 to about 1943, he worked as the house pianist for the jam sessions at Minton's Playhouse in Harlem. Although these sessions are now famous because of their role in the emergence of bebop, Monk was in all other respects on the periphery of jazz activity of the time—living at home with his mother, shunning the usual route for professional advancement through the swing bands for the low pay and relative obscurity of the Harlem jam session scene. During this period, he began writing many of the compositions for which he would become famous. Some, like "Epistrophy" and "'Round Midnight," were performed and even recorded by other artists as early as 1942. But by the very nature of the job at Minton's, he was required to play an endless string of jam session favorites. Surviving recordings from Minton's, captured by amateur phonographer Jerry Newman on a diskrecorder during 1941, faithfully document the tastes of the time: tunes like "My Melancholy Baby," "Sweet Georgia Brown," "Star Dust," and "Nice Work if You Can Get It."

The few recordings on which one can hear the twenty-three-year-old Monk generally show him in a subsidiary role. His job as pianist at the jam session, after all, was to accompany other musicians in a compatible style. But one recording, featuring "Sweet Lorraine," a 1928 ballad that had gained renewed currency thanks to a recent recording by Nat "King" Cole, puts the spotlight on Monk in what must have been a regular Minton's ritual.

The performance begins with Monk's unaccompanied piano rising above the background clatter at Minton's. As guitarist Danny Barker noted, "Monk generally started playing strange introductions going off, I thought, to outer space, hell knows to where. . . . Somewhere in Monk's intro there was the melody of the song to be played."[3] Indeed, in this eight-bar introduction (ex. 39-1) the melody of "Sweet Lorraine" is easy enough to pick out. The disorienting quality of the passage stems instead from the harmony, in which the

3. Danny Barker, *A Life in Jazz* (New York: Oxford, 1986), pp. 171–172.

familiar chords are displaced by tritone substitutions (A-flat-7 for D7 in m. 1, D-flat-7 for G7 in m. 2) and drifting half-diminished chords in first inversion (mm. 7-8).

For the tune statement proper, Monk is joined by his Minton's bandmate Joe Guy and by an unidentified bassist. While Monk continues to pursue his idiosyncratic harmonization, Guy takes over the melody on his trumpet. By contrast, the bassist,who seems not to have been "in the loop," struggles audibly for a foothold in Monk's slippery harmonies. Every so often he seems to have found one. When the harmony arrives in the fourth bar of the "A" section on the dominant of the relative minor (A7), for example, he plays with the confidence of a man who has finally found firm ground. But the unexpected harmonic twists consistently frustrate him, forcing him to retreat to the musical equivalent of mumbling. Only with the entrance of the drummer at the beginning of a new thirty-two bar cycle is order finally restored.

Monk's "weird chords" are part of the bebop legend. One of their purposes was to challenge and disorient musicians like the poor bass player. Jam sessions throughout the period routinely contained musical obstacles—fast tempos, unusual keys, reharmonizations—designed to weed out the inept and the uninitiated.[4] But critics and historians have also seized upon Monk's

39-1 *Thelonious Monk, "Sweet Lorraine" (1941), mm. 1-8.*

4. Scott DeVeaux, *The Birth of Bebop: A Social and Musical History* (Berkeley: University of California, 1997), pp. 208–217.

fondness for alternative harmonizations as a turning point. For many, the real significance of the revolution at Minton's Playhouse is that jazz finally severed its long and intimate association with popular song. In the wake of bebop, we no longer think of jazz improvisation as a *way* of playing tunes, but as an exacting art form in itself that happens, as a rule, to use popular music as a point of departure. In the hands of a jazz improviser, a copyrighted popular song is less text than pretext. Its crucial identifying feature—melody—is erased in the heat of improvisation, leaving behind the more abstract and malleable level of harmonic pattern. Out of the ashes of popular song comes a new structure, a new aesthetic order, shaped by the intelligence and virtuosity of the improviser; and it is to that structure, and that structure alone, that our attention should be drawn.

This view of jazz improvisation is linked to the broader project of elevating jazz as art by setting it apart from, and even in an adversarial relationship to, mere commercial music. Jazz criticism had, from its inception, characterized jazz as "anticommercial," but such rhetoric became particularly vehement when used in defense of bebop.[5] As Ross Russell wrote in an essay originally published in 1948: "Bebop is the music of revolt. . . . It is especially the intransigent opponent of Tin Pan Alley. Indeed the war against the horrible products of the tunesmiths . . . has been brought to a successful conclusion only by the beboppers, who take standard melodies at will, stand them on their heads, and create new compositions retaining only a harmonic relationship with the original."[6]

Any number of early bebop recordings can be heard as conforming to Russell's description. One of the most famous is "Ko Ko," the Charlie Parker/Dizzy Gillespie collaboration from1945 that is based on the 1938 pop song "Cherokee." "Cherokee" had been a favorite vehicle for Parker since the early 1940s; but as Frank Tirro notes, "If we compare the opening of Parker's "Ko Ko" with the opening of Noble's "Cherokee" we find the bebop transformation is complete. No vestige of the original remains visible on the surface of the performance."[7] The listener is confronted instead by a disorienting, lightning-fast introduction, half composed, half improvised, that leads directly into Charlie Parker's improvised solo. In Gary Giddins's words, this "explosion

5. Scott DeVeaux, pp. 529–530, in "Constructing the Jazz Tradition: Jazz Historiography," *Black American Literature Forum* 25, Fall 1991, pp. 525–560.
6. Ross Russell, "Bebop," in *The Art of Jazz*, Martin Williams, ed. (New York: Oxford, 1959), pp. 187–214.
7. Frank Tirro, *Jazz: A History*, second edition (New York: W.W. Norton, 1993), pp. 301–302.

of sound, [this] mad scramble of notes. . . . [h]elped to confirm jazz's emergence from the shadows of Tin Pan Alley tunesmiths."[8]

But does it make sense to draw from this the conclusion that the beboppers were unremittingly hostile toward popular song? In an earlier, incomplete version of "Ko Ko" from the same recording session, the musicians follow the explosive introduction by quietly intoning the melody to "Cherokee." At this point, the performance is abruptly cut off by whistling, the impatient clapping of hands, and a voice shouting "Hold it!" Was this Charlie Parker, who had just stopped playing a few seconds before? Perhaps; but the honor has also been claimed by record producer Teddy Reig.[9] According to Reig, he interrupted the session not out of intransigent opposition to Tin Pan Alley, but for more practical considerations. His boss, Herman Lubinsky, the grasping owner of Savoy Records, had advanced Charlie Parker the sum of $300 for four original compositions. In the subsequent take, "Cherokee" was disguised as "Ko Ko" (the title was apparently Reig's), with composer credit assigned to Parker, who got his $300. What was in it for Lubinsky? Aside from not having to pay out royalties to a Tin Pan Alley composer, each original composition would be "published" by Lubinsky on terms that would bring him substantial royalty income. (Royalty income was also due the composer, but Lubinsky was notorious for evading payment: as one musician said of him, "To Herman . . . if he could beat you out of $5, that was a great achievement."[10]) Out of such seedy economic incentives did the independence of bebop from popular song arise.

In general, to characterize bebop as a revolt of musicians against popular song misses the point. To be sure, the emergence of bebop as a genre depended upon the creation of a new repertory; musicians needed to establish at least some autonomy in the marketplace. But the sensibilities of the bebop generation were still intimately connected to the music of Tin Pan Alley. Playing the music of Gershwin, Kern, and Arlen was "nice work." The purpose of their improvisations was not so much to displace or erase the original, but to offer a personal interpretation of it. These interpretations, of course, were designed to display the artistry of the improviser through dizzying displays of virtuosic passage work, ingenious harmonic substitutions, and the like. All of this, admittedly, led in the direction of obscuring the original tune.

8. Gary Giddins, *Celebrating Bird: The Triumph of Charlie Parker* (New York: Oxford, 1987), pp. 87, 90.

9. Teddy Reig, *Reminiscing in Tempo: The Life and Times of a Jazz Hustler* (Metuchen, New Jersey: Scarecrow, 1990).

10. Ibid. p. 81.

39-2 *Thelonious Monk and Joe Guy (vocalist), "Nice Work if You Can Get It" (1941).*

Monk's method, however, led in the opposite direction. He preferred, even while improvising, to hold on firmly to the melody. Consider his performance at Minton's in 1941 of the 1935 Gershwin tune, "Nice Work if You Can Get It." The excerpt begins with a vocal chorus (by trumpeter Joe Guy), with a piano obbligato by Monk that is not so much a countermelody as a variation on the original tune. In many places, the relationship between his improvised line and the vocal line would be better described as heterophony than polyphony (ex. 39-2). The solo chorus that follows could similarly be described as melodic paraphrase.

The solo piano versions of standards from later in his career have an even more exaggerated respect for melodic content. These performances have an introspective mood quite removed from the noisy sociability of the Minton's recordings. They reflect a time when, as manager Teddy Hill remembered, "he'd come in here at any time and play for hours with only a dim light."[11] As Albert Murray has put it:

> Monk . . . is in a sense a very special descendant of the old downhome honky-tonk piano player who likes to sit alone in the empty ballroom and play around with unconventional chord combinations and rhythms for his own private enjoyment. There is something of the empty ballroom etude in almost all of Monk's compositions.[12]

Before he began writing his own compositions, Monk reshaped popular songs. Later in life, he enjoyed presenting distilled versions of these private

11. Ira Peck, "The Piano Man Who Dug Be-bop," *PM's Sunday Picture News*, February 22, 1948. [Reprinted here on p. 41. *Ed.*]
12. Albert Murray, *Stomping the Blues* (New York: McGraw-Hill, 1976), p. 228.

"empty ballroom etudes" in the recording studio or on the concert stage. Although Monk never offered any justification for these performances, I hear them as a kind of public confession of the centrality of these songs in the shaping of his aesthetic.

Monk continued to perform "Nice Work" throughout his career, including an extended piano-solo version on his penultimate recording session thirty years later for the London label Black Lion. The most striking aspect of the opening of this 1971 performance is its straightness. The tune statement is almost unsyncopated, the piano texture very conventional. It conveys the feeling of someone sight-reading the tune directly from the sheet music; and indeed, the similarity to the published version is striking (ex. 39-3 and 39-4).

But that exaggerated straightness is quite deliberate. It makes the few unexpected details stand out with particular clarity. For the most part, these details are matters of dissonant intervals. Monk had a well-known fondness for major and minor seconds, major and minor sevenths, minor ninths, tritones—intervals that he liked to present in an exposed, unadorned fashion. This, of course, was a trait that he shared with many other twentieth-century composers. Had he grown up in a different environment, he might simply have composed in a non-triadic idiom. Instead, he found ways to arrange popular songs so as to arrive on these sonorities.

39-3 *Gershwin, "Nice Work if You Can Get It," refrain, mm. 1-4 (transposed from G major).*

39-4 *Thelonious Monk, "Nice Work if You Can Get It" (1971), opening theme statement, mm. 1-4.*

A good example is the A-flat major chord in m. 7 (ex. 39-5). When I learned jazz piano, I was specifically advised by my teacher (bebop pianist Frank Cunimondo) not to harmonize a melody with the major seventh chord in first inversion because too much attention was thrown thereby to the exposed interval of a major second. Apparently this is why it appealed to Monk! Similar jolts are provided by the A-natural in m. 2.

These details serve to defamiliarize the familiar: they make the performance simultaneously a faithful rendering and unmistakably Monk. To an extent, one can regard Monk's fondness for certain sonorities as a "manner" that can be applied to virtually any tune. Every time he gets to a dominant chord, it seems, he can't resist the temptation to insert a tritone—usually deep in the left-hand voicing, where it fundamentally alters the sound of the chord. And his weakness for whole-tone scales is particularly well-known, and often deplored as a cliché.

But it is important to recognize the extent to which the tunes he chose to play *invite* these interpolations. "Nice Work," like so many tunes of the period, is built around the sound of the augmented dominant seventh chord—as a look at the sheet music confirms (ex. 39-3). It is a short step from there to the tritone-based, whole-tone idiom that Monk uses in the beginning of the second chorus (ex. 39-6). Monk brings starkly out in the open dissonant

39-5 *Thelonious Monk, "Nice Work if You Can Get It" (1971), opening theme statement, mm. 7–8.*

39-6 *Thelonious Monk, "Nice Work if You Can Get It" (1971), chorus 1, mm. 1–2.*

intervallic relations that in the original were cloaked in a generally mellifluous texture.

Take, for example, the B-natural in the melody line in m. 24. In Gershwin's tune, the arrival of this note is both ingenious and coy (ex. 39-7). For the first time, the interval of an augmented fifth appears in the melody rather than the harmonization, and in a structurally important spot: the half-cadence at the end of the bridge. At the same time, this B-natural serves as the leading tone for the C chord that sets the circle-of-fifths pattern of the A section in motion once again. Monk's treatment of this dissonance (ex. 39-8) is the opposite of coy. He pounces on it with a relish that has something of the flavor of vindication, as if he were announcing: "This is the sound I like—and look, I found it *right in the melody*!"

Some of the most arresting harmonic combinations in Monk's vocabulary can be found in his reworkings of standards. In many cases, they are not so much imposed on the tunes as *derived* from them through an ingenious reordering of musical materials. A particularly ingenious example is Monk's 1957 version of "(I Don't Stand) A Ghost of a Chance." It is not hard to see why Monk liked this tune, for like "Nice Work" it, too, prominently features the sonority of an augmented dominant chord (ex. 39-9). But a more interesting moment comes in mm. 3-4, in which a lusciously sentimental chromatic descent is accompanied by the harmony of a minor subdominant.

39-7 Gershwin, "Nice Work if You Can Get It," refrain, mm. 22–25 (transposed from G major).

39-8 Thelonious Monk, "Nice Work if You Can Get It" (1971), opening theme statement, mm. 22–24.

39-9 *"(I Don't Stand) A Ghost of a Chance," refrain, mm. 1–4 (transposed from C major).*

39-10 *Thelonious Monk, "(I Don't Stand) A Ghost of a Chance" (1957), mm. 1–4.*

Monk's recasting of this passage is elegant, if wholly unexpected (ex. 39-10). In the third measure, he simply reverses the bass line from F-D-flat to D-flat-F. In the following measure, the bass moves up a fourth, as before. The result of this sleight-of-hand is that the melody note in m. 4 now lands a major seventh away from the root of B-flat minor—tooth-rattling dissonance heightened immeasurably by Monk's decision to accompany the melody (doubled by an octave) by a left-hand "shell" of a *minor* seventh.

In the original, the minor IV chord collapses immediately to the tonic. Monk's replacement harmony, by contrast, is unnervingly static: it has nowhere that it wants to go, nowhere that it *can* go. Our attention is drawn straight to the intervallic combinations that Monk wants us to hear. All of this emerges from a subtle alteration to an otherwise "straight" rendering. One can imagine the "wrong turn" in m. 3 happening accidentally the first time, but thereafter becoming part of Monk's conception of the tune—and perhaps adding a new sonority to his vocabulary in the bargain.

An equally unsettling chord figures prominently in "April in Paris," another tune recorded on the same April 1957 session. As before, the sonority—an unusually-voiced left-hand chord made up solely of root, minor seventh, and minor-ninth—emerges from a collision between melody and harmony. This time, the immediate catalyst is the penchant in modern jazz for harmonic substitution.

39-11 *Duke Ellington, "April in Paris," refrain, mm. 7–10.*

39-12 *Duke Ellington, "April in Paris," mm. 9–12 (from* The Real Book*).*

39-13 *Thelonious Monk, "April in Paris," mm. 11–12.*

In its original sheet-music arrangement, the second eight bars of "April in Paris" begins with a leisurely movement from the subdominant to a gently dissonant second-inversion tonic (ex. 39-11). Such leisurely, contrapuntal bass lines, while not uncommon in commercial arrangements, were typically discarded by improvising jazz musicians in favor of more vigorous root-position progressions, the better to serve as the basis for new improvisations. While no two musicians would necessarily recast this passage in exactly the same way, a consensus of sorts is represented by the version printed in *The Real Book*, probably the most widely distributed "fake book" in circulation (ex. 39-12). In *The Real Book*, m. 12 is reinterpreted as a tonicization of the relative minor, A minor. And this, indeed, is the way Monk plays it—albeit with a singular twist of his own (ex. 39-13).

To see the logic behind Monk's unorthodox harmonization, one must keep in mind that since at least the 1940s jazz musicians have been fond of displacing

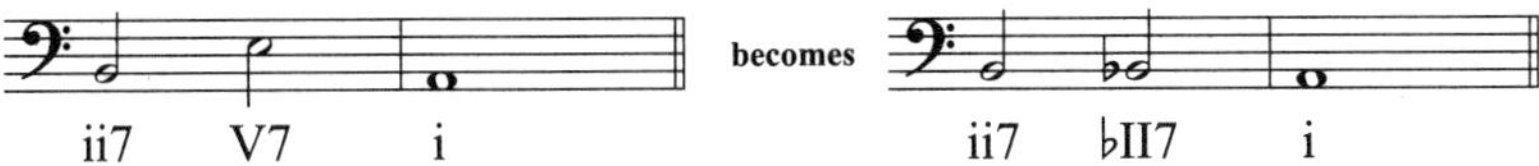

39-14 Tritone substitution for ii⁷–V⁷–i progression.

39-15 Tritone substitution for ii⁷–V⁷–i combined with melody of "April in Paris," mm. 11–12.

dominant seventh chords with chords a tritone distant—the so-called "tritone substitution."[13] In theory, such a procedure should work well enough in mm. 11–12 of "April in Paris" (ex. 39-14). But as occasionally happens, the substituted harmony clashes with the melody, in this case resulting in a grating cross-relation (an augmented octave, B-natural against B-flat) (ex. 39-15). Few jazz musicians—besides Monk—would choose this option. Once again, we are led by Monk to unfamiliar intervals that he manages to "discover" within the framework of the tune.

Having once established this felicitous dissonance, Monk uses it several more times. In mm. 17–20, it substitutes for the diminished chords in the original (ex. 39-16 and 39-17). Here, if anything, the clash between melody and harmony is even more pronounced. Because the B-natural in the melody is embellished with a lower chromatic neighbor, a single pitch class (A-sharp/B-flat) is simultaneously the root of the chord and a melodic dissonance! Finally, in m. 21, where the original harmonization specifies a move to A minor, Monk seizes the occasion for *parallel* minor ninths—the C in the first chord nicely harmonizing the melody in tenths (ex. 39-18).

"April in Paris" is not the only tune in which Monk evinces his fondness for this particular chord. It shows up, note-for-note as a passing dissonance in the December, 1956 recording of "I Surrender, Dear" (ex. 39-19) and more prominently in m. 4 of "Don't Blame Me" (from 1963) (ex. 39-20). Probably

13. Scott DeVeaux, *The Birth of Bebop: A Social and Musical History* (Berkeley: University of California, 1997), pp. 104–106.

39-16 *Duke Ellington, "April in Paris," refrain, mm. 17–18.*

39-17 *Thelonious Monk, "April in Paris" (1957), mm. 17–18.*

39-18 *Thelonious Monk, "April in Paris" (1957), mm. 21–22.*

the most memorable example, however, comes not in a re-harmonized Tin Pan Alley standard but as part of one of his best-known compositions. At the beginning to "Ruby, My Dear," also recorded in 1957, one can hear a pair of oddly-voiced parallel minor ninths just before the main melody enters, in precisely the same pitch and register as had occurred in m. 21 of "April in Paris" (ex. 39-21).[14]

What can one make of this coincidence? The tendency, I think, would be to give priority to Monk as composer: to assume that this innovative stroke was integral to his conception of "Ruby, My Dear," and that his use of it else-

14. To be precise, these two chords come at the very end of the tune, serving as a transition into the next chorus, or (as in the first recorded performance in 1947) into a repetition of the bridge in an abbreviated AABA-BA performance. In the 1957 recording, this ending is also used as an introduction.

39-19 *Thelonious Monk, "I Surrender, Dear" (1956), mm. 1–3.*

39-20 *Thelonious Monk, "Don't Blame Me" (1957), mm. 3–5.*

39-21 *Thelonious Monk, "Ruby, My Dear" (1957), mm. 1–2.*

where amounts to an after-the-fact, probably ironic, application of biting dissonance to bland popular songs. But to my mind, the close fit of harmonic sonority to the idiosyncrasies of "April in Paris" argues, if anything, for the reverse: that Monk may have first uncovered the sonority in the process working out his own version of the pop song, and only subsequently incorporated it into his own composition.

This scenario, of course, is only a hypothesis, and moreover one impossible to test, since by 1957 Monk had been playing both "April in Paris" and "Ruby, My Dear" for at least a decade (he recorded both tunes with a piano trio on his second recording session for Blue Note in October, 1947). Were it to turn out to be true, however, it would by no means diminish the importance or originality of Monk's achievement. By raising the issue, I suggest that his aesthetic was forged not in some idealized space, like the backroom of

Minton's, shielded from the corrupting influence of "commercial" music, but through an *engagement* with popular song. One cannot approach this important jazz composer and improviser without acknowledging his deep affinity for the popular songs he grew up with. That respect and affection, measured in part by fidelity to the original, is more nakedly exposed in Monk's solo-piano performances than elsewhere, but I strongly suspect it is shared by most other musicians of Monk's generation, and more deeply embedded in jazz as a whole than its most ardent champions might care to admit.

Index